# Microsoft® Expression Blend® 4 Step by Step

*Elena Kosinska*
*Chris Leeds*

Published with the authorization of Microsoft Corporation by:

O'Reilly Media, Inc.
1005 Gravenstein Highway North
Sebastopol, CA 95472

1 2 3 4 5 6 7 8 9  QG  6 5 4 3 2 1

**Acquisitions and Developmental Editor:** Russell Jones
**Production Editor:** Adam Zaremba
**Editorial Production:** Online Training Solutions, Inc.
**Technical Reviewer:** Kathleen Anderson
**Illustrator:** Robert Romano
**Indexer:** Ginny Munroe
**Cover:** Karen Montgomery

978-0-735-63901-0

## Dedication

*This book is dedicated to my lovely family—my husband, Konstantin, who always believes in me and lends moral support to all my projects, and my beautiful newborn son, Leo, who gave me inspiration for this book.*

*–Elena Kosinska*

# Contents at a Glance

# Table of Contents

**What do you think of this book? We want to hear from you!**

Microsoft is interested in hearing your feedback so we can continually improve our books and learning resources for you. To participate in a brief online survey, please visit:

**microsoft.com/learning/booksurvey**

---

**What do you think of this book? We want to hear from you!**

Microsoft is interested in hearing your feedback so we can continually improve our
books and learning resources for you. To participate in a brief online survey, please visit:

**microsoft.com/learning/booksurvey**

# Acknowledgements

A book of this size, about a product with wildly broad capabilities such as Microsoft Expression Blend, requires more than an author, or two. It requires a solid publishing team, and with this book we were lucky enough to have a great team: Kathy Krause (Top-Notch Content Editor), Kathleen Anderson (Technical Reviewer), Russell Jones (Acquisitions and Developmental Editor), and all the good folks at Microsoft Press and O'Reilly Media who put in so much effort and brought so much experience to the production of this book.

We would also like to thank all the Expression Blend users who have helped us design exercises and answer questions that we hope will be of maximum benefit to the user community. And we would like to thank the management and participants in the Microsoft MVP community who have helped us gain deeper contacts and understanding of the Microsoft Expression Studio product group.

Thank you all!

# Introduction

Microsoft Expression Blend 4 is Microsoft's newest interactive design tool. It's intended for designers and developers who need to create user interfaces for rich Internet, desktop, and mobile applications—and it offers tools that support the design of such applications, from conception to completion.

Expression Blend 4 is part of Microsoft Expression Studio 4 Ultimate, a suite of design tools that includes the impressive SketchFlow feature, which helps designers rapidly experiment with dynamic user experiences and create compelling functional prototypes.

Expression Blend provides powerful tools for integrating sample data into your application. If you're just beginning an application design and have no existing sample data to fill it with, Expression Blend provides sample data sources that you can use to populate the application with temporary (but realistic) data. If you do have sample data, Expression Blend lets you use that. In both cases, you'll be able to view the sample data while you design the user interface—even before the application gets connected to the final "live" data source.

With Expression Blend, you can even integrate graphics created in other design tools, such as Microsoft Expression Design, Adobe Illustrator, and Adobe Photoshop. The easiest source for integrating external graphic assets is Expression Design. The Expression Design + Expression Blend combination provides simple integration paths, because both applications are in the Expression Studio family. But you aren't limited to that combination. There are powerful importing tools that integrate assets from Adobe products as well. With Expression Blend, the choice of graphic design tools is up to you.

Expression Blend also makes it easy to enable interactivity without writing code. Behaviors, which are powerful interactivity building blocks, were developed expressly so that designers could add interactivity to applications without writing code. To use behaviors, you simply drag them onto objects in Expression Blend, set their properties, and enjoy the resulting interactivity.

The most common task for user interface designers—skinning controls—involves understanding the structure of common controls and creating reusable styles for applications. Powerful Expression Blend style/template editing capabilities help designers to carefully modify the look and feel of default Microsoft Silverlight or Windows Presentation Foundation (WPF) controls while retaining their functionality.

Expression Blend 4 also makes design workflow easier than ever before. Designers and developers can work seamlessly, sharing projects, code, and designs for better productivity and higher quality results.

# How to Access Your Online Edition Hosted by Safari

The voucher bound in to the back of this book gives you access to an online edition of the book. (You can also download the online edition of the book to your own computer; see the next section.)

To access your online edition, do the following:

1.  Locate your voucher inside the back cover, and scratch off the metallic foil to reveal your access code.

2.  Go to http://microsoftpress.oreilly.com/safarienabled.

3.  Enter your 24-character access code in the Coupon Code field under Step 1.

(Please note that the access code in this image is for illustration purposes only.)

4.  Click the CONFIRM COUPON button.

    A message will appear to let you know that the code was entered correctly. If the code was not entered correctly, you will be prompted to re-enter the code.

5.  In this step, you'll be asked whether you're a new or existing user of Safari Books Online. Proceed either with Step 5A or Step 5B.

    **5A.** If you already have a Safari account, click the EXISTING USER – SIGN IN button under Step 2.

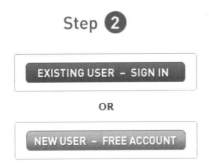

**5B.** If you are a new user, click the NEW USER – FREE ACCOUNT button under Step 2.

- You'll be taken to the "Register a New Account" page.

- This will require filling out a registration form and accepting an End User Agreement.

- When complete, click the CONTINUE button.

**6.** On the Coupon Confirmation page, click the My Safari button.

**7.** On the My Safari page, look at the Bookshelf area and click the title of the book you want to access.

# How to Download the Online Edition to Your Computer

In addition to reading the online edition of this book, you can also download it to your computer. First, follow the steps in the preceding section. After Step 7, do the following:

**1.** On the page that appears after Step 7 in the previous section, click the Extras tab.

**2.** Find "Download the complete PDF of this book," and click the book title.

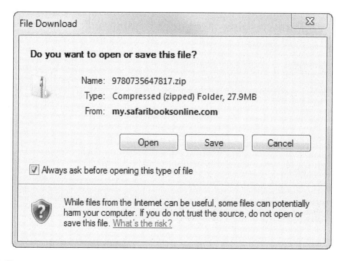

A new browser window or tab will open, followed by the File Download dialog box.

3. Click Save.

4. Choose Desktop and click Save.

5. Locate the .zip file on your desktop. Right-click the file, click Extract All, and then follow the instructions.

**Note** If you have a problem with your voucher or access code, please contact *mspbooksupport@ oreilly.com*, or call 800-889-8969, where you'll reach O'Reilly Media, the distributor of Microsoft Press books.

# System Requirements

To perform the exercises in this book, your computer should meet the following requirements:

- Windows XP with Service Pack 3, Windows Vista, Windows 7, or Windows Server 2008 operating system

- Computer with 1 GHz or faster processor

- 1 GB of RAM or more

- 2 GB or more of available hard-disk space

- Microsoft .NET Framework 4

- Silverlight 4

- Support for Microsoft DirectX 9.0 graphics with Windows Vista Display Driver Model (WDDM) Driver, 128 MB of graphics RAM or more, Pixel Shader 3.0 in hardware, 32-bits per pixel

- 1024 × 768 or higher resolution monitor with 24-bit color

- Internet functionality, which requires Internet access (additional fees may apply)

 **Important** Actual requirements and product functionality may vary based on your system configuration and operating system.

# Who Should Read This Book?

This book is intended for existing or new User Interface/User Experience designers, developers, and design integrators, as well as those who need some basic knowledge of the tools and capabilities used by designers. Although the book is expressly intended to provide information and step by step examples for new designers, experienced practitioners can use this book as well, to quickly gain familiarity with the Expression Blend 4 user interface and features. The book will also serve Adobe Flash designers who want to expand their professional repertoire into the Silverlight and WPF arena.

# Assumptions

The authors expect that you have at least a minimal understanding of the computer you will be using as well as familiarity performing file operations with your chosen operating system. You do not need deep experience in design or development, although a general familiarity with common computer graphics tools is helpful.

# What's New in Expression Blend 4

**Silverlight 4 and WPF4 projects**    Expression Blend provides powerful features for designing and developing applications based on Silverlight 4 and Windows Presentation Foundation 4 technologies.

**Shapes**    Expression Blend 4 now includes presets to help designers easily create arcs, arrows, callouts, and polygons, in both sketch and other styles. You can find this feature in the Assets panel within the new Shapes category.

**SketchFlow improvements**    SketchFlow Player now enables panning, scrolling, and screen resizing of SketchFlow prototype applications. The SketchFlow map is available as an overlay on selected screens. SketchFlow can generate documentation as Microsoft Word files, and can even include feedback from your team and customers.

**Layout States for the *ListBoxItem***    Designers can animate the process of items being added and/or removed from a *ListBox* in Silverlight 4 projects. The new states group includes *BeforeLoaded*, *AfterLoaded*, and *Loaded* states.

**Easing functions and Transition Effects**    Easing functions for animations and Visual State changes are now available for WPF 4 projects. Transition Effects such as *Fade*, *Pixelate*, *Slide In*, and many others are available through the States panel. Designers can easily combine visual effects.

**New behaviors**    Expression Blend 4 has a set of new behaviors, such as *DataStateBehavior*, *SetDataStoreValueAction*, *CallMethodAction*, *FluidMoveBehavior*, and others, which Microsoft added to help designers work with data.

**Data Store**    Designers can now store application variables in Data Store. Variables can be read and written to that storage so that they will be available for different parts of the application.

**Adobe Photoshop import improvements**    Expression Blend now has a faster and improved Photoshop import dialog box that enables designers to easily choose layers to be imported and merge effects for Photoshop files.

**Development using the MVVM Pattern**    Expression Blend 4 supports a new type of project: Silverlight Databound Application. This project type builds on the Model View ViewModel (MVVM) design pattern, which uses data and command bindings to support a loose coupling between a View (a user interface) and a ViewModel (code that coordinates the state of a View with an underlying Model).

**Development for Windows Phone Platform**    With Expression Blend for Windows Phone, available when you install the Windows Phone Developer Tools and Expression Blend 4 Service Pack 1, you can quickly and easily design Silverlight applications for Windows Phone by using the design tools in Expression Blend. As you create your Windows Phone applications, you can easily test them on either the Windows Phone emulator, included as part of the Windows Phone Developer Tools, or in a Windows Phone device attached to your computer.

# Acquiring Expression Blend 4

Expression Blend 4 is available as part of Expression Studio 4 Ultimate, which is an integrated group of applications that includes:

- **Expression Blend 4 and SketchFlow**    Using industry-proven technologies and languages such as Silverlight, WPF, XAML, Microsoft Visual C#, and Microsoft Visual Basic, Expression Blend enables you to deliver applications that are stable, scalable, accessible, reliable, and highly secure, while maintaining optimum performance. SketchFlow, a feature of Expression Blend 4, revolutionizes how quickly and efficiently designers can demonstrate their vision for an application. SketchFlow projects provide an informal way to quickly explore, iterate, and prototype user interface scenarios, and enable designers to evolve their concepts from a series of rough ideas into an interactive and functional prototype that can be made as realistic as a client or project demands.

- **Expression Web 4 and SuperPreview**    Expression Web is a professional design tool used to create engaging, web-connected multimedia experiences. SuperPreview speeds browser compatibility testing by not only showing a high-fidelity rendering of how pages will look on various browsers, but also by identifying an element's tag, size and position, applied styles, and location in a convenient Document Object Model (DOM) tree, so you can quickly remedy any cross-browser issues you uncover.

- **Expression Design 4**    Microsoft Expression Design 4 is the perfect companion to Expression Blend or Expression Web. Take advantage of existing artwork, or use intuitive vector drawing tools to quickly build sophisticated vector and image assets. Seamlessly transfer them to your Expression Blend or Expression Web projects knowing that their fidelity and effects will be maintained throughout the entire designer-developer workflow.

- **Expression Encoder 4 Professional**    Microsoft Expression Encoder simplifies publishing video to Silverlight. With Expression Encoder, you can encode a wide array of video file formats, stream live from webcams and camcorders, or even record screen videos on your computer. You can also make simple edits to video files as well as add overlays and advertising. Users can choose encoding settings, choose a video player interface from a range of player templates, and publish rich media experiences with Silverlight directly to the web. The professional version of Expression Encoder contains more import and export codecs and unlimited screen recording duration.

Expression Studio 4 Ultimate is also available as an upgrade—and the upgrade isn't limited to users of just Expression Blend 3. It is available to owners of any previous Microsoft Expression product as well as any version of Adobe Creative Suite or Microsoft Visual Studio 2005 or later.

Beyond that, you can get Expression Studio 4 Ultimate as part of the Microsoft Partner program, at *https://partner.microsoft.com/40043420*, and through the WebsiteSpark program at *http://WebSiteSpark.com*.

Finally, if you're a student, you can get Expression Studio 4 Ultimate and a huge collection of other Microsoft development software through DreamSpark, at *downloads.channel8.msdn.com/ Default.aspx*. Microsoft DreamSpark lets students download Microsoft developer and design tools at no charge, making it easier for them to learn the skills they need to excel both during school and after graduation.

# Sample Projects

Most of the chapters in this book include exercises that let you interactively try out new material learned in the main text. All the sample projects are available for download from the book's page on the web site for Microsoft's publishing partner, O'Reilly Media:

*http://oreilly.com/catalog/9780735639010*

Click the Companion Content link on that page under the book cover image. When a list of files appears, locate and download the SampleProjects.zip file.

## Installing the Sample Projects

Unzip the SampleProjects.zip file that you downloaded from the book's website to a location on your hard drive. To simplify locating and using the sample files, unzip them to your desktop.

## What's in the Sample Projects?

This book's sample projects contain Silverlight projects, videos, images, Expression Design, and other graphic assets that are required to complete the chapter exercises that you will encounter in the book.

# Organization of This Book

- Chapter 1: Welcome to the Silverlight and WPF World

  - Identify the basics of Silverlight and WPF technologies.

  - Differentiate between designer and developer roles.

  - Recognize products in Expression Studio 4.

  - Understand how Visual Studio can fit into your design process.

- Chapter 2: Exploring the Expression Blend 4 IDE

  - Download and install Expression Blend 4.

  - Open and run your first Silverlight project.

  - Use and customize the Expression Blend 4 user interface.

- Chapter 3: Designing an Interface

  - Create a new project.

  - Place visual elements and common controls in your project.

  - Use layout panels as containers for arranging objects.

  - Use image and video elements.

- Chapter 4: XAML and C#

  - Understand what Extensible Application Markup Language (XAML) is.

  - List basic XAML objects and properties.

  - Use the XAML editor and IntelliSense in Expression Blend.

  - Understand the basics of C#.

  - Explain the relationship of code-behind files to XAML files.

  - Create objects in C#.

  - Change properties of existing objects by using C# code.

  - Respond to events with event handlers.

- Chapter 5: Animations and Transformations

  - Resize user interface (UI) elements.

  - Scale, rotate, skew, and translate your objects.

  - Change the center point of an object.

  - Flip objects.

  - Simulate three-dimensional space via projection.

- ❑ Add storyboards.

- ❑ Use timelines and keyframes.

- ❑ Add animations and change object properties over time.

- ❑ Modify storyboards.

- ❑ Apply behaviors and run storyboards in response to events.

- ■ Chapter 6: Adding Interactivity

  - ❑ Use default Expression Blend behaviors.

  - ❑ Run storyboards based on behaviors.

  - ❑ Use behaviors to change properties of objects.

  - ❑ Use the *ToggleButton* control.

  - ❑ Modify the properties of behaviors.

  - ❑ Create visual states and switch between them.

- ■ Chapter 7: Creating Design Assets

  - ❑ Use Expression Design and its tools and panels.

  - ❑ Create graphic assets in Expression Design.

  - ❑ Export Expression Design assets as XAML to integrate into Expression Blend.

  - ❑ Import objects from Photoshop and Illustrator.

- ■ Chapter 8: Resources

  - ❑ Create color resources and use them in Expression Blend applications.

  - ❑ Create and apply gradient and image brushes.

  - ❑ Convert property values to resource values and apply them to properties of the same type.

  - ❑ Modify existing resources.

  - ❑ Organize resources by using dictionaries.

- ■ Chapter 9: Skinning Controls

  - ❑ Create and use styles for controls and visual elements.

  - ❑ Modify existing control templates and create custom templates for controls.

  - ❑ Use states to change the behavior of controls.

  - ❑ Create a theme for basic controls.

  - ❑ Use color, brush, and other types of resources.

  - ❑ Use implicit and key-based styles.

❑ Optimize resources and styles.

❑ Set template binding for object properties within custom templates.

■ Chapter 10: Working with Data

❑ Generate sample data.

❑ Use styles and templates on data display controls.

❑ Work with sample data.

❑ Bind object properties to data.

❑ Change data templates.

❑ Use element property binding.

❑ Use Master/Details scenarios to display data.

■ Chapter 11: Using SketchFlow

❑ Create and run a SketchFlow application.

❑ Navigate between SketchFlow screens.

❑ Create an application flow.

❑ Add controls and use sample data for prototyping.

❑ Make your SketchFlow projects interactive.

❑ Understand the SketchFlow Player settings.

❑ Package your application prototype.

❑ Use the feedback functionality to collect new ideas and comments.

❑ Generate documentation in Word format.

■ Chapter 12: Designer/Developer Collaboration

❑ Identify key points in a typical design workflow.

❑ Differentiate between designer and developer tasks and roles within the workflow.

❑ Identify mixed tasks.

❑ Share projects between Expression Blend and Visual Studio.

❑ Understand the benefits of using source control.

# Conventions and Features in This Book

This book has been designed to lead you step by step through all the tasks you are most likely to want to perform in Microsoft Expression Blend 4. If you start at the beginning and work your way through all the exercises, you will gain enough proficiency to be able to create rich user interfaces for your applications. Each topic is self-contained, but some of them are united with the same theme. If you need a fast way to find the information to perform a procedure, the following features of this book will help you locate specific information:

- **Detailed table of contents**   Scan this listing of the topics and sidebars within each chapter to quickly find the information you want.

- **Detailed index**   Look up specific tasks and features and general concepts in the index, which has been carefully crafted with the reader in mind.

- **Companion content**   Install the practice files needed for the step-by-step exercises through this book's website. See the "Sample Projects" section of this Introduction for instructions on getting and installing the practice files.

In addition, this book presents information using conventions designed to make the information readable and easy to follow:

- Most chapters include step-by-step exercises that you can follow to get guided exposure and practice to completing tasks.

- Each exercise consists of a series of tasks, presented as numbered steps (1, 2, and so on) listing each action you must take to complete the exercise.

- Boxed elements with labels such as "Note," "Troubleshooting," and so on provide additional information, directions for starting or ending the step by step exercises, or alternative methods for completing a step successfully.

- Text that you are supposed to type (apart from code blocks) appears in bold.

- A plus sign (+) between two key names means that you must press those keys at the same time. For example, "Press Alt+Tab" means that you hold down the Alt key while you press the Tab key.

- Tool icons that you need to recognize to work with Expression Blend appear where they are first mentioned. You should strive to memorize these icons and their locations in the Blend user interface as you work through the exercises.

# Errata & Book Support

We've made every effort to ensure the accuracy of this book and its companion content. If you do find an error, please report it on our Microsoft Press site at *oreilly.com*:

1. Go to *http://microsoftpress.oreilly.com*.

2. In the Search box, enter the book's ISBN or title.

3. Select your book from the search results.

4. On your book's catalog page, in the list of links under the cover image, click View/Submit Errata.

You'll find additional information and services for your book on its catalog page. If you need additional support, please send an email message to Microsoft Press Book Support at *mspinput@microsoft.com*.

Please note that product support for Microsoft software is not offered through these addresses.

The authors also maintain a support site for this book and Expression Blend in general. Visit *http://ExpressionBlendStepByStep.com*.

# We Want to Hear from You

At Microsoft Press, your satisfaction is our top priority, and your feedback our most valuable asset. Please tell us what you think of this book at:

*http://www.microsoft.com/learning/booksurvey*

The survey is short, and we read every one of your comments and ideas. Thanks in advance for your input!

# Stay in Touch

Let's keep the conversation going! We're on Twitter: *http://twitter.com/MicrosoftPress*.

# Chapter 1
# Welcome to the Silverlight and WPF World

**After completing this chapter, you will be able to:**

- Identify the basics of Silverlight and Windows Presentation Foundation (WPF) technologies.

- Differentiate between designer and developer roles.

- Recognize products in Expression Studio 4.

- Understand how Visual Studio can fit into your design process.

New and continually evolving technologies have always been, and will always be, attractive to cutting-edge people. To touch and use them is almost like touching the future. The most fortunate among us get to design and develop something based on these technologies and produce amazing new software. Contemporary end users are bored with the static nature of previous development norms and increasingly expect friendly, good-looking, and interactive interfaces. Design is a competitive advantage in many of the products we use today. Software with a beautiful interface is always more viable than similar software with an unattractive interface. Design can provide a substantial return on investment in software applications.

 **Important** There are no exercises in this chapter, so no accompanying practice files are required.

## Introducing Silverlight and WPF

Windows Presentation Foundation (WPF) is a comprehensive user interface platform with which developers and designers can create amazing, visually stunning Windows applications. With WPF, developers and designers can build rich desktop applications based on vector graphics, and WPF maintains a clear separation between the user interface and the business logic. Basically, WPF is the graphics subsystem in the Microsoft .NET Framework 3.0 and .NET Framework 4. Developers who have some programming experience in .NET languages such as Microsoft Visual C# and Microsoft Visual Basic .NET can easily start working in this area. WPF uses a markup language known as Extensible Application Markup Language (XAML) that's based on Extensible Markup Language (XML). With XAML, designers and developers alike are free to create user interfaces in a very flexible way, which is the reason why .NET developers and designers all over the world have begun to move their work to this platform.

Designers can start with small information kiosks or simple games and move to data visualization and multi-touch applications. Without a doubt, WPF is a platform for the creation of friendly and attractive interfaces for today's world, as well as the natural user interfaces of tomorrow.

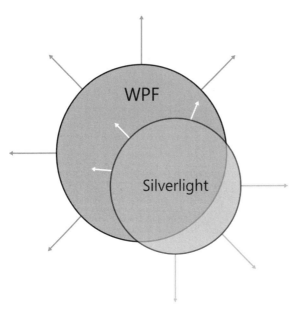

WPF is aimed primarily at developers of Windows desktop applications. Microsoft decided to create a new platform that would extend WPF to the web in order to widen application boundaries and allow developers to create applications that could run everywhere with a subset of the complete WPF features. This new platform was originally called *WPF/E* (which stood for *Windows Presentation Foundation/Everywhere*) but, fortunately, it was later renamed to *Microsoft Silverlight*. This small subset of WPF extends the platform to the web via a small runtime—a cross-browser plug-in that provides powerful features to deliver text and media content, rich vector and bitmapped graphics, animations, and more to multiple operating systems, including Windows, Mac OS, and Linux.

> **Note** Third-party developers sanctioned by Microsoft are working on ports for Linux, FreeBSD, and other open-source platforms. For example, Novell, in cooperation with Microsoft, has developed a Linux implementation named Moonlight.

Silverlight is a lightweight platform for building Rich Internet Applications (RIAs). RIAs usually run inside the browser and can provide a rich experience similar to traditional desktop applications. Silverlight doesn't have *all* the features of WPF; it's missing some features, such as the ability to work in real three-dimensional space without third-party plug-ins. Also, for security reasons, it typically does not have access to local devices and other system components—those that are not usually available through a browser. Don't think of that as a deficiency, though; Silverlight has other great advantages. For example, designers can build mobile applications in Silverlight and run them on the new Windows Phone 7 series of devices. Silverlight applications can also run as connected or disconnected desktop applications. All these platforms have commonalities—but each has its own niche and needs as well.

Fortunately, Silverlight has been around long enough that it has a large and comprehensive standard of controls—and when those aren't enough, both free and commercial kits are available to satisfy the requirements of even the most hard-to-please developers. Based on the historical development progression of Silverlight, it appears that future versions will likely have an even smaller downloadable runtime, and Microsoft will continue to reduce the differences between Silverlight and the full WPF platform.

# The Designer/Developer Workflow

It's no secret that creating a great user experience takes two types of people, each of whom thinks differently: designers and developers. Until recently, designers and developers didn't usually work closely together, and they used tools from totally different families. But that's rapidly becoming a thing of the past. The WPF and Silverlight platforms unify and simplify the designer/developer workflow. Designers work on the front end—creating beautiful user interfaces, adding interactivity, and creating all sorts of cutting-edge elements. Developers work on the back end—writing code that enables application functionality. Both designers and developers can use the same type of project, have a common point of tangency—XAML—and work within one platform.

# Expression Studio: The Designer's World

Designers need a design suite optimized for their role, one that lets them collaborate effectively with developers, create high-quality interfaces, and add interactivity to WPF and Silverlight applications. To meet this need, Microsoft created Expression Studio—a professional suite of front-end design tools for both the WPF and Silverlight platforms.

Expression Studio 4 Ultimate consists of four interrelated products:

- **Microsoft Expression Blend + SketchFlow**    Expression Blend is an interactive design tool with which designers can create front ends for both RIAs and desktop applications, taking applications from concept to completion. With SketchFlow, designers can rapidly experiment with dynamic user experiences and create functional prototypes.

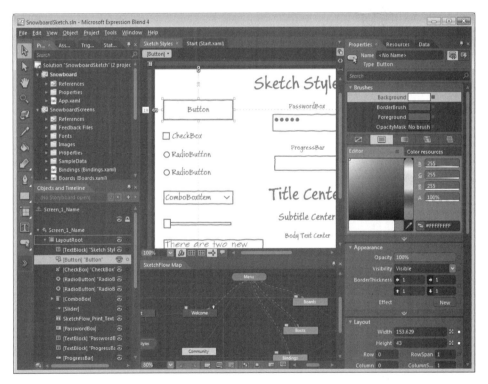

- **Microsoft Expression Design**    This is an easy-to-use graphic design tool for creating and exporting graphics for WPF and Silverlight applications and websites. It contains powerful import tools that designers can use to import files from Adobe products such as Photoshop and Illustrator.

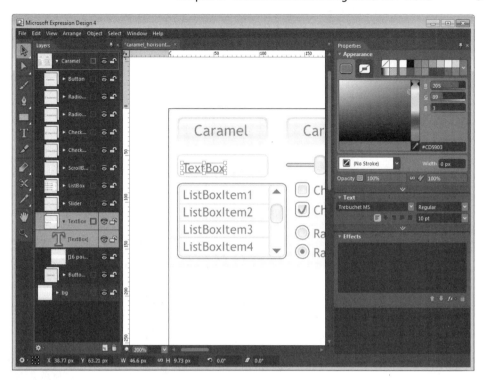

■ **Microsoft Expression Web + SuperPreview**   Expression Web is a professional web design tool that produces high-quality, standards-based websites based on common server languages and web standards such as PHP, Microsoft ASP.NET, ASP.NET AJAX, HTML/XHTML, DHTML, cascading style sheets, and JavaScript. Developers and designers can preview, test, and debug their pages in multiple browsers on the same computer with the help of SuperPreview and the Microsoft Expression Development Server.

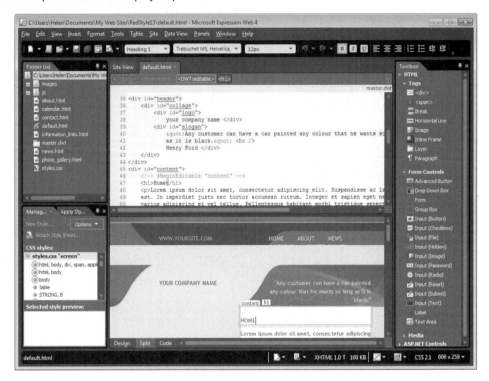

- **Microsoft Expression Encoder 4 Pro** Expression Encoder can encode, enhance, and publish videos across the web by using the Silverlight platform. With its Screen Capture feature, you can record any activity on the computer screen.

The following is an example of the process a designer might follow when using Expression
Studio to design and develop a Silverlight application.

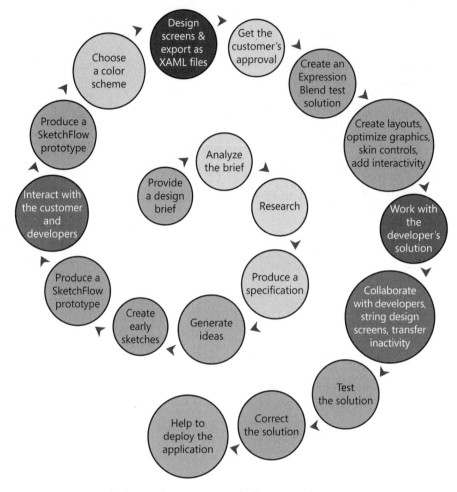

Here are some typical steps in a common design scenario:

1. Provide a design brief to the customer.

2. Analyze the brief and understand the client's needs and goals.

3. Research design solutions that address needs similar to the client's.

4. Produce a specification or list of design requirements.

5. Generate a range of ideas to satisfy the requirements.

6. Create early sketches with pen and paper.

7. Produce a prototype by experimenting with ideas in SketchFlow.

8.  Interact with customers and developers to choose the best idea.

9.  Correct and finalize the SketchFlow prototype.

10. Choose an application color scheme to meet the customer's requirements or reflect the corporate identity.

11. Design application screens and control styles in Expression Design and then export the work as XAML files.

12. Get the customer's approval on the design screens.

13. Create an Expression Blend test solution and import the XAML files.

14. Create layouts for the application screens, transfer and optimize background graphics, skin controls, and add interactivity.

15. Connect to the source control system and work with the developer's solution.

16. Collaborate with the developers, string design screens, transfer interactivity, and implement data binding.

17. Test the solution.

18. Modify and correct the solution.

19. Help to deploy the application to the customer's environment.

It's important to understand that these steps illustrate only one possible scenario. The process followed by any given set of designers might be different: some steps might be ignored, combined, or expanded depending on the particular scenario. Designers will also add or change steps based on their specific requirements, habits, and goals. You'll learn about this topic in greater detail in Chapter 12, "Designer/Developer Collaboration."

This book focuses primarily on Expression Blend as the designer's main tool, but along the way you will also explore Expression Design and Expression Encoder.

# Visual Studio: The Developer's World

Developers have had their own tailored world almost since the beginning of software development as a discipline. The .NET developer's tool of choice is Microsoft Visual Studio. This integrated development environment (IDE) simplifies designing, developing, testing, debugging, and deploying applications. With Visual Studio, developers can be more productive while building their products.

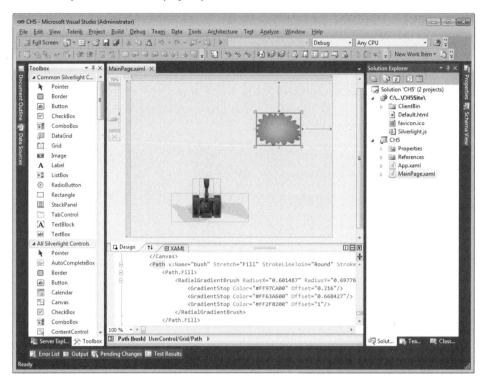

Although design tools and development tools traditionally occupy very different worlds, when Expression Blend and Visual Studio are used to design WPF and Silverlight applications, these two separate worlds have several points of overlap. Both Expression Blend and Visual Studio use the same project structure and use XAML as a shared file format—which effectively separates programming code from application design. Designers can create SketchFlow prototypes in Expression Blend, do their user interface (UI) mockups in Expression Design, convert graphics into controls, and add interactivity in Expression Blend. Developers can create compatible projects in Visual Studio, open and work on the designer's projects, and add their code to make a fully functional application.

To work much more effectively and productively, both designers and developers can share project files by using the check-in and check-out functionality of Microsoft Visual Studio Team Foundation Server. Team Foundation Server ensures that the work of both designers and developers is versioned, up to date, and available to the whole team. To connect to Team Foundation Server, you must have a Client Access License (CAL). If you have an edition of Visual Studio 2010 that includes an MSDN subscription[1], you will already have a CAL.

---

1   See the MSDN subscription site for details: http://msdn.microsoft.com/subscriptions/.

# Key Points

- WPF is a comprehensive UI platform used to design and create Windows desktop applications.

- WPF is a graphics subsystem in the .NET Framework from version 3.0 to 4.

- Silverlight is a subset of WPF that extends the platform to the web via a downloadable runtime mechanism.

- With Silverlight, designers and developers can create Rich Internet Applications (RIAs).

- Both WPF and Silverlight use the XAML markup language.

- Designers can work on the front end, creating user interfaces and adding interactivity.

- Developers can work on the back end, writing code that enables application functionality.

- Expression Studio is a professional suite of front-end design tools that includes Expression Blend + SketchFlow, Expression Design, Expression Web + SuperPreview, and Expression Encoder + Screen Capture.

- Visual Studio is an IDE for developers that simplifies designing, developing, testing, debugging, and deploying applications.

- Both Expression Blend and Visual Studio use the same project file format, so they can open and work on the same WPF and Silverlight projects.

- Stay in sync with your team by using Team Foundation Server integration in Expression Blend and Visual Studio.

## Chapter 2
# Exploring the Expression Blend 4 IDE

**After completing this chapter, you will be able to:**

- Download and install Microsoft Expression Blend 4.
- Open and run your first Microsoft Silverlight project.
- Use and customize the Expression Blend 4 user interface.

Rapidly evolving and recently released, the fourth version of Microsoft Expression Studio is a suite of front-end design tools with which designers can bring their creative ideas to life. Expression Blend 4, part of Expression Studio 4, is aimed at interactive designers and developers who design for industry-proven technologies such as Silverlight, Microsoft ASP.NET, and Windows Presentation Foundation (WPF).

This book will give you the information you need to start using Expression Blend 4 to design and create beautiful interfaces. You don't need to be a developer or an expert in behind-the-scenes code. You can start from the beginning and move forward rapidly. If you are a developer seeking to improve collaboration with your designers or learn the basics of designing user experiences, this book will help you start that process right now. If you are interested in building dynamic prototypes for your applications, you'll appreciate the information in this book about SketchFlow, which is a component of Expression Blend 4 that is useful for demonstrating ideas, application flows, screen layouts, and functionality with your team and with clients.

In this chapter, you will learn how to set up Expression Blend 4 and other accompanying tools. You'll explore and customize the integrated development environment (IDE), and you will create and test your first Silverlight project.

 **Important** The exercises in this chapter do not require any accompanying practice files.

# Downloading and Installing Expression Blend 4 and Supporting Tools

Expression Blend 4 is a part of Expression Studio 4 Ultimate, and it's available in packages that match the way you work. If you don't have Expression Studio 4 Ultimate, you can download a trial version from the Microsoft Expression product site.

## Downloading Expression Blend 4, Trial Version

### Downloading Expression Blend 4

1.  Browse to the Expression product site at *http://www.microsoft.com/expression/*, and find Expression Studio 4 Ultimate in the download section.

2.  Click the appropriate download link to navigate to the download page at the Microsoft Download Center.

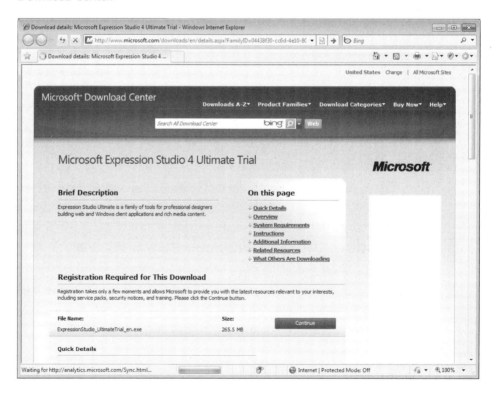

**3.** Click the Continue button. You'll be forwarded to the Microsoft sign-in page, where you can sign in with your Windows Live ID. Sign in or click the Sign Up Now button to register if you don't have a Windows Live ID.

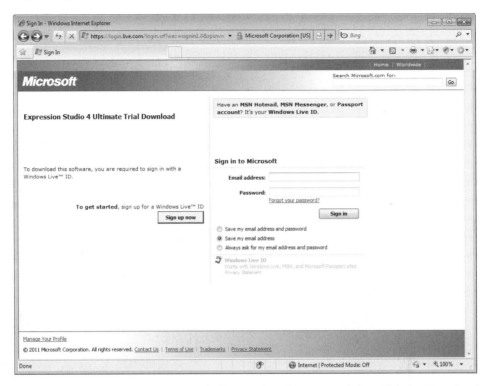

**4.** Fill in the form on the next page, click the Continue button, and then click the Download button. You'll see a dialog box that asks whether you want to run or save the file. Click Save, and save the file to a folder on your local computer.

## Downloading the .NET Framework 4 Runtime

Before navigating to your download location and running the setup program for Expression Blend 4, you need to ensure that you have installed the Microsoft .NET Framework 4 runtime, which is required by the Expression software suite. With the .NET Framework 4 runtime, you can develop and run applications that target .NET Framework 4.

**Tip** You can check which version of the .NET runtime is installed by using Windows Explorer to browse to the C:\<*Windows*>\Microsoft.NET\Framework folder. Check for a subfolder that starts with v.4.0.x. If the version 4 folder is present, you can skip the download and installation of the .NET Framework 4 runtime.

If you have not yet installed .NET Framework 4, follow this procedure.

### Downloading the .NET Framework 4 runtime

1. Navigate to the folder on your hard drive in which you saved the trial version of Expression Studio 4 Ultimate, and double-click the setup file.

2. Expression Studio 4 Ultimate requires the Microsoft .NET Framework 4 and asks whether you want to download and install it. Click Yes. The setup program forwards you to the Microsoft Download Center, which displays information about the Microsoft .NET Framework 4 (Web Installer).

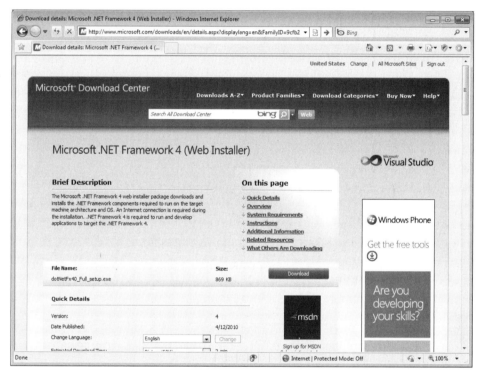

3. Locate the Download button, and click it to start the download. You will be asked whether you want to run or save the dotNetFx40_Full_setup.exe file. Click Save, and save the file to your local computer in the same folder in which you saved the Expression Studio 4 Ultimate setup file.

## Downloading Silverlight 4

If you don't have Silverlight installed on your computer, you will need to install the Silverlight runtime, which is available for test machines, for the Windows platform, and for your applications.

### Downloading Silverlight 4

1. Go to the Microsoft Silverlight site and locate the Silverlight 4 information page, at *http://www.silverlight.net/getstarted/*.

2. Download Silverlight 4 by clicking the *Silverlight Runtime (Install now)* link or by typing **http://cut.ms/Xv2** in your browser. Save the file locally in the same folder in which you saved the .NET Framework 4 and Expression Blend 4 setup files.

Next, you will install the .NET Framework 4, Silverlight 4 and Expression Blend 4 with SketchFlow as part of Expression Studio 4 Ultimate.

## Installing the .NET Framework 4 Runtime

Follow the steps in this section to install the .NET Framework 4 runtime on your computer.

### Installing the .NET Framework 4

1. Navigate to the folder on your hard drive in which you saved the .NET Framework 4 setup file, and double-click it.

2. Read and accept the license terms.

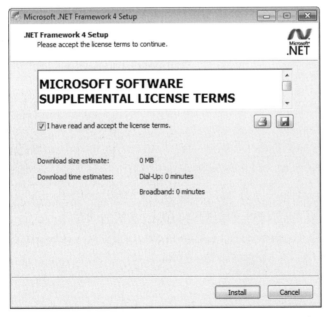

3. Click Install and wait while the .NET Framework is installed. After a successful installation, you'll see a dialog box confirming that the .NET Framework 4 has been installed.

**4.** Click the Finish button.

## Installing Expression Studio 4 Ultimate with Expression Blend 4

This section describes the installation procedure for the trial version of Expression Blend 4.

> **Note**  If you have a retail copy of Expression Studio 4 Ultimate, you should use it, instead of the trial version.

### Installing the trial version of Expression Studio 4 Ultimate with Expression Blend 4

**1.** Navigate to the folder on your hard drive in which you saved the trial version of Expression Studio 4 Ultimate, and double-click the setup file.

**2.** Read the end-user license agreement, and accept it by clicking the Accept button.

**3.** Click Yes if you'd like to help improve Microsoft Expression Studio 4 Ultimate.

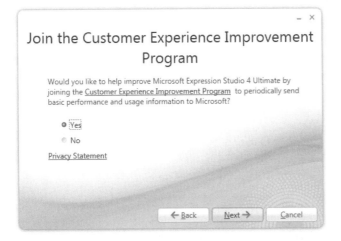

**4.** Click Next.

**5.** In the next dialog box, you will choose which programs from the Expression Suite to install. From here you can also change the installation location. The small icon near each package indicates which programs will be upgraded from older versions. It's better to install all of the programs as new rather than upgrading previous versions.

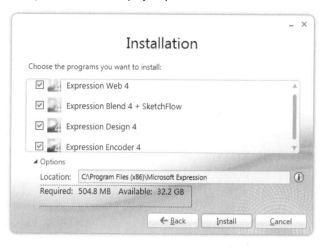

**6.** Click Install, and then click Finish after setup completes the installation.

# Installing Silverlight 4

Silverlight is a technology with which you can run .NET-based applications in a browser or on the desktop.

### Installing Silverlight 4

**1.** Navigate to the folder on your hard drive in which you saved the developer runtime for Silverlight 4, and double-click the setup file. Click Run when the Open File dialog box appears.

**2.** Click Install Now. Wait while the setup program installs Silverlight on your computer.

**3.** Click Next when the Enable Microsoft Update dialog box appears.

**4.** Finish the setup by clicking the Close button.

Next you will run Expression Blend 4, open an existing project, and explore the IDE.

# Opening and Testing Your First Silverlight Project

Now that you have installed Expression Blend 4 and the other supporting tools, you can launch Expression Blend 4 for the first time.

> **Important**  Be sure you have installed the .NET Framework, Expression Blend 4, and the Silverlight plug-in before beginning this exercise.

### Running a Silverlight project

1. On the Windows taskbar, click Start, then click All Programs, and then click Microsoft Expression.

2. Click Microsoft Expression Blend 4. The program starts, and a welcome dialog box appears.

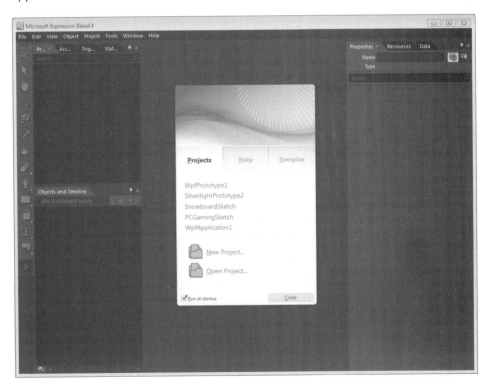

There are three tabs in the welcome dialog box:

- ❑ Projects
- ❑ Help
- ❑ Samples

3. To explore Silverlight projects, we recommend that you start with the amazing samples provided in Expression Blend 4. Click the Samples tab.

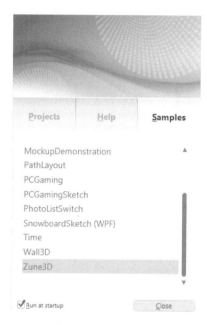

4. Click the Silverlight project called Zune3D. Expression Blend loads the sample project, and its environment comes to life.

To ensure that you have installed all of the tools, as well as Silverlight, correctly, you need to test the application.

5. Press F5 on the keyboard to run the application. In a few seconds, a browser containing the running Silverlight application opens.

**Tip** In Internet Explorer, press F11 on your keyboard to view the project in full-screen mode. This will give you more screen space to see the entire project. You can exit full-screen mode by pressing F11 again.

**6.** Take a few minutes to fully examine the Zune3D project in your browser. When you move your mouse pointer over the picture of the Zune, the pointer changes. Note that you can drag the picture left or right by using your mouse. You'll see the Zune rotate through 360 degrees. Also note that there are several different images that, when selected, become integrated into the Zune object. In addition, the color buttons at the bottom of the Zune object change both the color of the main object and the background color of the page. This is a fairly complex sample project that does a good job of demonstrating many of the features that you will be able to incorporate into your own projects as you progress through the learning curve of this powerful technology.

**7.** When you have finished exploring the Silverlight application, return to Expression Blend 4 to examine the user interface.

# Exploring the User Interface

The user interface in Expression Blend 4 closely matches the interface of the other products in the Expression Studio; it is compact, elegant, and intuitive. The workspace enables you to design your own applications quickly. It's well-organized and consists of these main visual interface elements:

- Artboard
- Menus
- Tools panel
- Authoring views
- Panels

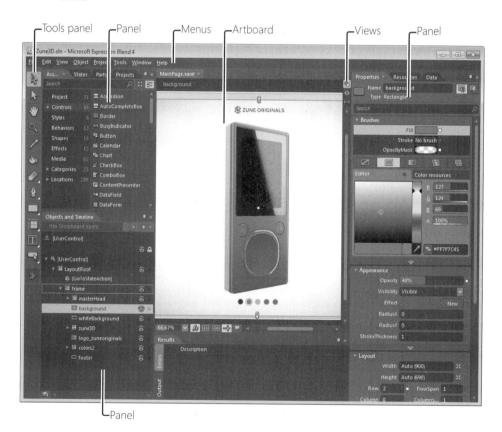

The last element, panels, includes several commonly used panels, each of which provides special-purpose functionality:

- Assets
- Objects And Timeline
- Projects
- Properties
- Resources
- Results

Expression Blend 4 includes additional panels that are not specified in the preceding list, but they are less commonly used. You'll see more about them later in this book. All the panels are part of your workspace. You can resize, move, dock, and undock these panels, arranging them to meet your needs.

## Exploring the Panels

In this exercise, you will start Expression Blend 4, familiarize yourself with the panels that are available, and manipulate those panels. There are no practice files for this exercise.

> **Note**  If Expression Blend is still open, skip the first two steps.

### Exploring panels in Expression Blend 4

1. On the Windows taskbar, click Start, then point to All Programs, point to Microsoft Expression, and click Microsoft Expression Blend 4. Expression Blend 4 starts, and the welcome dialog box is displayed.

2. Click the Samples tab in the welcome dialog box, and then click the Zune3D project. The MainPage.xaml file opens when you start this project in Expression Blend 4 for the first time. When you open your project next time, Expression Blend will start with the last active file, or nothing if you have closed all files.

3. The center area in Expression Blend 4 is the main work surface called the Artboard, on which you design a document by drawing objects and modifying them. Note the Document tab (currently titled MainPage.xaml) at the top of the visual design surface. When you have more than one document open on the Artboard, each document's name appears on a separate tab. You can switch between documents by clicking its corresponding tab.

4. Click Object on the menu bar. The menus in Expression Blend 4 are of the "Smart Menu" variety, which activates or deactivates items based on the current work context. If an item or subitem in the menu can't be used in your current context, it won't be available.

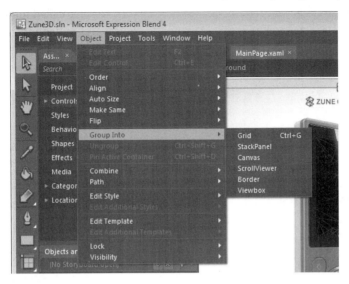

Almost everything you might need to do within Expression Blend 4 is available from the eight menus on the menu bar.

**5.** Click the Projects tab to activate its panel.

> **Tip** If you have trouble locating a panel, or if it isn't visible in your workspace, click Window on the menu bar, and then click the name of the panel you're looking for. You can also reset your workspace, which returns the user interface to the default settings. To do so, click Reset Current Workspace on the Window menu.

**6.** In the Projects panel, you can see the structure of the project you currently have open—the Zune3D project, in this case. The top level presents the Solution, which consists of one or more projects. The Projects panel conveniently helps organize all the files and folders of a project.

Solutions frequently contain both a Silverlight application project and the corresponding website project—but Expression Blend 4 might also create the website project automatically, which you might already have noticed when you pressed F5 in the Zune3D sample earlier in this chapter. If the solution contains only a Silverlight project, Expression Blend 4 creates an application that can be run in the Silverlight runtime viewer, inside or outside of a browser window. The Silverlight project itself contains several files, including the Extensible Application Markup Language (XAML) files with their code-behind files, a sample page with its code-behind files, the application manifest, the assembly information file, reference files, images, sample data, folders, and other files.

Expression Blend 4 documents are based on a unique markup language, XAML. As mentioned earlier, Expression Blend 4 opens the MainPage.xaml file by default. This file contains default application XAML content. In the Project panel, the code-behind file for an XAML document appears as a child item under its respective XAML document. You can open the MainPage.xaml.cs code-behind file to see programming logic in C#.

7. Below the active Project panel is the Objects And Timeline panel. In this panel, you can view the hierarchical structure of all objects on the Artboard, select objects to modify through other panels (Properties, for example), create storyboards, and more.

**8.** In the Objects And Timeline panel, click the arrow beside LayoutRoot, then the one beside Frame. Then click the Background object. The view in the Properties panel changes.

**9.** In the Properties panel, you can view and modify the properties of a selected object. All of the selected object's properties are organized in expandable categories. Look at the Brushes category for the selected background object. The Color Editor allows you to set solid color and gradient brushes. Change the Fill property by clicking red within the Color Editor.

Notice that the property changes are reflected in the Artboard. The red color you selected in the Color Editor is now visible in the corners of your open document and has changed from olive to pink.

Why pink and not red? Look below the Brushes category at the Appearance category. The Opacity property is set to 40 percent, so you're not really seeing pink; you're seeing the red you picked in the Color Editor but at only 40 percent opacity.

 **Tip** Some categories of properties in the Properties panel have an expandable Advanced section, which you can open by clicking Show Advanced Properties. The advanced properties are categorized separately, because they're less commonly used than other properties.

**10.** At the top of the Properties panel, click the tab for the Resources panel. The Resources panel shows all the resources used in the open project.

**Tip**  Resources might include different types of brushes, styles, and templates. Resources can also be organized in resource dictionaries. For more information, see Chapter 8, "Resources."

11. Press F12 on your keyboard to view the Results panel, which appears below the Artboard. It displays information that you can use to view and debug errors in your application.

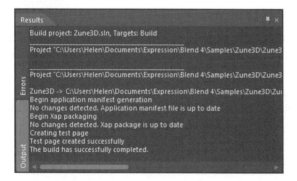

# Understanding the Tools Panel, Authoring Views, and Workspace Configurations

You have just examined some of the panels available in the Expression Blend 4 workspace. In the following exercises, you will examine the Tools panel, authoring views, and workspace configurations. There are no practice files for the exercises in this section. You can continue to use the Zune3D sample.

## The Tools Panel

On the left side of the Expression Blend 4 workspace is a vertical panel called the Tools panel. This set of tools helps you create new objects and modify existing objects in your application. For instance, to draw on the Artboard, you first select a tool and then use it to draw.

The first section contains the selection tools: Selection and Direct Selection. You use the Selection tool to select elements on the Artboard to change their properties through the Property panel or directly on the Artboard. With the Direct Selection tool, you can select and edit nested objects and path segments.

The next section contains the view tools, Pan and Zoom, which you use to pan and zoom to adjust the portion of the Artboard that you can see.

The next section contains the brush tools: the Eyedropper, Paint Bucket, and Gradient tools. These tools are used for selecting colors, filling objects with a selected color, and manipulating an object's gradient. Notice the small triangle in the lower-right corner of the Gradient tool. If you click it, you'll see that there are more tools available. Expression Blend 4 often groups similar tools under a single icon, which both saves space and displays the most recently used tool.

The next section is a very powerful and important part of the Tools panel. It contains the object tools—the Pen, Rectangle, Grid, TextBlock, and Button tools. Each of these primary icons contains additional tools grouped within it, such as those for creating and manipulating shapes, paths, layout panels, text objects, and simple and complex controls. You use the object tools to draw various objects and other controls on the Artboard.

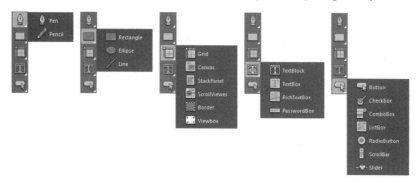

The final button in the Tools panel is Assets, which gives you access to various assets used in your project.

### Using the Assets tool

*Assets button*

1. Click the Assets button Expression Blend 4 automatically places your cursor in the search box.

2. Type **Flu** into the search box. As you type each letter, Expression Blend 4 filters the available assets, showing only those that match your entry. When you type the final **u**, the filter shows only two items: FluidMoveBehavior and FluidMoveSetTagBehavior.

   This tool's ability to rapidly access assets will be of great use to you as you learn how to work with projects and assets in Expression Blend.

3. Click the Assets button again to close the Assets dialog box.

**Tip** You'll also find an Assets tab beside the Projects tab that you examined in previous steps. The Assets tab provides similar functionality in a panel, to provide workspace layout flexibility.

## Authoring Views

Authoring views are another important feature of the Expression Blend 4 workspace. So far, you've looked at a project on the Artboard in only one view: Design view; however, to design and develop various projects In Expression Blend 4, you will need more than just Design view. Expression Blend 4 has three real-time authoring views, each with a corresponding button in the upper-right corner of the Artboard.

The available views are Design view, XAML view, and Split view. In Design view, you view your document on the Artboard in a completely visual way. In XAML view, you can view and edit the document's XAML code. Split view provides both Design and XAML views in a split window.

> **Tip**  Don't overlook the value of using Split view to learn how XAML works as you create the visual design of your documents. Because selections in either the XAML pane or the Design pane are synchronized to the other pane, you can use Split view to quickly gain an understanding of the fundamental relationship between the XAML and the design.

## Using Split view

1. Click Split View. The Artboard switches to Split view, with both Design and XAML views in separate panes.

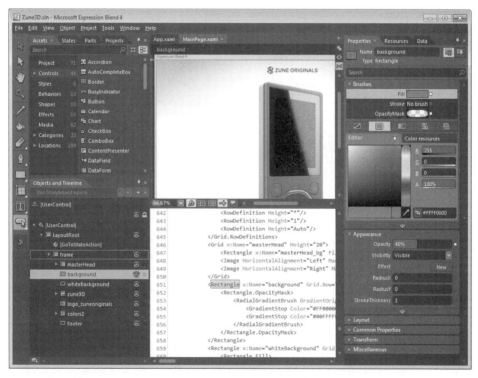

2. Scroll the Design pane down so that you can see the set of colored buttons below the Zune player image, and click the first button on the left (the black one).

**3.** Notice that the XAML pane focuses on the element you just clicked in the Design pane. You can see in the XAML pane that you've selected a *RadioButton*. If you look just above that element, you can see that this *RadioButton* set is inside a *StackPanel* on the Artboard. Also notice how the Objects And Timeline and Properties panels on the sides of your workspace change in response to the selected element.

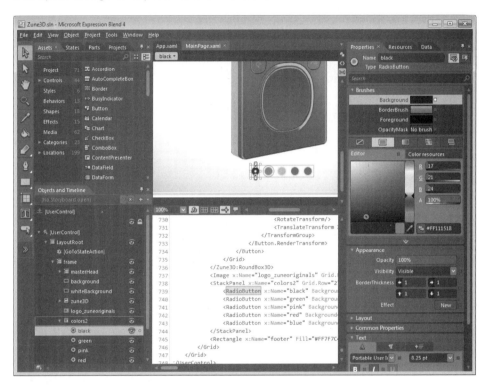

As you begin to examine the objects on the Design pane in conjunction with the XMAL pane, you can begin to see how a Silverlight project works. The visual elements are completely described in text form by the XAML code. This is the very essence of Extensible Application Markup Language: the ability to describe extremely complex objects with reasonably simple text markup. In the past, descriptive language for complex objects was limited to desktop applications, but with Silverlight, this power is available to designers for use on a variety of devices and formats, not the least of which is the web browser.

**Tip** Press F11 to cycle the active document through its available views. You can also find these views by clicking Active Document View on the View menu. It's also possible to split the screen horizontally. On the View menu, select Split View Orientation, and then select Arrange Panes Horizontally.

## Workspace Configuration

The last feature you will explore in this section is workspace configuration. Expression Blend 4 has two default workspaces: the Design workspace and the Animation workspace. By default, Expression Blend 4 loads the Design workspace configuration, which lets you focus on general authoring. The Animation workspace provides more space for design and animation by moving the Objects And Timeline panel below the Artboard so that the timeline has more room to be displayed.

### Modifying the workspace configuration

1. From the Window menu, choose Workspaces, and then select Animation. Your workspace changes from Design to Animation.

   The Animation workspace is intended to provide the tools necessary for creating complex animations in Expression Blend. You will learn more about this workspace and how to use it in Chapter 5, "Animations and Transformations."

   If you customize your workspace and would like to retain the new configuration, select Save As New Workspace from the Window menu. Give your custom workspace a name, and then click the Save button in the dialog box.

2. From the Window menu, choose Workspaces, and then select Design to return to the previous (default) Design workspace.

**Tip** The Animation workspace is ideal for creating storyboard animations. You can switch between workspaces by pressing F6.

# Customizing the User Interface

To help you work efficiently and comfortably, you can adjust the Expression Blend 4 workspace to suit the workflow required for the job you're doing. Because it provides different workspaces, sufficient free space for its various panels, and multiple views of your Artboard, Expression Blend 4 lets you work the way you want to and doesn't force you to adapt to its default workspace layouts.

## Changing the Color Scheme, Artboard Background, and Other Options

In this exercise, you will set a different color scheme for your workspace, change the Artboard background, and use other options to improve ease of use.

### Changing workspace settings

1. From the Tools menu, select Options. The Options dialog box opens.

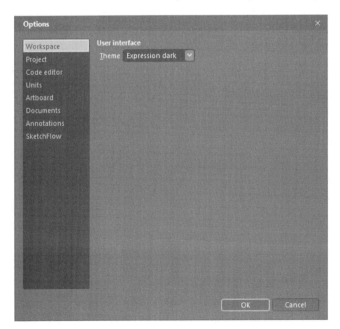

**2.** Click the arrow to the right of Theme, and then click Expression Light.

**3.** Click OK to accept the change. The Options dialog box closes.

Examine the user interface with the newly applied theme. Sometimes it's more comfortable to use one theme instead of the other; the one that works best at any given time depends on your project and working environment.

> **Note** The graphics in this book use the Expression Dark theme. If you prefer your screen to match this book's images, keep the Expression Dark theme.

If you are creating a project that uses dark colors, it's often more convenient to set the background of the Artboard to a light color. Conversely, when your artwork is very light, you might find it easier to work with a dark Artboard background. The default background for the Artboard is checkered.

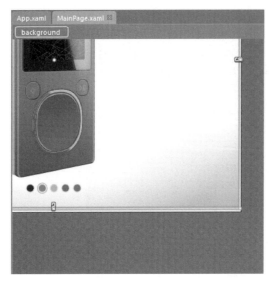

**4.** From the Tools menu, select Options. The Options dialog box appears. In the categories list on the left side, click Artboard.

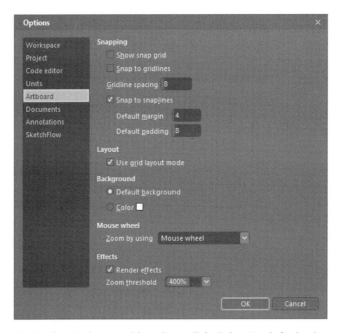

**5.** Under the Background heading, click Color. By default, the color is set to white. Click the white Color square. The Color Picker opens.

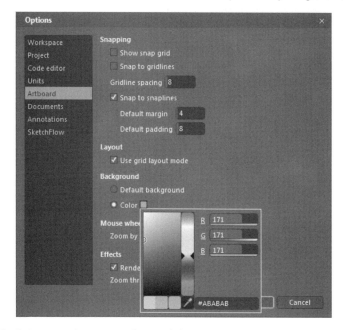

**6.** Select an alternate color, and then accept the change by clicking OK.

*Zoom tool*

Another important feature for working with objects on the Artboard is zoom level. By altering the zoom level of the Artboard, you can see large artwork without having to scroll or pan, and you can zoom deeply into finely detailed objects so that you can work more precisely. The Zoom tool is available in the lower-left corner of the Artboard.

**7.** Click the arrow on the right side of the Zoom box. A list of predefined zoom levels appears, as well as a Fit Selection option.

**8.** Click the arrow again to hide the list of zoom levels. Point to the numeric value in the Zoom box. The numerical adjust pointer appears. Alter the zoom by dragging when the numerical adjust pointer appears. Drag up to increase the zoom level and down to decrease it.

 **Tip** You can press Ctrl+9 to make the selected object fill the entire view so that you can work on it in detail. To zoom back to actual size, press Ctrl+1. You can change the Artboard zooming keyboard shortcuts in the Options dialog box. From the Tools menu, choose Options, and then click the Artboard category. Select one of the options next to the Zoom By Using field.

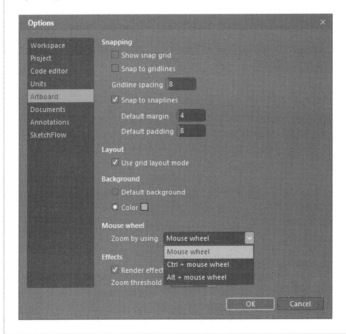

# Controlling Expression Blend's Panels

AutoHide

In the previous exercises in this chapter, you accessed Expression Blend's panels via the Window menu—but that's not the only way to work with them. They also have an interesting feature called AutoHide, which lets you collapse individual panels.

### Using AutoHide

1. Click the Turn On AutoHide button in the upper-right corner of the Properties panel. The entire group of panels collapses, leaving the panel names visible as tabs along the right edge of the Artboard. Now, point to one of these tabs. The panel reappears, and you can access functionality within it. When you point away from the panel, it collapses again.

   AutoHide is a helpful feature that lets you access all of your panels easily, yet doesn't crowd your workspace, leaving more room for the Artboard.

Turn Off
AutoHide

2. Click the Properties tab for the collapsed panel, and then click the Turn Off AutoHide button in the upper-right corner of the panel.

> **Tip** You can show or hide any panel except the Tools panel, which cannot be hidden. You can hide all panels at once by using the F4 keyboard shortcut.

*Close*

3. When you don't need panels, you can close them at any time. For example, click Close in the upper-right corner of the Properties panel, beside the AutoHide icon. The panel closes and disappears from your workspace.

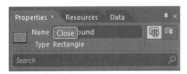

4. To return the Properties panel to the workspace, choose Properties from the Window menu. The Properties panel reappears in the workspace.

**Tip** You can return the workspace to its default layout by selecting Reset Workspace from the Window menu.

Another way to organize your workspace is by floating, docking, or moving panels. You can move any panel or group of panels to a different location in the workspace.

## Arranging panels

1. By default, the Properties panel is on the right side of the Artboard. Drag the title tab of the Properties panel to undock it from its default location, and then release it in a new location in the center of the screen. The Properties panel is now a *floating* panel.

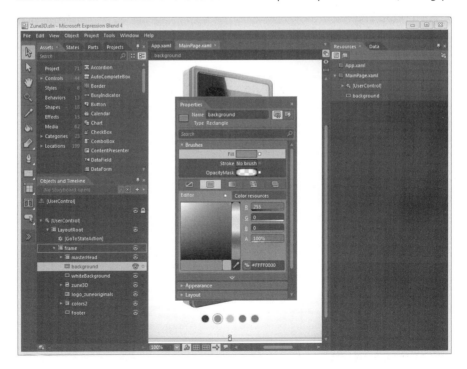

**2.** Next, dock the Properties panel to a new location near the Projects, Assets, and States panels. Drag the title tab of the floating Properties panel to the left side of the workspace. You'll see blue lines appear around it when it has moved over a docking area.

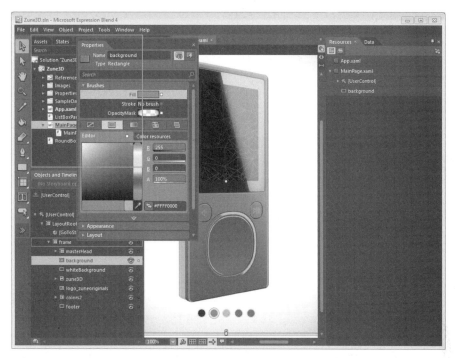

**3.** When the panel is in position, release the mouse button to dock it with the others.

**Tip** You can reorder tabs within a panel by dragging a tab to new position at the top of the panel.

# Switching Between Workspaces

In the previous exercises, you examined two workspaces in Expression Blend: Design and Animation. For maximum user customization, with Expression Blend 4 you can create and save one or more workspaces. You can also switch between workspaces easily.

### Saving and switching workspaces

1. From the Window menu, select Save As New Workspace.

2. In the Save As New Workspace dialog box, enter a name for your workspace; for example, **My Workspace**.

3. Click OK to accept the name and save the workspace.

   You can save multiple workspaces that are suitable for various tasks. For example, many designers like to have one customized workspace for design work, another for animation work, and so on.

4. To switch between the newly saved custom workspace and the default Design workspace, point to Workspaces on the Window menu, and then select Design. The workspace changes to the default Design workspace.

**Tip**  You can press F6 to quickly cycle through all the default and saved workspaces.

At this point, you should have a basic understanding of the Expression Blend 4 user interface; however, to become proficient with Expression Blend, you'll need to spend some additional time moving panels around; examining the XAML pane/Design pane relationship as you select objects in the project; familiarizing yourself with the locations of various tools and features; and with accessing, customizing, and controlling the workspace. Gaining this level of familiarity with a new program comes only after you spend considerable time learning it, so if you feel a little overwhelmed at first, don't worry; that's normal, and it won't last very long.

# Key Points

- The Expression Blend 4 workspace contains all of the program's visual interface elements, including the Artboard, panels, menus, tools, and authoring views.

- The visual design surface is called the Artboard.

- Almost everything you might need to do within Expression Blend 4 is available from the eight menus on the menu bar.

- The Tools panel lets you add new objects and modify existing objects on the Artboard.

- The Objects And Timeline panel lets you view the hierarchical structure of all objects on the Artboard.

- By using the Properties panel, you can view and modify the properties of a selected object.

- The Projects panel represents the structure of your solution and the projects within it.

- The Resources panel includes all the resources used in the currently open project.

- The Results panel displays information that you can use to view and debug errors in your application.

- The Assets panel shows all of the controls available to your project.

- There are three authoring views in Expression Blend: Design view, XAML view, and Split view.

- Expression Blend 4 has two default workspaces: the Design workspace and the Animation workspace.

- You can customize the Expression Blend 4 user interface by using either of two built-in themes: Expression Dark or Expression Light.

- You can change the Artboard background while designing applications.

- You can reorganize your workspace by moving panels.

- You can increase the space available for the Artboard by resizing, changing, showing, hiding, adding, and removing panels.

- You can save unique customized workspaces and switch between workspaces easily.

# Chapter 3
# Designing an Interface

**After completing this chapter, you will be able to:**

- Create a new project.

- Place visual elements and common controls in your project.

- Use layout panels as containers for arranging objects.

- Use image and video elements.

In this chapter, you will complete exercises that help you build your skills in creating projects with Microsoft Expression Blend 4. Even if you're not an artist, you will be able to create a multimedia project and run a website—all from within the Expression Blend user interface. The previous chapters dealt mostly with the workspace itself and where you could find the Expression Blend tools. This chapter will help you use the tools and features you learned about in the previous chapters to produce amazing results.

 **Important** Before you can complete the exercises in this chapter, you need to install the downloadable practice files to their default location. For more information about the practice files, see the instructions at the beginning of this book.

## Visual Elements

Expression Blend operates with both vector and bitmap graphics. You can draw both simple and complex vector paths, use built-in shapes, and paste high-quality images into your project. When you place or draw each vector element of your application visually, at the same time Expression Blend creates the XAML markup language that defines those elements. For those who like to draw and work visually, Expression Blend provides a wide variety of design tools.

The Expression Blend 4 Tools panel contains an Objects section that helps you choose the right element and place it on the Artboard.

In addition to layout panels and controls, which you will learn about later in this chapter, this section of the Tools panel includes some common vector tools:

- *Rectangle*    For drawing squares and rectangles with straight or rounded corners
- *Ellipse*    For drawing ellipses and circles
- *Line*    For drawing straight lines

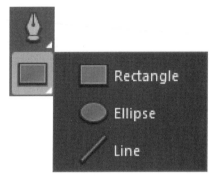

- *Pen*    For creating simple and complex paths in which you define each node
- *Pencil*    For drawing lines, curves, or freehand paths, such as signatures and pencil drawings

There are two elements in the Selection section of the Tools panel that help you select and move individual nodes or entire paths and change the attributes of existing shapes:

- *Selection*    Use this tool to select shapes, paths, and objects so that you can change their properties through the Properties panel or directly on the Artboard.
- *Direct Selection*    This tool lets you select and edit nested objects and path segments.

In the next exercises, you will create a new project, drawing its elements by using paths and basic and custom shapes.

# Creating a New Project

Before you can draw and add elements on the Artboard, you must create a new project.

### Starting a new project

1. On the Windows taskbar, click Start, then click All Programs, Microsoft Expression, and then Expression Blend 4. The Expression Blend welcome dialog box opens. Click New Project on the Projects tab to open the New Project dialog box.

2. By default, the New Project dialog box has two project tabs on the left side: Silverlight and WPF. In this exercise, you'll create a Silverlight project. Click the Silverlight tab if it's not selected yet.

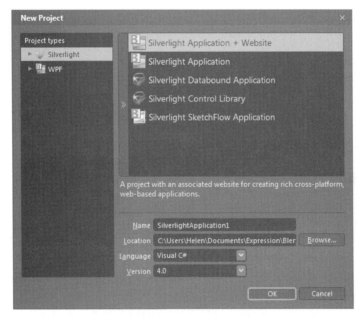

The Silverlight tab contains the following project options:

- ❑ **Silverlight Application + Website**   A project with an associated website that you can publish to a web server.

- ❑ **Silverlight Application**   A project that creates an application that can be run in the Silverlight runtime viewer, inside or outside of a browser window.

- ❑ **Silverlight Databound Application**   A project that uses data and command bindings to support a loose coupling between a View (a user interface) and a ViewModel (code that coordinates the state of a View with an underlying Model).

- ❑ **Silverlight Control Library**   A project for creating custom controls that can be reused in other Silverlight projects.

- ❑ **Silverlight SketchFlow Application**   This option allows you to create prototype applications in a very visual manner.

**3.** Click Silverlight Application + Website. Type the project name **CH3** in the Name field. Accept the default settings in the other fields,

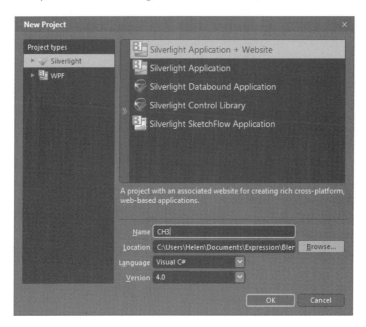

**4.** Click OK. Expression Blend creates a new project.

 **Important** By default, Expression Blend saves projects to the folder Users\<*user*> \Documents\Expression\Blend 4\Projects\. You can change this location by clicking the Browse button next to the Location field and choosing a different location.

By default, your new project's MainPage.xaml document visually defines an area 640 pixels wide and 480 pixels high on the Artboard.

 **Note** Expression Blend uses *WPF (Windows Presentation Foundation) pixels* when setting size-related properties. WPF pixels are virtual units (device-independent pixels or device-independent units) that are equivalent to the size of a pixel on a monitor set to a screen resolution of 96 dots per inch (DPI). Each unit is approximately 1/96 inch, regardless of monitor size or screen resolution.

The Objects And Timeline panel shows the top-level element of your document, represented by a *UserControl*. The next element, a layout panel, was created by Expression Blend automatically and is named *LayoutRoot* in the visual tree. This layout panel forms a grid into which you can place, arrange, and group elements. Consider the *LayoutRoot* as a container in which you can organize elements in a flexible way.

# Using Basic Shapes

Although you can draw basic shapes manually on the Artboard in Expression Blend, it's often faster and more accurate to insert basic shapes rather than drawing them in a free-form style. Expression Blend provides three basic shape tools in the Tools panel: Ellipse, Rectangle, and Line. They share the same button, but clicking the small triangle in the lower-right corner of the button makes all the options visible.

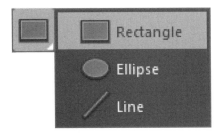

## Creating some basic shapes

1. In the Tools panel, click Ellipse.

 **Tip** If you can't find the Ellipse button, click the small triangle in the lower-right corner of the Rectangle or Line tool. These three shapes share the same button.

2. On the Artboard, draw an elliptical shape by dragging with your mouse.

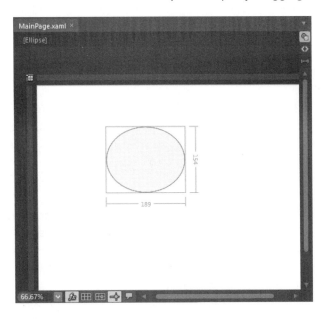

In the Objects And Timeline panel, the element you just added has appeared and is the active selection.

3. In the Properties panel, click the arrow to expand the Layout category (if it isn't already expanded). The Properties panel expands and displays the properties for the newly added *Ellipse* object. You are going to change some of them.

4. Set the width to **100** and the height to **150**. The ellipse you drew on the Artboard changes shape to match the changed width and height.

5. In the Properties panel, find the Brushes category. If it's collapsed, expand it. Notice that the ellipse has a default fill and uses a solid brush by default.

6. Click the Gradient brush tab just above the Color Editor. Expression Blend applies a basic gradient to your ellipse. Below the Color Editor and the Color Bar, click the Radial Gradient button to switch the fill style from a linear gradient to a radial gradient.

*Gradient button*

7. In the Properties panel, at the bottom of the Brushes category, click the Show Advanced Properties icon (the small white square to the right of the gradient stop offset field). The advanced properties appear. Set the *GradientOrigin* fields to **0.7** and **0.3**.

8. Click the Hide Advanced Properties icon to close that panel area.

9. Now you will change the color of each gradient stop. Click the right stop on the Color Bar, type the hexadecimal (hex) color value **#FF00B6BA** into the color field, and then press Enter on your keyboard. The object's color changes.

10. Click the left stop on the Color Bar, type the hex value **#FFBFFEFF** into the color field, and then press Enter. The secondary color of your object changes, and the object now has a three-dimensional appearance.

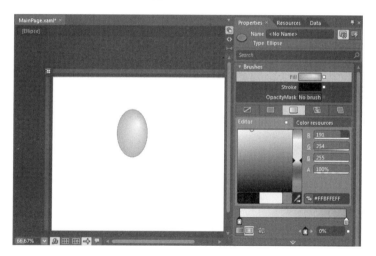

**Tip** You might find it easier to use the Color Editor and color eyedropper tool for manipulating colors in most situations. But when you need to set accurate values, typing the hex value in the color field will be your best choice.

11. On the Properties panel, in the Brushes category, click the Stroke horizontal tab. You'll find it grouped with the Fill and OpacityMask horizontal tabs. Select the No Brush subtab. Now the ellipse has no edge border (stroke) and looks even more three dimensional.

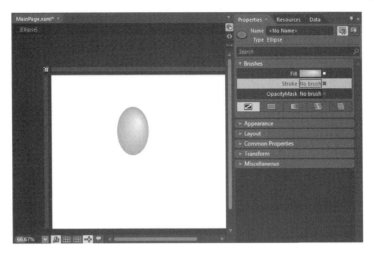

**12.** Press Ctrl+C to copy the balloon, and then press Ctrl+V to paste it onto the Artboard.

Notice that there's another entry in the Objects And Timeline panel. That's the balloon object you just pasted.

*Selection tool*

**13.** On the Tools panel, click the Selection tool button, and then drag the newly pasted balloon to the right and a little lower on the Artboard.

**14.** In the Layout category of the Properties panel, set the *Height* property to **120**.

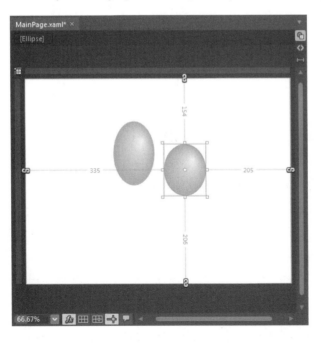

15. Next you will change this object's color for each gradient stop. Click the right stop on the Color Bar, type the hex value **#FFFFE100** into the color field, and then press Enter. The object's color changes.

16. Click the left stop on the Color Bar, type the hex value **#FFFFFFFF** into the color field, and then press Enter. You should now have two balloons, one blue and one yellow.

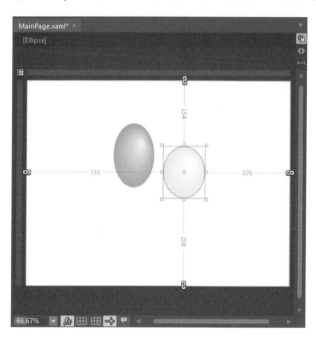

# Drawing Paths

When a predefined shape won't work even with the various manipulations you can apply, you will need to draw it manually. In Expression Blend, you draw shapes by creating paths on the Artboard with Expression Blend's drawing tools. In the following exercise, you will draw strings hanging from the bottom of your balloon shapes.

## Drawing free-form paths

*Pen tool*

1. On the Tools panel, select the Pen tool. Click the Artboard a little below the blue balloon to position the first node. Move the Pen tool downward about an inch, and click again to position the second node. Move the Pen tool down about two inches more, and click the Artboard again to position a third node.

> **Tip**   Don't worry if it seems that your path is not ideal. The shape of the curve can be modified during drawing and after the path has been drawn. You can change the position of nodes or redefine the arches of the curve with the help of the Direct Selection tool.

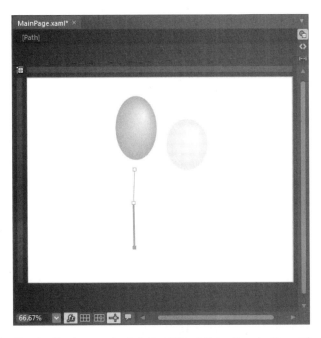

*Direct
Selection*

*Convert
point
pointer*

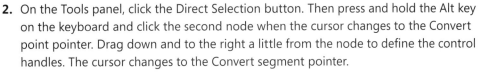

2. On the Tools panel, click the Direct Selection button. Then press and hold the Alt key on the keyboard and click the second node when the cursor changes to the Convert point pointer. Drag down and to the right a little from the node to define the control handles. The cursor changes to the Convert segment pointer.

*Convert
segment
pointer*

> **Tip**   Dragging defines the control handle of the node, which describes the tangent of the line at that point.

Notice that your string has the same brush and gradient properties you used when you created the second balloon shape.

*Solid brush*

**3.** With your newly drawn path still selected, click the Stroke tab in the Brushes category of the Properties panel, and then click the Solid brush tab.

**4.** Beside the Color Bar, enter **#FF4D4D4D** into the color field, and then press Enter.

*No Brush*

**5.** In the Brushes category, click the Fill tab, and then select the No Brush sub tab. Now your path has only a stroke property for the curve.

*Select button*

**6.** In the Tools panel, click the Selection button. Expression Blend displays a bounding box around the object. Drag the string shape upward until a red dashed line appears under the balloon shape.

The red dashed line indicates that the two paths have touched. This is a feature called *Snapping To Snaplines*. Snapping is very useful for lining objects up to each other on the Artboard.

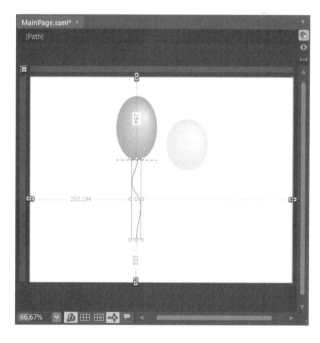

 **Tip** When Snapping To Snaplines is enabled, red dashed lines appear when you drag an object on the Artboard. The feature enables objects to snap to baselines and alignment boundaries.

*Snap to*
*Snaplines*

**Troubleshooting** By default, Snapping To Snaplines is turned on, but if you don't see red dashed lines and the string path doesn't snap to the balloon, click the Snapping To Snaplines button in the lower-left corner of the Artboard. Alternatively, you can select Options from the Tools menu. In the Options dialog box, make sure that the Artboard category is selected on the left, select the Snap To Snaplines check box, and then click OK.

**7.** Press Ctrl+C to copy the path, and then press Ctrl+V to paste the copy to the Artboard. Move the second path to the right and snap it to the bottom of the yellow balloon.

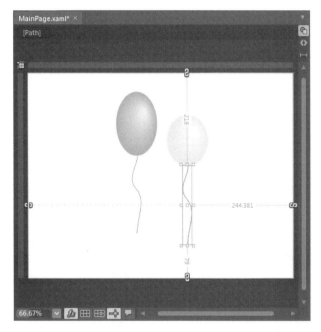

In the next steps, you will create triangles to serve as the tails of the balloons.

**8.** In the Tools panel, click the Pen tool. You are going to draw a very small triangle by creating its *geometric apexes*.

*Zoom box*

**9.** Increase the Artboard zoom level by selecting the 200% preset zoom value from the Zoom box at the bottom of the Artboard. Zooming makes drawing small objects much easier.

**10.** Click the Artboard to position the first node at the top apex of the triangle.

**11.** Move the Pen tool down and to the right, and then click the Artboard to position the second node at the lower-right apex of the triangle.

**12.** Move the Pen tool to the left and click the Artboard to position the third node of the triangle.

*Pen tool*

**13.** Point to the first node. The Pen tool will change to include a small circle to indicate that you are going to close the path. Click the first node you created to close the shape and complete the triangle. Your object should look similar to this one.

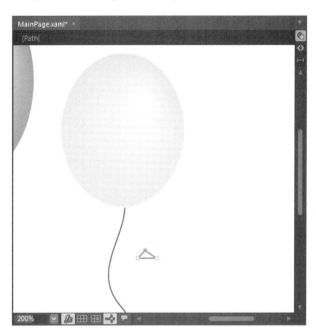

**14.** On the Properties panel, click the Fill tab in the Brushes category, and then select the Solid color brush tab. Beside the Color Bar, type **#FFFFE100** into the color field, and press Enter. The triangle is now filled with a solid yellow color.

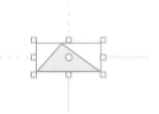

**15.** Click Stroke in the Brushes category, and then click the No Brush tab.

**16.** Click the Selection Tool and move the triangle under the yellow balloon until a red dashed line appears.

**17.** Press Ctrl+C to copy the triangle, then press Ctrl+V to paste it onto the Artboard. Move and snap the duplicate triangle to the bottom of the blue balloon.

**18.** In the Brushes category, click Fill and then enter **#FF00B6BA** into the color field. The triangle's fill color changes to blue.

**19.** Press Ctrl+- (Ctrl+minus sign) twice to zoom out to the original zoom level.

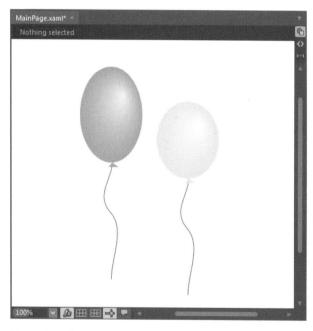

**20.** From the File menu, select Save or press Ctrl+S to save your project.

To create these balloons you used a few simple shapes, drew a curved path for the strings, and drew a triangle-shaped path for the tail.

# Using Custom Shapes

Among the new features in Expression Blend 4 is the ability to easily add and modify custom shapes in your projects. Custom shapes are ideal for meeting requirements that are too detailed for a simple shape such as the one you inserted in the previous section, especially when you need these shapes often enough that it would be inefficient to draw them by hand every time.

You can find *Shapes* on the left side of the Assets panel. Clicking Shapes displays a list of existing shapes on the right side of the panel that includes arrows, callouts, arcs, polygons, and more.

 **Note**  Use the CH3 project you created and modified in the previous exercise.

### Adding a custom shape

1. Click the Shapes tab on the left side of the Assets panel, and then double-click the Star shape. A star appears in the upper-left corner of your document.

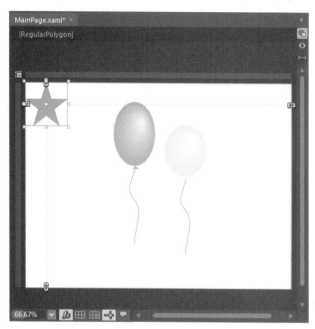

2. In the Tools panel, click the Selection button, and then find the Appearance category in the Properties panel.

3. Enter **70%** in the InnerRadius field, and enter **70%** in the Opacity field.

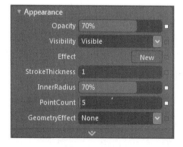

   **Tip**  This method is a quick way to apply a basic three-dimensional depth appearance to any object. Try different values in the fields for different appearances.

4. In the Layout panel, enter **30** in the *Width* field and **30** in the *Height* field.

5. In the Brushes category, click Stroke, and then click the No Brush tab. The edge stroke color will disappear from the star. In the Brushes category, click Fill and set the color to white. Move the star until it is on top of the blue balloon.

6. In the Assets panel, double-click the Callout Cloud shape. A new object appears in the upper-left corner of your document. In the Brushes category, select Stroke and click the Solid color Brush tab. Enter **#FF00B6BA** into the color field and **#FF00B6BA** into the *Foreground* field. These values set the color of the border and the text of the *Callout* shape, respectively. On the Artboard, drag the cloud shape to the right of the yellow balloon.

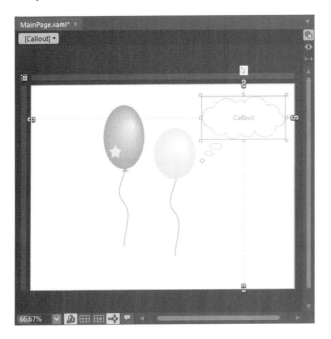

**Tip** Notice the blue boundaries and margin handles that appear around an object when you select it on the Artboard. The margin properties show the amount of space between the outside edges of the selected element and its parent element.

7. Double-click the cloud shape, type **Hi from Expression Blend** inside of it, and then click the Artboard outside of the *Callout* shape to exit text-editing mode.

8. In the Objects And Timeline panel, select LayoutRoot.

9. In the Properties panel, click the *Background* property, and then click the Gradient brush tab.

10. Click the black stop of the Color Bar, type **#FFA7F0F1** into the color field, press Enter on your keyboard, and then save the document.

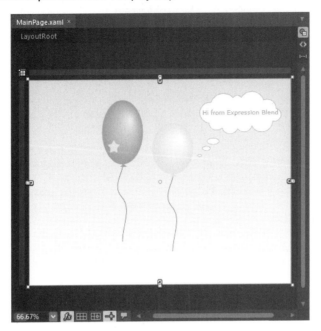

**11.** Press F5 on your keyboard. Expression Blend builds the project, starts the Expression Development Server, and displays the page in your default browser.

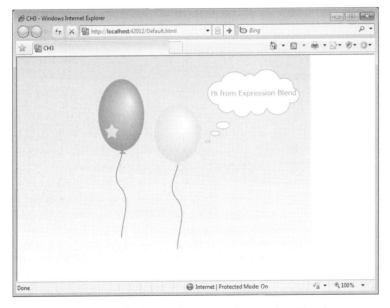

**12.** Close your browser window and return to Expression Blend.

# Using Controls

There are hundreds of controls available for use in your Silverlight projects, both free, open-source controls and commercially made controls. From the simple *Button* and *CheckBox* controls to complex controls such as the *DataGrid* and *Dataform*, controls help you add functionality to your applications quickly and easily.

The Tools panel contains some of the most commonly used controls, but the Controls tab on the Assets panel contains many more.

Adding a control to your document in Expression Blend is very similar to adding any other visual element.

 **Tip**  You can find additional controls at Microsoft's Expression Gallery (*http://gallery.expression .microsoft.com/*), and even more ship with the Silverlight toolkit, which can be downloaded from *http://silverlight.codeplex.com/.*

 **Note**  Use the CH3 project you created and modified earlier in this chapter.

## Adding controls to a project

*Button
icon*

1. On the Tools panel, double-click the Button icon. A *Button* control appears in the upper-left corner of your document.

2. Choose the Selection tool from the Tools panel, double-click the *Button* control on the Artboard, and type **Hello!**. Click the Artboard somewhere outside the *Button* to exit text input mode, and then drag the *Button* below the *Callout* shape.

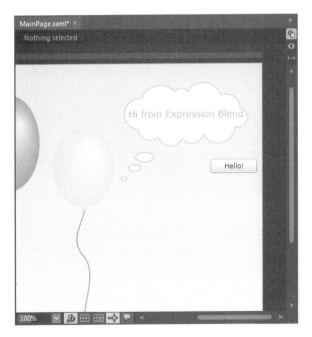

 **Tip** You can double-click a control icon in the Tools or Assets panel to insert that control at its default size. Alternatively, you can click the control icon once to select that control, and then draw the control on the Artboard with your mouse at whatever size you want.

**3.** In the Assets panel, in the Control group, double-click Calendar to insert a *Calendar* control at its default size, and then move the new *Calendar* control to the lower-right corner of the document.

**4.** Press F5 to view these newly added controls in your browser. Take a few minutes to examine how your browser renders the controls, especially the *Calendar* control.

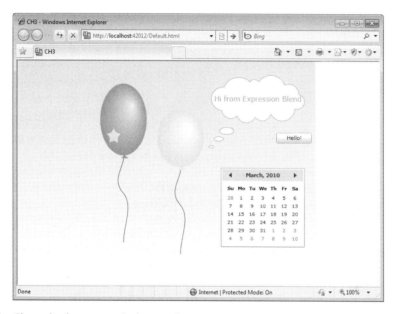

**5.** Close the browser window and return to Expression Blend.

# Using Layout Panels

Layout elements serve as containers for the objects in your project. With layout elements you can control the size, positioning, and arrangement of their child elements. If you are familiar with laying out HTML pages, you can think of a layout element as similar to a div tag, table cell, or other container element. There are several types of layout panels available for use in your Silverlight projects:

*Grid*

- **Grid**   This is the most common layout panel. It looks like a flexible next-level table. The *Grid* is composed of rows and columns that have numerous properties useful in layout, such as *MinWidth*, *MinHeight*, *MaxWidth*, and *MaxHeight*. It's also possible to set sizing options such as *Fixed*, *Star*, and *Auto* with the *Grid*. Objects that you place in a *Grid* layout panel will automatically resize when you resize your application. That's the main advantage of this element.

Canvas

- ■ ***Canvas*** This layout panel has limited capabilities. The *Canvas* will never change the positioning of its child elements. Objects that you place in this panel will not automatically resize when you resize your application, but sometimes it's very useful, such as for background elements in a project.

StackPanel

- ■ ***StackPanel*** You can use this layout element to stack its child objects either horizontally or vertically, depending on its *Orientation* property.

Scroll
Viewer

- ■ ***ScrollViewer*** This layout element can hold content bigger than it is! Users can scroll to view portions of the contents that extend beyond the edges of the control. The *ScrollViewer* allows only a single child element, so you need to use other layout elements to include multiple objects. Scroll bars appear when the content exceeds the bounds of this panel.

Border

- ■ ***Border*** As its name implies, this element provides a way to create borders around another element. It can also be used to set a background for bordered areas. Like the *ScrollViewer*, the *Border* layout element can only have one child element.

Viewbox

- ■ ***Viewbox*** With this layout element you can stretch and scale a single child element to fill the available space.

# Arranging Objects

In the preceding exercise, you placed all of the objects in one container: the *LayoutRoot*. The *Button* and *Calendar* controls, the balloons, and the small details are all child elements of the LayoutRoot. But imagine that you need to move all of these small parts together and maintain their positions relative to each other. To accomplish this higher level of layout control, you will have to use grouping, which will enable you to easily select, move, and transform the group as if all of the objects in the group were one object.

> **Note** Use the CH3 project you created and modified in the previous exercises.

### Using layout elements to arrange objects

1.  In the Tools panel, click the Selection tool icon. Drag on the Artboard to draw a marquee around the blue balloon and all of its elements. Expression Blend selects all the elements within the marquee.

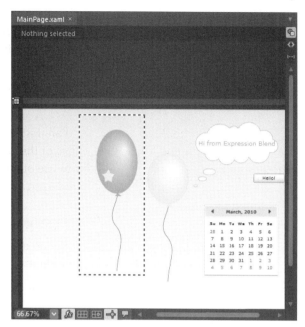

The Objects And Timeline panel also lists the selected elements.

**Tip** You can also use the Objects And Timeline panel to select multiple objects. Just hold down the Ctrl key on your keyboard and click the label for each object you want to select.

2. On the Artboard, right-click the selected objects to see the shortcut menu.

3. Point to the Group Into menu, and then click Canvas. Expression Blend groups the blue balloon along with the other selected individual component parts into a *Canvas* layout element.

   Look in the Objects And Timeline panel. You'll see a new element named *Canvas* that contains the selected elements. The *Canvas* layout element will never change the positions of the child elements it contains.

4. Group the yellow balloon and its component parts onto their own *Canvas* element by repeating the steps you just performed on the blue balloon.

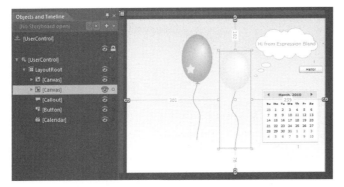

As a project becomes more complex, it also becomes difficult to identify objects in the Objects And Timeline panel. It's a good practice to give your project elements names that make them easier to identify.

5. Double-click the first *Canvas* element in the Objects And Timeline panel, type **BlueBalloon**, and then press Enter on your keyboard. Double-click the second *Canvas* element in the Objects And Timeline panel, type **YellowBalloon**, and then press Enter.

**Tip** Don't use spaces in element names. Expression Blend will replace spaces with underscores.

**6.** On the Artboard, click the *Button* control, and then hold down the Ctrl key and click the *Calendar* to select both controls at the same time.

**7.** Right-click the selected objects to view the shortcut menu. Point to the Group Into menu, and then click StackPanel. Notice that the *StackPanel* object arranges your elements vertically by default.

When you first add it, the *StackPanel* looks like it takes up more space than necessary. This happened here because you placed the *StackPanel* around both of the controls, so it kept their positions relative to each other. You can contract the *StackPanel* so that it tightly contains its child elements.

**8.** On the Properties panel, in the Layout category, set the vertical alignment to center and enter **0** into the top and bottom *Margin* fields.

**Tip** Change the *Orientation* property in the Layout category to orient elements horizontally or vertically in a *StackPanel*. You can achieve the same effect by setting the margins for an element relative to its layout element. To do that, click the margin (link) icons that appear around the element on the Artboard when the element is selected and is in Grid layout mode.

9. In addition to the Group Into command on the shortcut menu, you'll also see an Ungroup command. To ungroup the grouped set of objects, click the *StackPanel* element in the Objects And Timeline panel, and then right-click it to view the shortcut menu.

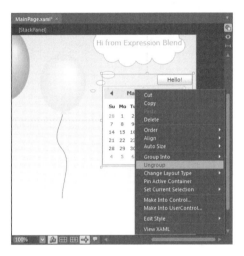

10. Select Ungroup. Expression Blend deletes the *StackPanel* that contained the *Button* and the *Calendar* controls.

 **Tip** If you prefer not to use a shortcut menu, you can access the Group Into and Ungroup options from the Object menu.

11. The next layout element is *Border*. Click the *Calendar* and, on the Object menu, point to Group Into, and then click Border. Visually, nothing happens.

12. In the Background category on the Properties panel, click the Solid color brush tab and enter **#FF00B6BA** in the color field. In the Layout category, enter **5** into all of the *Padding* property fields.

13. In the Appearance category on the Properties panel, enter **2** into all of the *BorderThickness* fields.

14. Click the Solid color brush tab for the *BorderBrush* property on the Properties panel, and set the color to white. Now you have a double-border effect.

15. A *Calendar* is a non-scalable control by default. Select the *Calendar* in the Objects And Timeline panel and try to scale it by using the on-object handles that appear on the Artboard when you point to one of the corners of its blue bounding box. Only the width and height properties change.

16. Press Ctrl+Z (Undo) on your keyboard as many times as necessary to undo your attempt to scale the *Calendar*.

    Expression Blend provides a *Viewbox* layout element that enables you to scale one or more objects simultaneously.

17. Click the *Border* element in the Objects And Timeline panel to select it, and then right-click it to view the shortcut menu. Point to the Change Layout Type menu, and then click Viewbox. The background and borders disappear, because the *Viewbox* element doesn't have *Background* or *Border* properties.

18. Press Shift on your keyboard and scale the *Viewbox* a little by using the on-object handles that appear on the Artboard.

**19.** Click LayoutRoot in the Objects And Timeline panel.

The *Grid* layout element lets you create a resizable application that can adjust to various client screen sizes and resolutions. It automatically resizes (or auto-sizes) according to the available window size. A *Grid* layout panel organizes its contents in rows and columns. There are several ways you can add or modify the rows and columns. The easiest method is by drawing visual boundaries between the rows and columns on the Artboard.

**20.** Expression Blend places rulers on the top and left of the *Grid* layout panel; the rulers look like blue lines. If you point to the top ruler, you'll see the pointer change to an arrow with a plus sign, and Expression Blend draws an orange line that shows where it will add a new column separator. Click the top ruler to add a column to the *Grid* layout panel so that the blue and yellow balloons are separated by the orange line.

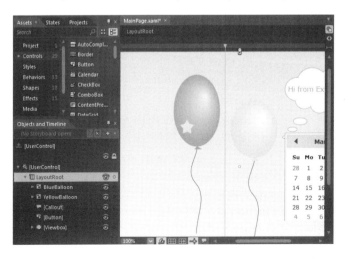

> **Tip**  The *Grid* layout element has only one column and one row by default.

When you created this application at the beginning of the chapter, the main page had fixed sizes. You will now change this behavior.

**21.** Click the *UserControl* element in the Objects And Timeline panel, and then click the Show Advanced Properties icon at the bottom of the Layout category on the Properties panel.

*Set To Auto*

**22.** Enter **640** in the *MinWidth* field, and **480** in the *MinHeight* field. In the Layout category, click the Set To Auto icon next to both *Width* and *Height*.

**23.** Press F5 to run your application and display it in your default browser. Resize the browser several times to see the strange effect: elements move depending on the browser size, and the *Callout* shape might change in width.

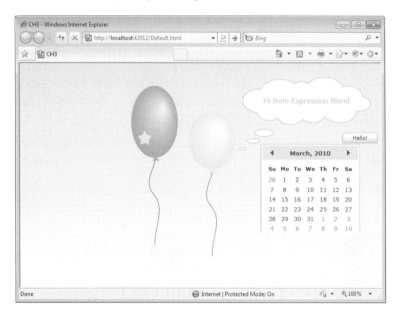

> **Tip**  If your application is resizable at runtime, you can prevent your elements from disappearing by setting the minimum width and minimum height properties.

In the next steps, you will modify the grid so that the browser will place objects correctly when you resize the browser. The blue balloon will remain close to the yellow balloon and stay on the right side of the first column. The yellow balloon and the cloud will stay on the left side of the second column, and the *Button* and *Calendar* controls will stay on the right side of the second column.

Link

**24.** On the Artboard, click the *Callout* object, and then click the right margin (link) icon that appears to the right of this object on the Artboard.

**25.** Click the *Viewbox* object in the Objects And Timeline panel, and then click the left and bottom margin (link) icons that appear to the left and at the bottom of this object on the Artboard.

**26.** Click the *BlueBalloon* object in the Objects And Timeline panel. Make sure that the value of the left margin is set to 0 in the Properties panel; if it is not, click the left margin icon on the Artboard to unbind the *BlueBalloon* object from the left.

**27.** Press F5 to run the application and view it in your default browser. Try resizing the window of your browser now. You can see the power that the *Grid* layout element gives you to control what happens when the screen size changes.

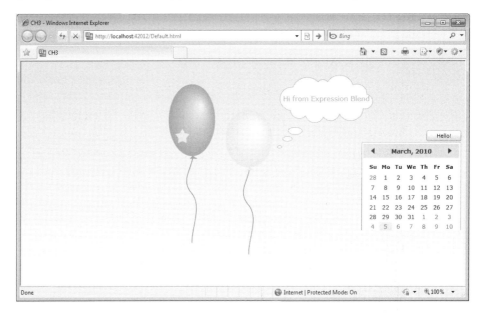

**Tip** You can delete a grid divider by double clicking that divider on the ruler at the top or left of the Artboard.

Congratulations! You have just finished the introduction to layout elements. You will work with layout elements often in the following chapters.

# Using Images and Video

In addition to drawing visual elements and adding controls and layout elements to your project, you can also insert images, video, and other media elements. These capabilities of Expression Blend help you create meaningful projects that can take advantage of existing media assets and help you convey a message to the viewer.

## Using Images

In this exercise, you will add a basic image to a Silverlight project. Because many businesses and sites already have an inventory of creative assets such as images, the skills you will develop in this exercise are important in repurposing existing creative assets.

> **Note**  Use the CH3v sample project from the CH3 folder located in the \Sample Projects folder.

### Adding and modifying images in a project

1. Click Open Project/Solution on the File menu. The Open Project dialog box opens. Click Browse and browse into the CH3v folder, then double-click the CH3v.sln file. (Solution files always have an .sln extension.) Click the Projects panel for your solution.

2. In the folder list for the CH3v project, click the Images folder.

3. On the Project menu, click Add Existing Item. The Add Existing Item dialog box opens. Click Browse, and then browse to the CH3\CH3-Import folder in this book's companion files.

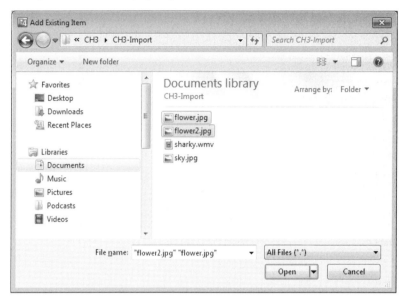

4. In the CH3-Import folder, select the flower.jpg file, press and hold the Ctrl key on your keyboard, and then click the flower2.jpg file to select both files. When both files are selected, click Open.

The two images will now appear in the Images folder of the CH3v project.

 **Tip** It's a good practice to segregate your project's files into folders with names that reflect their contents, such as Images, Video, Audio, and so on. This practice will help keep your projects manageable over the long term.

5. Click the MainPage.xaml file in the CH3v project folder. Drag the flower.jpg image from the Images folder of the Projects panel onto the Artboard.

*Advanced
Options*

**6.** In the Layout category of the Properties panel, click the Advanced Options icon beside each of the *Margin* fields, and then click Reset. Expression Blend sets all the margins to zero, and your image fills its allocated space.

> **Tip** You can make many changes to your objects right on the Artboard. Click an object on the Artboard to select it, and then use the on-object handles that appear when you point to the corners of its blue bounding box. These handles let you rotate, resize, flip, and move your image.

Be sure to set the *Width* and *Height* fields to Auto in the Layout category. If you don't set a width or height value for an Image, it will be displayed at the image's original dimensions.

**7.** In the Common Properties category of the Properties panel, click the *Stretch* property.

Expression Blend provides four different stretching options:

❑ **None** This option doesn't stretch the image at all.

❑ **Fill** The image is scaled to fit the output dimensions. Because the content's height and width are scaled independently, the original aspect ratio of the image might not be preserved, and the image might be distorted when it completely fills the output area.

❑ **Uniform** This is the default option. The image is scaled to fit the output dimensions, and its aspect ratio is maintained.

❑ **UniformToFill** The image is scaled so that it completely fills the output area but preserves its original aspect ratio.

8. Set the *Stretch* setting to None, and see how image appearance changes on the Artboard. Try setting the *Stretch* property to Uniform and UniformToFill, and then set it back to the Fill value.

9. In the Common Properties category of the Properties panel, click the drop-down list next to the *Source* property field, and then click the flower2.jpg file. Notice that the image on the Artboard changes.

> **Tip**  You can easily change the source of an image by selecting it from the drop-down list next to the *Source* property field in the Common Properties category of the Properties panel. That list displays all the images available in a project.

This introduction to using images in Expression Blend would be incomplete if it didn't teach you how to apply some simple effects to pictures in your projects. There is only one property available in the Brushes category of the Properties panel: *OpacityMask*. *OpacityMask* is a brush type for which color is ignored; instead, the brush transfers opacity to the masked object.

**10.** Click the image on the Artboard to make sure it is selected, and then click Gradient Brush for the selected *OpacityMask* property, under Brushes.

**11.** Enter **0%** in the *Alpha* field for the left gradient stop. Notice how the image on the Artboard changes.

Wherever the opacity mask is opaque, the masked object will be opaque, and wherever the opacity mask is transparent, the masked object will be transparent. That's why you can see the background through the top part of the image but not through the bottom part. Expression Blend makes many such image effects available, including drop shadow, blur, and more. You will see more about all of these effects in subsequent chapters.

## Using Video

Using media elements in your project can help you deliver information to your visitors in an easy-to-consume way and goes far beyond the visual impact afforded by static elements such as text and images. Over the past few years, video use on the web has exploded. Expression Blend provides tools that help designers provide high-end media experiences.

### Media File Formats

Expression Blend supports most common video file types, including .asf, .avi, .dvr-ms, .ifo, .m1v, .mpeg, .mpg, .vob, .wm, and .wmv. Expression Blend also supports audio file types such as .aif, .aifc, .aiff, .asf, .au, .mid, .midi, .mp2, .mp3, .mpa, .mpe, .rmi, .snd, .wav, .wma, and .wmd. In fact, Expression Blend supports the full list of video and audio file formats that Windows Media Player 10 supports.

The process for adding media elements to a project is very similar to the one you've already seen for adding images. In this exercise, you will add a basic video to the project you worked with in the previous exercise.

**Note**  Use the CH3v sample project from the CH3 folder located in the \Sample Projects folder.

### Adding video to a project

1. Click the Projects panel for your solution. In the CH3v project folder list , click the Media folder to select it.

2. Click Add Existing Item on the Project menu. In the Add Existing Item dialog box, click Browse, and browse to the …\CH3\CH3-Import folder.

3. In the CH3-Import folder, click the sharky.wmv file, and then click Open. A video file appears in the Media folder of your CH3v project.

**Tip**  Organize your videos by placing them in special folders such as Video, Media, and so on. Practicing folder segregation now will save you from difficulties later on.

4. Drag the sharky.wmv video from the Media folder of the Projects panel onto the Artboard, and snap it to the bottom boundary.

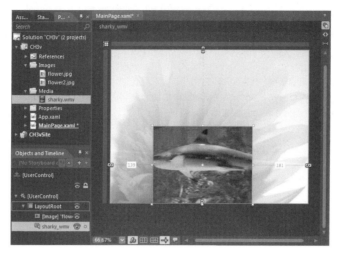

**5.** Press F5 on your keyboard. Expression Blend builds the project and displays it in your default browser. You'll see the video playing in your running project.

 **Tip** To apply stretching features to video (like the ones you used for images in the preceding section), click the Show Advanced Properties button in the Media category of the Properties panel.

By default, when Expression Blend inserts a new video, the *AutoPlay* function is enabled and the volume is set to half volume.

6. To make sure that the video doesn't play automatically, in the Media category of the Properties panel, clear the check box beside the *AutoPlay* field, and then press F5 on your keyboard to view the project in your browser.

> **Troubleshooting**  This video example doesn't include an audio track. You can test changing the volume property by using your own video files.

7. Close the open browser and return to Expression Blend.

8. In the Media properties category of the Properties pane, click the check box beside the *AutoPlay* field to re-enable the automatic behavior.

9. Click the video on the Artboard to make sure it is selected, and then click Gradient Brush for the selected *OpacityMask* property under Brushes.

10. Below the Color Editor and the Color Bar, click the Radial Gradient button to switch the fill style from linear gradient to radial gradient.

11. Enter **0%** in the *Alpha* field for the right gradient stop. Observe how the image on the Artboard changes.

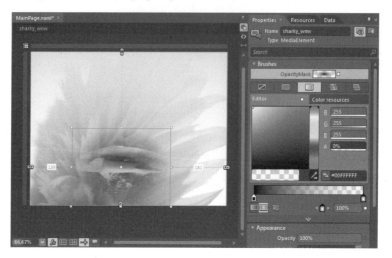

12. Press F5 to build the project and view it in your default browser.

Using visual effects on video files is a fast, easy way to make the video seem more integral to the project. You will learn more about controlling and working with video later in Chapter 4, "XAML and C#," Chapter 5, "Animations and Transformations," Chapter 6, "Adding Interactivity," and Chapter 9, "Skinning Controls."

## Key Points

- With Expression Blend, you can work with a variety visual elements.

- You can create basic shapes, draw your own paths, or use built-in shapes.

- There are hundreds of free, open-source and commercial controls you can use in Silverlight projects.

- Layout elements work as containers and control the positioning, size, dimensions, and arrangement of their child elements.

- You can use Grid, Canvas, StackPanel, ScrollViewer, Border, and Viewbox layout panels for arranging objects.

- Images and media elements can make a project more compelling.

- Expression Blend provides tools to add visual effects to objects in a project.

Chapter 4
# XAML and C#

**After completing this chapter, you will be able to:**

- Understand what XAML is.

- List basic XAML objects and properties.

- Use the XAML editor and IntelliSense in Expression Blend.

- Understand the basics of C#.

- Explain the relationship of code-behind files to XAML files.

- Create objects in C#.

- Change properties of existing objects by using C# code.

- Respond to events with event handlers.

Designers can no longer be only visual designers. Of course, they should be professionals in that area—but it's no longer enough to add and work with elements solely by using a mouse. An understanding of how solutions and projects are organized, how generated code works, and how to use that code efficiently helps everyone who builds Microsoft Silverlight or Windows Presentation Foundation (WPF) applications.

> **Important** Before you can complete the exercises in this chapter, you need to install the downloadable practice files to their default location. For more information about practice files, see the instructions at the beginning of this book.

## XAML—What Is It?

You know from the previous chapters that Silverlight and WPF use a markup language known as XAML (Extensible Application Markup Language). Both technologies use XAML to construct user interfaces (UIs) in markup instead of in a programming language such as Microsoft Visual C# or Microsoft Visual Basic .NET. Because XAML is declarative, it requires additional code to support logic and interactivity for your application. You can draw beautiful elements and animate them, skin controls and create amazing states for them, add interactivity by using behaviors, or modify the timelines of video. But your application cannot perform and respond to calculations, display data from a database, or dynamically create new UI elements without relying on some executable code.

While working with Expression Blend, you've probably discovered its project structure—and you might have noticed that any code added to a XAML application is stored in a separate file. Microsoft Expression Blend displays this file as a child item under the application's XAML document file. This separation of UI design from the underlying code enables developers and designers to work on the same project without delaying its overall development progress and prevents developers and designers from interfering with each other's work.

The XAML used in Silverlight differs somewhat from the XAML in WPF projects because Silverlight is focused primarily on web features, whereas WPF targets desktop applications. But the XAML markup for both platforms shares many common aspects. You can examine and compare objects in XAML files from both technologies by using Split view in Expression Blend. This view synchronizes and displays the Design and XAML views and can help you quickly gain an understanding of how XAML works to create the visual design of your documents. It's also always possible to edit generated code in XAML view, even if the elements were originally added visually in Design view.

Here's what a typical XAML element looks like:

```
<Rectangle
    Fill="#FF49C2DA" Stroke="Black"
    Height="100"  Width="100"
    VerticalAlignment="Center" HorizontalAlignment="Center" />
```

Visually, the preceding XAML creates a simple rectangle in the center of your document. In essence, XAML gives rendering instructions to Silverlight or WPF, telling the engine what to render, and capturing the instructions for the UIs of your applications.

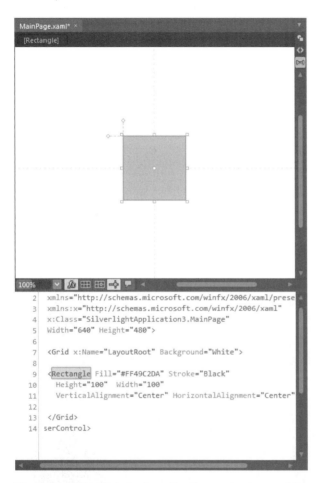

The goal of XAML is to describe the content unambiguously. There are many different types of XAML elements, and you can change their view, appearance, position, and behavior by using a set of element properties known as *attributes*.

Consider the previous example that describes a *Rectangle* object. The object has several properties (attributes), such as a blue fill color (*#FF49C2DA*), a black stroke, and a width and height of 100 pixels. Also, it's vertically and horizontally centered, which helps define its position. After you have become familiar with the general layout and terminology, you'll find XAML easy to read and understand. Without needing to consider the order in which they're set, you can change the values of existing properties as well as add new properties.

# Using the XAML Editor in Expression Blend

In the previous chapter, you worked with objects visually, grouping and organizing them in panels such as *StackPanel*, *Grid*, and *Border*. You can accomplish exactly the same result by working in XAML view, entering code directly into the XAML editor. The XAML view editor color-codes XAML elements so they're easy to identify.

You can also customize some aspects of the XAML editor.

 **Note** Use the CH4 sample project from the CH4 folder located in the \Sample Projects folder.

### Customizing the XAML editor

1. Select Open Project/Solution from the File menu. The Open Project dialog box appears. Click Browse, browse into the CH4 folder, and then double-click the CH4.sln file. Expression Blend opens your project and loads the MainPage.xaml document.

2. Select Options from the Tools menu, and then select Code Editor from the list of components on the left side of the Options dialog box.

3. If you have limited accessibility or trouble viewing the default XAML code formatting, you can change the *Font* and *Size* properties on this page. Expression Blend displays the result in the Sample box. Click OK when you've finished customizing the code editor's appearance, or click Cancel to close the dialog box.

You can use XAML view to make changes directly in the XAML files in your projects. It's easy to select existing code and then cut or copy it, or to set a cursor and paste new code into it. With the XAML editor, you can type in new code elements and add new attributes to existing elements—all of which is made much simpler with the help of an autocompleting feature called *IntelliSense*. IntelliSense is designed to make application development much easier by helping you automatically generate code.

## Using the XAML editor

1. If your workspace isn't already in Split view, click the Split button in the upper-right area of the Artboard.

> **Tip**  Press F11 to cycle through all three views: Design, XAML, and Split.

2. Press F4 to hide all unnecessary panels. You'll have more screen space and, because you'll be focusing on the code itself, the panels won't be of much help anyway.

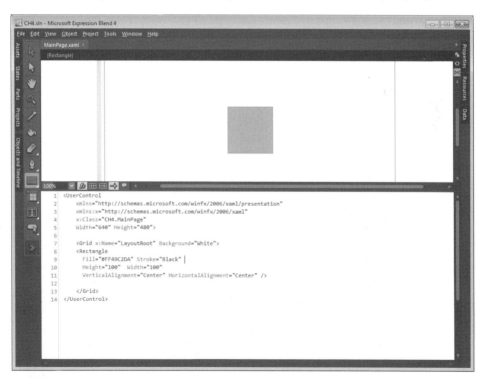

3. In the XAML pane, select the lines that correspond to the *Rectangle* element.

**Tip** Click the rectangle element in the Design pane to automatically select the XAML code in the Code pane.

```
100%
 1  <UserControl
 2      xmlns="http://schemas.microsoft.com/winfx/2006/xaml/presentation"
 3      xmlns:x="http://schemas.microsoft.com/winfx/2006/xaml"
 4      x:Class="CH4.MainPage"
 5      Width="640" Height="480">
 6
 7      <Grid x:Name="LayoutRoot" Background="White">
 8      <Rectangle
 9          Fill="#FF49C2DA" Stroke="Black"
10          Height="100"  Width="100"
11          VerticalAlignment="Center" HorizontalAlignment="Center" />
12
13      </Grid>
14  </UserControl>
```

**4.** Copy the XAML code to the Clipboard and paste it below the selected element.

```
100%
 1  <UserControl
 2      xmlns="http://schemas.microsoft.com/winfx/2006/xaml/presentation"
 3      xmlns:x="http://schemas.microsoft.com/winfx/2006/xaml"
 4      x:Class="CH4.MainPage"
 5      Width="640" Height="480">
 6
 7      <Grid x:Name="LayoutRoot" Background="White">
 8      <Rectangle
 9          Fill="#FF49C2DA" Stroke="Black"
10          Height="100"  Width="100"
11          VerticalAlignment="Center" HorizontalAlignment="Center" />
12      <Rectangle
13          Fill="#FF49C2DA" Stroke="Black"
14          Height="100"  Width="100"
15          VerticalAlignment="Center" HorizontalAlignment="Center" />
16
17      </Grid>
18  </UserControl>
```

Nothing happens visually in Design view because both elements have the same sizes and positions. Next you will vertically align your second *Rectangle* element to the one above it.

**5.** Change the value of the *VerticalAlignment* attribute by deleting the word *Center* and typing **Top** in its place. Make sure you keep the quotation marks.

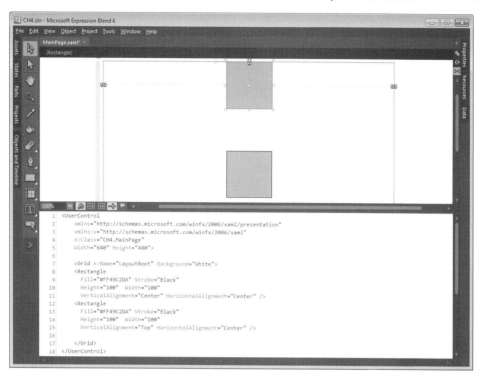

You can delete unnecessary properties if they have default values. For example, you can delete the character string *HorizontalAlignment="Center"* without affecting the visual result, because the parent container already centers fixed-sized elements horizontally and vertically by default. The *Rectangle* element's width and height properties maintain its size within the *Grid* cell. At this point, you can see that one of the main advantages of using the XAML editor is to clarify the intent of your code.

**6.** Delete the unnecessary *HorizontalAlignment="Center"* property for both *Rectangle* elements and the *VerticalAlignment="Center"* property for the first *Rectangle*.

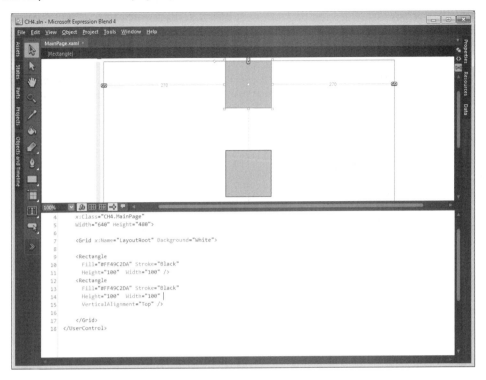

## XAML Objects

Both *Rectangle* elements are XAML objects. The parent container *Grid* (named *LayoutRoot*) and the top-level element, *UserControl,* are also XAML objects. Object element syntax always starts with an opening angle bracket (<) and the element type name. After entering the element type name, you have the option of declaring properties (attributes) within the object element. To complete the object element tag, you must end it with a closing angle bracket (>).

You must "close" all XAML tags. There are two ways to close an element tag. You can either write an opening angle bracket followed by a forward slash (</), followed by the element type name and a closing angle bracket—for example, *</Grid>*. Alternatively—but only for elements that have no child elements—you can use a shorter, self-closing form by completing the opening tag with a space (the space is required), a forward slash, and a closing angle bracket in succession (/>).

The previous example shows both ways of closing object elements. The code for the simple *Rectangle* element uses the shorthand form and ends with />. The parent element, *Grid*, has a start tag, *<Grid>*, and content (two *Rectangle* elements), so it uses the full closing tag *</Grid>* after the *Rectangle* child tags.

You can add new object elements or group existing objects in the proper containers (layout panels) directly in the XAML code.

> **Important**  Some layout panels can have only one child element, so in some cases you'll find that you can't group existing objects into those layout panels without placing them in another container.
>
> For example, before grouping objects into a *Border*, you should place them into a *Grid* or a *Canvas*, because the *Border* layout element can only have one child element.

### Adding and grouping objects

1. Click in the empty line between the *Grid* object element and the first *Rectangle* (or create an empty line after the *Grid* element by pressing Enter on your keyboard).

2. Type an opening bracket (<). The IntelliSense feature appears, showing a list of possible elements.

3. Type **St**. The XAML editor finds the *StackPanel* element in this list and displays it with a description.

4. Press Enter. The XAML editor completes the word *StackPanel* so that you don't have to type the full word.

```
100%
 1  <UserControl
 2      xmlns="http://schemas.microsoft.com/winfx/2006/xaml/presentation"
 3      xmlns:x="http://schemas.microsoft.com/winfx/2006/xaml"
 4      x:Class="CH4.MainPage"
 5      Width="640" Height="480">
 6
 7      <Grid x:Name="LayoutRoot" Background="White">
 8      <StackPanel
 9      <Rectangle
10          Fill="#FF49C2DA" Stroke="Black"
11          Height="100" Width="100" />
12      <Rectangle
13          Fill="#FF49C2DA" Stroke="Black"
14          Height="100" Width="100"
15          VerticalAlignment="Top" />
16
17      </Grid>
18  </UserControl>
```

5. Close the *StackPanel* object element by typing a closing bracket (>). The XAML editor completes the object element tag and automatically adds the closing *</StackPanel>* tag.

```
100%
 1  <UserControl
 2      xmlns="http://schemas.microsoft.com/winfx/2006/xaml/presentation"
 3      xmlns:x="http://schemas.microsoft.com/winfx/2006/xaml"
 4      x:Class="CH4.MainPage"
 5      Width="640" Height="480">
 6
 7      <Grid x:Name="LayoutRoot" Background="White">
 8      <StackPanel></StackPanel>
 9      <Rectangle
10          Fill="#FF49C2DA" Stroke="Black"
11          Height="100" Width="100" />
12      <Rectangle
13          Fill="#FF49C2DA" Stroke="Black"
14          Height="100" Width="100"
15          VerticalAlignment="Top" />
16
17      </Grid>
18  </UserControl>
```

6. Select the closing *</StackPanel>* tag and cut it by pressing Ctrl+X. Now paste it after the second *Rectangle* element but before the closing *</Grid>* tag. Now your two *Rectangle* elements are organized into a *StackPanel* layout panel. Because these elements are shown within the opening and closing *StackPanel* tags, they are called child elements of the *StackPanel*. Conversely, the *StackPanel* is the parent element of the two *Rectangle* tags.

> **Note** The *StackPanel* fills the entire space because it doesn't have *Width* and *Height* properties.

## XAML Properties

Properties can modify the appearance of an object. Each object property (attribute) has a value. The value of the attribute is always specified as a string surrounded by quotation marks. The equal sign (=) separates the property name and its value. You can set several properties for an object by separating the properties with spaces.

### Setting simple properties

1. In the opening *<StackPanel>* tag, click between the end of the word *StackPanel* and the closing bracket, and press the Spacebar on your keyboard. The IntelliSense window opens again.

2. Type an H and find the *HorizontalAlignment* property. You can scroll through the list directly and click any item to read its description.

Property
icon

> **Note** The list identifies properties by using a small property icon.

3. Double-click the *HorizontalAlignment* property to insert it into your XAML code.

```
100%
 1  <UserControl
 2      xmlns="http://schemas.microsoft.com/winfx/2006/xaml/presentation"
 3      xmlns:x="http://schemas.microsoft.com/winfx/2006/xaml"
 4      x:Class="CH4.MainPage"
 5      Width="640" Height="480">
 6
 7      <Grid x:Name="LayoutRoot" Background="White">
 8      <StackPanel HorizontalAlignment
 9      <Rectangle
10          Fill="#FF49C2DA" Stroke="Black"
11          Height="100"  Width="100" />
12      <Rectangle
13          Fill="#FF49C2DA" Stroke="Black"
14          Height="100"  Width="100"
15          VerticalAlignment="Top" />
16      </StackPanel>
17      </Grid>
18  </UserControl>
```

The XAML editor underlines the *HorizontalAlignment* property and informs you that there is an error in your code.

**4.** Point to the underlined text. The following message appears: "There is a missing equals ("=") character." To fix the error, type an equal sign (=) and select *Center* from the list of property values.

```
100%
 1  <UserControl
 2      xmlns="http://schemas.microsoft.com/winfx/2006/xaml/presentation"
 3      xmlns:x="http://schemas.microsoft.com/winfx/2006/xaml"
 4      x:Class="CH4.MainPage"
 5      Width="640" Height="480">
 6
 7      <Grid x:Name="LayoutRoot" Background="White">
 8      <StackPanel HorizontalAlignment="
 9      <Rectangle                          Center          Center
10          Fill="#FF49C2DA" Stroke="Black" Left
11          Height="100"  Width="100" />    Right
12      <Rectangle                          Stretch
13          Fill="#FF49C2DA" Stroke="Black"
14          Height="100"  Width="100"
15          VerticalAlignment="Top" />
16      </StackPanel>
17      </Grid>
18  </UserControl>
```

Now your *StackPanel* is horizontally centered.

## Compound Properties

For some object element properties, setting the property and its value directly in line with the tag is not possible, because the object or information necessary to provide the property value cannot be described in a simple string. Instead, you enter these properties as child elements, by using a different syntax known as *property element syntax*, which makes it possible to set compound properties.

For example, the syntax for the *Fill* property of a *Rectangle* object can be described in XAML by using property element syntax, as shown here:

```
<Rectangle  Stroke="Black" Height="100"  Width="100">
    <Rectangle.Fill>
         <SolidColorBrush Color="#FF49C2DA"/>
    </Rectangle.Fill>
</Rectangle>
```

> **Note**  It's not necessary to use property element syntax when assigning a solid color to the *Fill* property as shown here, but if you were, for example, assigning a gradient fill, the property element syntax approach makes more sense.

## Setting compound properties

1. Remove the *Fill="#FF49C2DA"* property from the first *Rectangle*.

2. Remove the */>* symbols from the end of the *<Rectangle>* tag, and type a closing bracket (>). The XAML editor autocompletes this structure by creating a closing *</Rectangle>* tag.

3. Press Enter between the opening and closing tags to create a new empty line.

```
 1  <UserControl
 2      xmlns="http://schemas.microsoft.com/winfx/2006/xaml/presentation"
 3      xmlns:x="http://schemas.microsoft.com/winfx/2006/xaml"
 4      x:Class="CH4.MainPage"
 5      Width="640" Height="480">
 6
 7      <Grid x:Name="LayoutRoot" Background="White">
 8      <StackPanel HorizontalAlignment="Center">
 9      <Rectangle Stroke="Black" Height="100" Width="100">
10
11      </Rectangle>
12      <Rectangle
13          Fill="#FF49C2DA" Stroke="Black"
14          Height="100" Width="100"
15          VerticalAlignment="Top" />
16      </StackPanel>
17      </Grid>
18  </UserControl>
```

4. Type the opening tag **<Rectangle.Fill>** and use autocomplete to create the closing tag, *</Rectangle.Fill>*. Press Enter between the opening and closing tags.

```
 1  <UserControl
 2      xmlns="http://schemas.microsoft.com/winfx/2006/xaml/presentation"
 3      xmlns:x="http://schemas.microsoft.com/winfx/2006/xaml"
 4      x:Class="CH4.MainPage"
 5      Width="640" Height="480">
 6
 7      <Grid x:Name="LayoutRoot" Background="White">
 8      <StackPanel HorizontalAlignment="Center">
 9      <Rectangle Stroke="Black" Height="100" Width="100">
10          <Rectangle.Fill>
11
12          </Rectangle.Fill>
13      </Rectangle>
14      <Rectangle
15          Fill="#FF49C2DA" Stroke="Black"
16          Height="100" Width="100"
17          VerticalAlignment="Top" />
18      </StackPanel>
```

5. Type the tag **<LinearGradientBrush>**. Again, create opening and closing tags, and then insert an empty line between them.

6. Type two **<GradientStop>** tags inside of the *LinearGradientBrush* structure. For the first *GradientStop*, set the *Color* attribute to **#FF6AE6FF** and the *Offset* attribute to **0**; for the second, set the *Color* attribute to **#FF004958** and the *Offset* attribute to **1**.

```
1  <UserControl
2      xmlns="http://schemas.microsoft.com/winfx/2006/xaml/presentation"
3      xmlns:x="http://schemas.microsoft.com/winfx/2006/xaml"
4      x:Class="CH4.MainPage"
5      Width="640" Height="480">
6      |
7      <Grid x:Name="LayoutRoot" Background="White">
8      <StackPanel HorizontalAlignment="Center">
9      <Rectangle Stroke="Black" Height="100"  Width="100">
10         <Rectangle.Fill>
11             <LinearGradientBrush>
12                 <GradientStop Color="#FF6AE6FF" Offset="0"/>
13                 <GradientStop Color="#FF004958" Offset="1"/>
14             </LinearGradientBrush>
15         </Rectangle.Fill>
16     </Rectangle>
```

Visually, the structure you just built inside the *Rectangle* element represents a linear gradient fill that runs from the upper-left corner to the lower-right corner. The gradient brush has two stop points, which you can see in the XAML as child elements of *<LinearGradientBrush>*.

**Tip** You will learn more about the various types of brushes in Chapter 8, "Resources."

# Attached Properties

XAML uses several different programming concepts, one of which is attached properties. Sometimes child elements must inform the parent element how they, the child elements themselves, will be presented inside of parents. The main idea of attached properties is to allow different child elements to specify values for a property that is actually defined by a parent element. The following example will help you understand how this concept works.

## Setting attached properties

1. Change the layout panel for the *Rectangle* elements from *StackPanel* to *Grid*. You can do this directly in the XAML editor by simply modifying the name of the opening and closing tags.

```
100%    ⌄  ƒx ⊞ ⊞ ⇨ ▣  ◄ ────────────────
  6
  7       <Grid x:Name="LayoutRoot" Background="White">
  8       <Grid HorizontalAlignment="Center">
  9         <Rectangle Stroke="Black" Height="100"  Width="100">
 10            <Rectangle.Fill>
 11               <LinearGradientBrush>
 12                  <GradientStop Color="#FF6AE6FF" Offset="0"/>
 13                  <GradientStop Color="#FF004958" Offset="1"/>
 14               </LinearGradientBrush>
 15            </Rectangle.Fill>
 16         </Rectangle>
 17         <Rectangle
 18           Fill="#FF49C2DA" Stroke="Black"
 19           Height="100"  Width="100"
 20           VerticalAlignment="Top" />
 21       </Grid>
 22       </Grid>
```

2. Press Enter before the first *Rectangle* element to create an empty line. Type a **<Grid.RowDefinitions>** tag, and be sure to add its closing tag, **</Grid.RowDefinitions>**.

3. Type two **<RowDefinition />** tags inside the structure you just created.

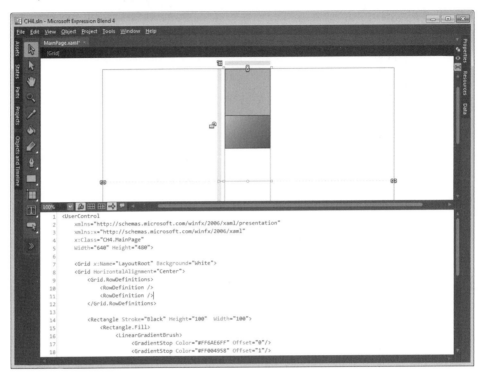

Now your *Grid* has two rows. But both *Rectangle* elements are placed inside the first row by default.

4. By using attached properties, you can specify where your *Rectangle* elements will be defined. Go to the second *Rectangle* and press the Spacebar before the closing />. Type **Grid.** and look at the list of options that IntelliSense suggests.

Because your *Grid* has two rows, it's logical to select the *Row* property.

5. Set the value of the *Row* property to **1**. In the Design pane, you can see that your second *Rectangle* has moved to the second row of the *Grid* layout panel.

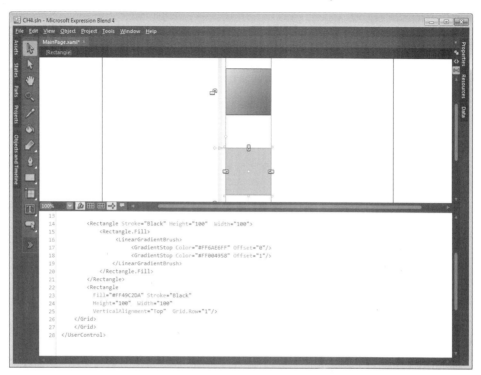

It's convenient to use the attached property *Grid.Row* to specify where your elements are to be placed within the *Grid*. Different attached properties appear in IntelliSense for child elements depending on the type and structure of their parent elements.

As you've seen, for *Grid* child elements, you can set the attached properties *Grid.Row*, *Grid.Column*, *Grid.RowSpan*, and *Grid.ColumnSpan*. Of course, you must define rows and/or columns for the *Grid* layout panel before you can use these attached properties for its child elements.

## The XAML Root Element

Perhaps you've already noticed the XAML root element—*UserControl*. Expression Blend creates this element by default, along with several predefined properties, when you create a new Silverlight project.

```
1  <UserControl
2      xmlns="http://schemas.microsoft.com/winfx/2006/xaml/presentation"
3      xmlns:x="http://schemas.microsoft.com/winfx/2006/xaml"
4      x:Class="CH4.MainPage"
5      Width="640" Height="480">
6
```

Here's a breakdown of the various property settings for the default *UserControl* tag:

- **xmlns="http://schemas.microsoft.com/winfx/2006/xaml/presentation"** This property defines the default XAML namespace, which provides your applications with the core Silverlight elements.

> **Tip** A XAML namespace is simply an extension of the concept of an XML namespace. A namespace provides a way of organizing related objects within a common grouping (a namespace). If you need to define multiple namespaces, each namespace must be uniquely prefaced.

- **xmlns:x="http://schemas.microsoft.com/winfx/2006/xaml"** This is the XAML language namespace. It provides functionality that's common across XAML. The *x* prefix (which appears after the colon, before the equal sign) is a shorthand way to refer to the namespace.

- **x:Class="CH4.MainPage"** This is the partial class declaration that connects markup to any code-behind defined for the partial class. The name of this class depends on the solution (project) name.

## Naming Objects

It's a good practice to name elements clearly—not only to identify them in your Objects And Timeline panel, but also because it gives you unambiguous access to named elements from your code-behind files. You can name your objects through the Objects And Timeline panel, or you can set their names directly in the XAML editor by setting the *x:Name* property value. The following procedure shows how to set or change an object's name in the XAML editor.

### Changing an object's name

1. Press the Spacebar after the object name inside of the *Rectangle* tag without the gradient fill. Add the attribute **x:Name** and set its value (after the equal sign) to **SolidRectangle**. Don't forget the quotation marks around the value.

2. Press F4 to see the corresponding changes in the Objects And Timeline panel.

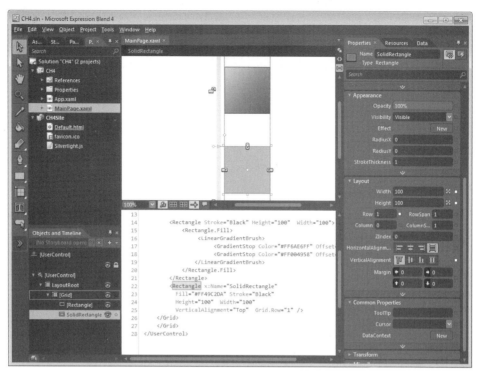

```
13
14          <Rectangle Stroke="Black" Height="100"  Width="100">
15              <Rectangle.Fill>
16                  <LinearGradientBrush>
17                      <GradientStop Color="#FF6AE6FF" Offset
18                      <GradientStop Color="#FF004958" Offset
19                  </LinearGradientBrush>
20              </Rectangle.Fill>
21          </Rectangle>
22          <Rectangle x:Name="SolidRectangle"
23              Fill="#FF49C2DA" Stroke="Black"
24              Height="100"  Width="100"
25              VerticalAlignment="Top"  Grid.Row="1" />
26          </Grid>
27          </Grid>
28 </UserControl>
```

**3.** Set the *x:Name* property for the first *Rectangle* to **GradientRectangle**.

**4.** Delete the *Grid* layout panel with the two rectangles. You don't need them for the rest of the procedures in this chapter. Keep only the *LayoutRoot* as the top layout panel.

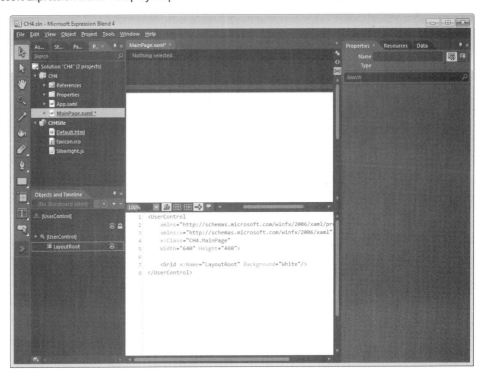

# Introducing C# for Designers

You might have the impression that you can do anything in XAML. But, as mentioned at the beginning of this book, each project needs both designers and developers, and there is a floating boundary between these two roles. Developers need to know about organizing and grouping objects, filling objects with different types of brushes, the basics of animations, and other similar design details. Developers typically do their work directly in the Microsoft Visual Studio XAML editor. Conversely, designers should know about project structure, events, and the basics of programming. When developers and designers each understand a bit about the other discipline, it fosters a more productive relationship between them.

It's important to understand what can and can't be done in XAML. You can use XAML to:

- Design the user interface of your application by adding objects, grouping them into panels, and transforming them in various ways.

- Create amazing animations for your objects.

- Add audio and video content to your project.

- Trigger the playing of animation timelines, audio files, and video files from user actions such as clicking a player's buttons or pointing to an object.

- Add interactivity to your application by using behaviors.

- Design custom user controls, such as voting controls, custom sliders, progress bars, and similar controls.

- Create reusable style templates and resources.

- Bind a property of an object to a value contained in another property.

Developers use C# (and other .NET languages that are not discussed here because the concepts are essentially identical) to build desktop and web applications. As you'd expect, there are some tasks that they (and you) can do only in C#:

- Write logic for an application.

- Define more complicated behaviors in event handlers that fire when a user interacts with elements of the user interface.

- Create new behaviors as pieces of packaged code that can be dragged onto any object and then customized by changing the properties.

- Create new custom controls, such as voting controls, custom sliders, progress bars, and similar controls.

- Customize the behavior of existing controls.

- Create elements or set their properties dynamically.

- Work with data from databases, such as Microsoft SQL Server.

So what is C#? It's a very popular object-oriented programming (OOP) language from the .NET family of languages developed by Microsoft. OOP is a programming methodology that defines the components of an application as objects that have properties and methods (functions) that are applied to them. The main purpose of this paradigm is to allow developers to build flexible applications that can be easily extended and modified. It doesn't matter which objects you operate: rectangles, images, buttons, windows, or abstract objects—with OOP, you don't need to fully rewrite the functionality and methods of your applications if you decide to substitute one object for another as your project progresses.

## Objects, Classes, and Other Terminology

Objects are not the only OOP concept that you need to be familiar with. *Class* is another, more abstract construct that is used as a template to create individual objects of that class. An object that belongs to a particular class is called an *instance* of that class. To keep these straight, you can think along these lines:

- Abstract definition: If *Cat* is a class, then the individual cat object *Tom* would be a representative of the *Cat* class.

- Abstract definition: If *Bike* is a class, then an object that represents your own bicycle would be an instance of the *Bike* class.

- Abstract Definition: The classes *Button*, *Rectangle*, *StackPanel*, *HitButton*, *HugeRectangle*, *VStackpanel*, for example, each have objects that you can include in your application.

In OOP terms, your Silverlight application consists of default .NET classes and custom classes created by application developers.

Developers also describe the properties and methods of classes. You can think of properties as *characteristics*; for example:

- Class *Cat* has characteristics such as color and type of fur.

- Class *Bike* has characteristics such as color, number of wheels, intended purpose, and number of gears.

- *Button* and *Rectangle* classes have now-familiar properties such as *Width*, *Height*, and *Margin*; the *StackPanel* class has an *Orientation* property.

Similarly, you can think of methods as behaviors that are common to all future objects that will be created from these classes. A method can be called one or many times, depending on its purpose:

- Think of *Meow*, *Chase*, *Sleep*, and *Touch* as methods for a *Cat* class. Each specific cat has these behaviors.

- The methods *Roll*, *Jump*, and *Park* could be appropriate methods for a *Bike* class.

- Because buttons can receive the input focus, *Focus* is an appropriate method for the *Button* class.

There is also a special type of method named *constructor* that is called when you create a new instance (a new object) of a class. It is used for the basic initialization of an object. You will see it in an example later in this chapter.

Classes also use *inheritance* in OOP. A class can be a child of another class and have children classes of its own. A class gains, or *inherits*, all of the characteristics of its parent. For example, the parent class *Cat* can have child classes *WildCat*, *SiameseCat*, and *PersianCat*. Each of these subspecies has and inherits all characteristics from its parent and is basically a *Cat*. Of course, subclasses can have their own properties and methods that their parent doesn't have. Also, this basic example can be widened by thinking about superclasses. Imagine that the *Cat* class also has a parent *Feline* class that has the derived classes *Cat*, *Tiger*, *Lion*, and *Lynx*.

In addition to objects, classes, properties, and methods, there is yet another interesting C# term that you should be familiar with: the *event*. An event is an action that can occur. It's usually initiated outside your application code, perhaps by a user, and can be handled by a piece of code inside the application. Here are some possible events:

- For a *Cat*, *Touching* and *Touched*

- *Riding*, *Stopped*, and *Stopping* for a *Bike*

- *Click*, *MouseEnter*, *MouseLeave*, and *GotFocus* for a *Button*

Methods created expressly to respond to these events are called *event handlers*. You can write code inside of event handlers to respond to the various events that can occur in your application. For example, it's easy to write an event handler that makes an initially hidden rectangle (or other object) become visible when a user moves the mouse over a specific area, to rearrange a set of objects vertically or horizontally when a user clicks the appropriate button, or launch a video or animation immediately after an application loads.

## XAML Code and Code-Behind Files

You can find C# code in the code-behind files for your project. These files are paired with XAML documents, have a .cs extension, and contain the logic that the document performs. You can use code-behind files to add code to control existing objects in your XAML file or to create new ones dynamically. It's easy to write code that will respond to different events, such as "when the user clicks a button, a rectangle appears," or "when the application loads, start this animation and change the background color smoothly." Basically, you use event handlers to make your application respond to user input and application changes. And the code that makes this interactivity happen will be in the code-behind files.

### Inspecting the structure of code-behind files in your project

1. Expand the arrow near the MainPage.xaml file of the CH4 project in the Projects panel.

2. Double-click the MainPage.xaml.cs file and take a look at the top.

   This file provides the default UI for your application. As you can see, there are several *using* statements at the beginning of the C# code-behind file that reference the needed namespaces. The Microsoft .NET Framework uses namespaces to organize its many classes. This section of *using* lines lists the namespaces that the application will be using frequently and saves the developer from having to specify a fully qualified name every time.

```
CH4.sln - Microsoft Expression Blend 4
File  Edit  View  Object  Project  Tools  Window  Help

Assets  States  Projects ×        MainPage.xaml.cs ×   MainPage.xaml        Properties ×  Resources  Data
Search                       1   using System;                              Name
Solution "CH4" (2 projects)  2   using System.Windows;                      Type
  CH4                        3   using System.Windows.Controls;
    References               4   using System.Windows.Documents;        Search
    Properties               5   using System.Windows.Ink;
    App.xaml                 6   using System.Windows.Input;
      App.xaml.cs            7   using System.Windows.Media;
    MainPage.xaml            8   using System.Windows.Media.Animation;
      MainPage.xaml.cs       9   using System.Windows.Shapes;
  CH4Site                    10
    ClientBin                11  namespace CH4
    Default.html             12  {
    favicon.ico              13      public partial class MainPage : UserControl
    Silverlight.js           14      {
                             15          public MainPage()
                             16          {
Objects and Timeline         17              // Required to initialize variables
(No Storyboard open)         18              InitializeComponent();
                             19
                             20
                             21          }
                             22      }
                             23  }
```

3. Look at the line *namespace CH4*.

   The *namespace* keyword is used to declare a *scope*—in this case, the namespace *CH4*. Declaring your own namespaces lets you organize code and can help control the scope of class and method names in larger programming projects. By default, the name of your project and your project namespace in .cs files are the same. You can define your own classes inside the curly brackets that delimit the namespace.

4. Look at the line *public partial class MainPage : UserControl*.

   Classes can inherit from other classes. This line defines a custom *MainPage* class that inherits from the *UserControl* class.

5. Look at the line *public MainPage()*.

   This line defines a built-in method that will act as the constructor of the class. Notice that it has the same name as the top class. This method will be called when an instance of that class is created.

   The last line in the code, *InitializeComponent()*, is a method call used to set everything up. If you want to set custom property values or call methods when the application starts, you should add your code after that line.

## Creating Objects in C#

Now that you've had an introduction to the code-behind file, you should understand that any object you create in XAML can also be, and in fact is, created in the C# code-behind file and added to the workspace. Earlier, as you created rectangles and organized them with various panels, you could have accomplished the same tasks, and much more, by writing C# code.

### Adding objects from XAML and C#

1. Open the MainPage.xaml document in Split view.

2. Expand the *LayoutRoot Grid* so that it has a starting *<Grid>* tag, an empty line for content, and a closing *</Grid>* tag after the empty line.

3. Add the following code to your document inside of *LayoutRoot Grid*:

```
<Rectangle x:Name="SolidRectangle" Height="100"
    Width="100" Fill="LightBlue"  HorizontalAlignment="Left" />
```

This XAML code creates a light blue *Rectangle* that is horizontally aligned to the left inside of the *LayoutRoot* layout panel. You can test and view your application by pressing F5.

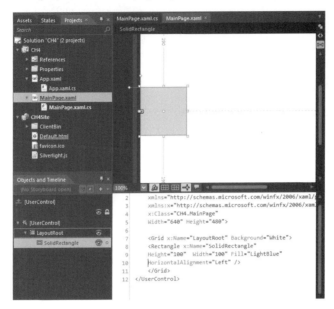

4. Open MainPage.xaml.cs and add the following code inside of the *MainPage()* constructor:

```
Rectangle SolidRectangle2 = new Rectangle();
SolidRectangle2.Width = 100;
SolidRectangle2.Height = 100;

SolidColorBrush myBrush = new SolidColorBrush(Colors.Orange);
SolidRectangle2.Fill = myBrush;

LayoutRoot.Children.Add(SolidRectangle2);
```

```
CH4.sln - Microsoft Expression Blend 4
File  Edit  View  Object  Project  Tools  Window  Help

Assets  States  Projects ×        MainPage.xaml.cs ×   MainPage.xaml
Search                          1   using System;
                                2   using System.Windows;
Solution "CH4" (2 projects)     3   using System.Windows.Controls;
  CH4                           4   using System.Windows.Documents;
    References                  5   using System.Windows.Ink;
    Properties                  6   using System.Windows.Input;
    App.xaml                    7   using System.Windows.Media;
      App.xaml.cs               8   using System.Windows.Media.Animation;
    MainPage.xaml               9   using System.Windows.Shapes;
      MainPage.xaml.cs         10
  CH4Site                      11   namespace CH4
    ClientBin                  12   {
    Default.html               13       public partial class MainPage : UserControl
    favicon.ico                14       {
    Silverlight.js             15           public MainPage()
                               16           {
                               17               // Required to initialize variables
Objects and Timeline           18               InitializeComponent();
(No Storyboard open)           19
                               20               Rectangle SolidRectangle2 = new Rectangle();
                               21               SolidRectangle2.Width = 100;
                               22               SolidRectangle2.Height = 100;
                               23
                               24               SolidColorBrush myBrush = new SolidColorBrush(Colors.Orange);
                               25               SolidRectangle2.Fill = myBrush;
                               26
                               27               LayoutRoot.Children.Add(SolidRectangle2);
                               28
                               29
                               30           }
                               31       }
                               32   }
```

 **Note** Make sure to add this code *inside* the curly brackets.

The C# code you just added creates a *Rectangle* similar to the one you added in XAML, but with a different name, color, and default alignment. When you add it, nothing seems to happen in the visual representation of your MainPage.xaml file. Run the project and you'll see both rectangles: the one you created in XAML and another that you just created in C#.

Examine the code you just added:

❑ The first line, *Rectangle SolidRectangle2 = new Rectangle();*, creates a new object of class *Rectangle* with name *SolidRectangle2*.

❑ The second and third lines set the *Width* and *Height* properties of this rectangle to *100*.

❑ The fourth line of code creates a new object named *myBrush*, which is an instance of the *SolidColorBrush* class, and assigns it the color *Orange* by using a parameter. Notice that the *SolidColorBrush(Colors.Orange)* in the right part of this line is a method constructor. Constructors can be parametric and have specific values as parameters to create objects with different initial states.

❑ The next line of code fills the rectangle by using the new brush.

❑ The last line adds the just-created rectangle as a child of the *LayoutRoot* root layout panel so that you can see it when your application is run.

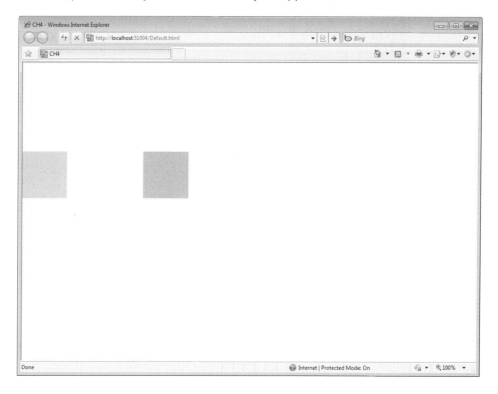

**5.** Now try changing the alignment of the light blue rectangle (the one you created in XAML) from C# code. After the line in which you added the rectangle as a child element of *LayoutRoot*, add this line:

```
SolidRectangle.HorizontalAlignment = System.Windows.HorizontalAlignment.Right;
```

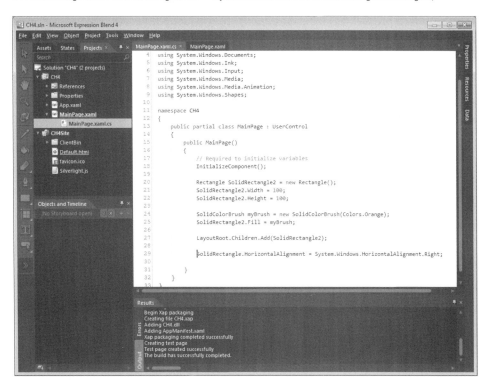

By adding this line, you change the value of the *HorizontalAlignment* property of the *SolidRectangle* object to *Right*. Press F5 to see the result.

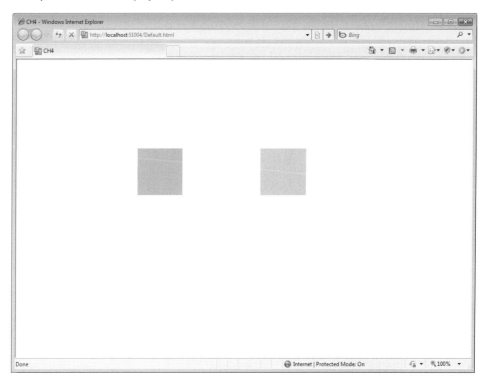

As you can see, you can use C# code to create objects and change the properties of existing objects, whether you originally created those objects in XAML or in C# code.

## Using Event Handlers

Users will interact with your application by clicking buttons, scrolling lists, expanding blocks, entering values into fields, dragging objects from one place to another, and more. All of these actions are called *events*. As discussed earlier, it's possible to respond to any (or all) of these events by using specific methods called *event handlers*. For example, you can respond to events by opening new pages, hiding or showing content, or loading new data. You can even configure your application so that it responds to changes in the application state itself.

With Expression Blend, you can add event handler methods easily in the Events view of the Properties panel. When you add an event handler, Expression Blend generates *stub code*, which is an empty method. Then you just need to add the specific code that determines what happens when the method fires.

### Adding an event handler

1. Add a button to the *LayoutRoot Grid* by double-clicking the *Button* object in the Tools panel.

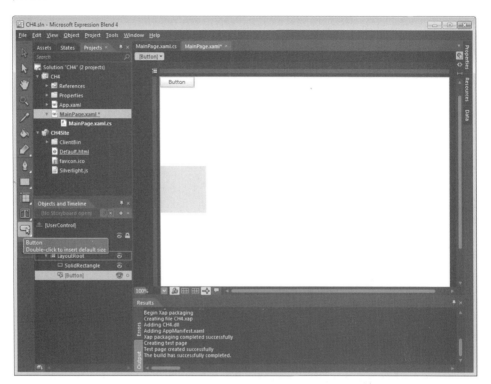

2. Double-click the *Button* object in the Tools panel again to add a second button.

3. Select both buttons in the Objects And Timeline panel. From the Object menu, choose Group Into, and then click the *StackPanel*.

4. Select the first button, and set the value of its *Content* property to **Hide** through the Properties panel. At the top of the Properties panel, set the name of this button to **Hide** as well.

5. Select the second button, and set the value of its *Content* property to **Show** through the Properties panel. Set its name to **Show** as well.

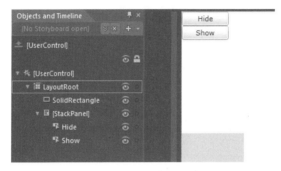

6. Select the *Hide* button, and switch the view of your Properties panel from Properties to Events.

A list of all available events for the selected button appears.

7. Find the *Click* event in the events list. You don't need to specify the name for an event handler (although you can); instead, just double-click the text box beside the *Click* event. Expression Blend will automatically generate a default name for your event handler method, place that name in the text box, and generate the stub code for the new empty method, which in this case is named *Hide_Click*.

Expression Blend switches the active document to MainPage.xaml.cs, and you can begin to add code to your method.

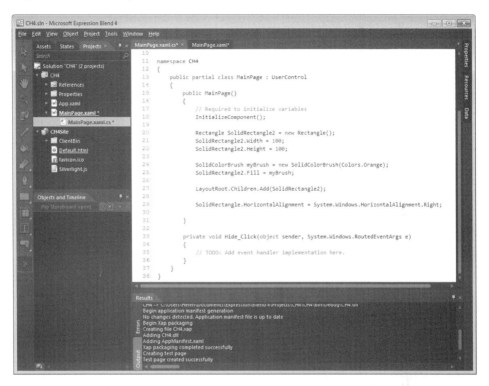

8. Set your cursor after the *TODO:* comment, and then press Enter to create an empty line.

9. Type **SolidRectangle**. You can see that the autocompleting IntelliSense feature works here, too. Type **.v** and select the *Visibility* property from the list.

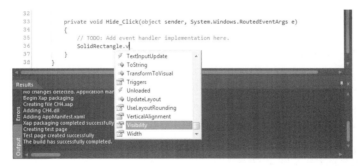

10. Type = and use the autocomplete feature to finish the line, which should now read:

```
SolidRectangle.Visibility = System.Windows.Visibility.Collapsed;
```

**Note** Don't forget to type the semicolon (**;**) at the end of the line.

11. Press F5 to run your application.

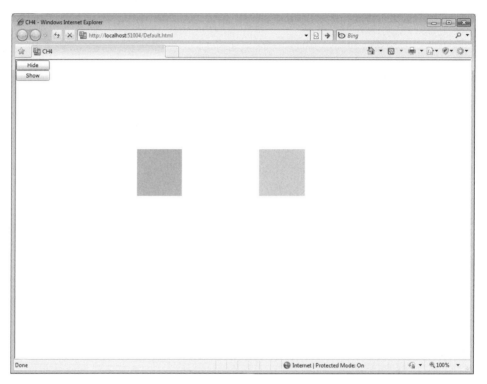

12. Click the *Hide* button to see how it works. The light blue rectangle should disappear. You just asked the *Hide* button to listen for the *Click* event and respond by running code in the *Hide_Click* event handler method. Your code for this method changes the value of the rectangle's *Visibility* property to *Collapsed*.

   Next you need to do the opposite action: show the rectangle when a user clicks the *Show* button.

13. Return to Expression Blend. Open MainPage.xaml and select the second button, the one named *Show*.

14. Make sure that Events view is active, and then double-click the text box beside the *Click* event in the Properties panel. Expression Blend creates a *Show_Click* event handler method and switches back to MainPage.xaml.cs.

```
32
33          private void Hide_Click(object sender, System.Windows.RoutedEventArgs e)
34          {
35              // TODO: Add event handler implementation here.
36              SolidRectangle.Visibility = System.Windows.Visibility.Collapsed;
37          }
38
39          private void Show_Click(object sender, System.Windows.RoutedEventArgs e)
40          {
41              // TODO: Add event handler implementation here.
42          }
43      }
44  }
```

**15.** Copy and paste the line you typed in the previous method to the body of the new *Show_Click* method.

**16.** After copying the line, change the last value from *Collapsed* to **Visible**.

```
32
33          private void Hide_Click(object sender, System.Windows.RoutedEventArgs e)
34          {
35              // TODO: Add event handler implementation here.
36              SolidRectangle.Visibility = System.Windows.Visibility.Collapsed;
37          }
38
39          private void Show_Click(object sender, System.Windows.RoutedEventArgs e)
40          {
41              // TODO: Add event handler implementation here.
42              SolidRectangle.Visibility = System.Windows.Visibility.Visible;
43          }
44      }
```

**17.** Run your application again by pressing F5. Click the *Hide* and then the *Show* button to see how the rectangle disappears and reappears.

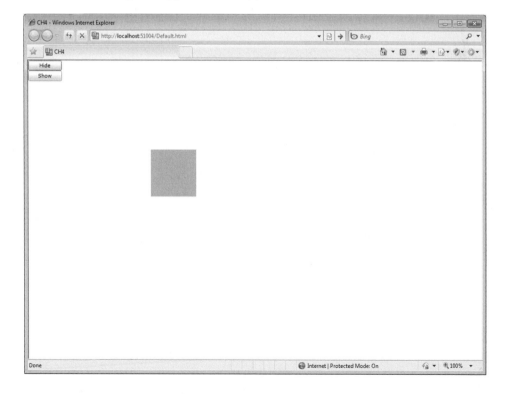

At this point, you have had a basic introduction to C# and have received a very small introduction to the possibilities inherent in objects, classes, events, and event handlers. More importantly, you now know that you can control the behavior and appearance of the objects in your project.

# Key Points

- XAML stands for Extensible Application Markup Language.

- Use XAML view to make changes to the XAML code files in your projects.

- Customize the XAML editor by using the Code editor tab in the Options dialog box.

- Use properties to modify the appearance of your XAML objects.

- Attached properties allow child elements to specify unique values for a property that is actually defined in a parent element.

- Name your objects appropriately to identify them easily and simplify access to them from code-behind files.

- C# is a very popular object-oriented programming (OOP) language from the .NET family of languages developed by Microsoft.

- OOP is a programming methodology that operates on objects with properties and methods (functions).

- Each C# code-behind file is paired with a XAML document, has a .cs extension, and contains the logic that the document performs.

- From C# code, you can create XAML objects and change the properties of existing objects.

- A *class* is a code construct used as a template to create objects of that class.

- An object of a particular class is called an *instance* of the class.

- An *event* is an action that can occur, often initiated outside of your application, that can be handled with code in a method inside your application called an *event handler*.

- With Expression Blend, you can easily add event handler methods through the Events view of the Properties panel by generating stub code for empty event handler methods.

# Chapter 5
# Animations and Transformations

**After completing this chapter, you will be able to:**

- Resize UI elements.

- Scale, rotate, skew, and translate your objects.

- Change the center point of an object.

- Flip objects.

- Simulate three-dimensional space via projection.

- Add storyboards.

- Use timelines and keyframes.

- Add animations and change object properties over time.

- Modify storyboards.

- Apply behaviors and run storyboards in response to events.

Transformations and animations are two great features in Microsoft Expression Blend 4 that allow you to create amazing effects in your user interface. These tools provide powerful capabilities that enable you to move, resize, scale, rotate, and transform objects in both simple and complex ways. Transformations modify the rendering of an element while maintaining its original values. Animations serve to make your applications more interesting, natural, and lively. Transformations and animations can work everywhere—in games as well as in educational, developmental, and business applications.

 **Important** Before you can complete the exercises in this chapter, you need to install the down-loadable practice files to their default location. For more information about practice files, see the instructions at the beginning of this book.

# Transformation

In Chapter 3, "Designing an Interface," you saw how to draw elements and move and reposition them on the Artboard. Transformation opens up a new world of expressive possibilities. In this chapter, you'll discover transformations such as scaling, rotating, skewing, translating, flipping, and more.

## Resizing (Not a Transformation)

Resizing is the simplest way to change the size of an object—you just change its *Width* and *Height* properties. You might have noticed that when you select an element you can directly change its size on the Artboard. It would seem logical that resizing is a type of transformation; however, that's not the case. Resizing changes only the dimensions of the object (its *Width* and *Height*) and doesn't apply a transformation.

**Note**  Use the CH5 sample project from the CH5 folder located in the \Sample Projects folder.

### Resizing objects

1. Click Open Project/Solution on the File menu. The Open Project dialog box appears. Click Browse, browse to the CH5 folder in the practice files for this book, and then double-click the CH5.sln file.

   Solution files always have an *.sln* extension.

2. Click the Project panel for the solution. In the folder list for the CH5 project, double-click the MainPage.xaml file.

3. In the Objects And Timeline panel, click *LayoutRoot*. You'll see two visible objects: a simple bush and a complex tank.

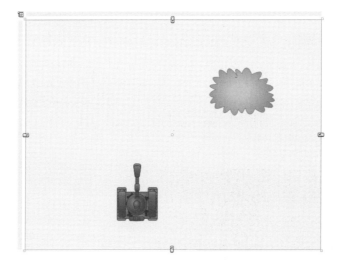

The document's visual tree also includes one hidden complex element called *sand*.

**4.** Select the *bush* object with the Selection tool, and then click the object on the Artboard. On the Artboard, point to one of the corner handles or midpoint handles of the *bush* object until the pointer becomes a double-ended arrow, and then drag the pointer to change the size of the object until its width is 150 and its height is 120.

> **Tip**  You can hold down the Shift key to constrain the proportions of the object when resizing it. Holding down the Alt key maintains the object's center point.
>
> You can also change an object's size by using the Layout category in the Properties panel. You do so by entering values in the *Width* or *Height* field.

You've now seen how to resize an object; but if resizing isn't a transformation, how does a real transformation work? Expression Blend applies transformations by using specific *transform properties*. To transform a user interface element, you need to specify which transformation Expression Blend should use by setting the *RenderTransform* property.

# Transformations

Expression Blend provides the following two-dimensional transformations:

- **RotateTransform**   Rotates an element by the specified angle
- **ScaleTransform**   Scales an element by the specified *ScaleX* and *ScaleY* values
- **SkewTransform**   Skews an element by the specified *AngleX* and *AngleY* values
- **TranslateTransform**   Moves an element by the specified *X* and *Y* values

Microsoft Silverlight 4, for example, includes a new feature, a class called *CompositeTransform*, which lets you easily apply multiple transformations such as scale, rotate, skew, or translate to an object. For example, to simply scale an object, you use the *CompositeTransform* to change its size based on a multiple of its initial *X* and *Y* values.

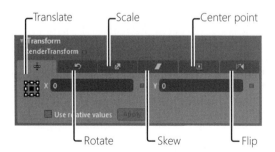

## Scale Transformation

Scaling is another way to change the size of an object.

### Applying a scale transformation

1. Select the *bush* object.

2. In the Properties panel, under the Transform category, click the Scale tab.

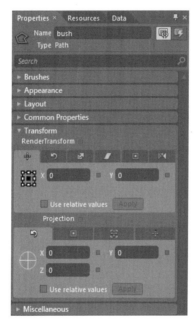

3. When the numerical adjust cursor appears near the *X* property field, drag to scroll through the values. You'll see the changes reflected on the Artboard. Set both the *ScaleX* and *ScaleY* properties to 0.8. Notice that the *Width* and *Height* properties don't change. You can also see this in the Layout category in the Properties panel.

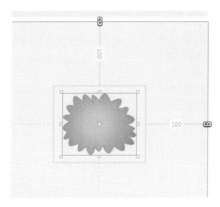

# Rotate Transformation

You can easily rotate your object through a full 360 degrees (from -180 degrees to +180 degrees) in two ways: by manipulating the object directly on the Artboard or by using the Rotate tab to rotate the object.

### Applying a rotate transformation

1. Select the *bush* object.

2. In the Properties panel, under Transform, click the Rotate tab.

3. Rotate the object to a 30-degree angle by dragging the pointer on the small circular diagram.

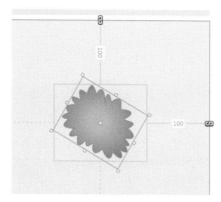

# Skew Transformation

Another type of transformation, *skewing*, allows you to distort an object by a specified angle from an x or y axis. It's also possible to use skewing to simulate three-dimensional effects.

### Applying a skew transformation

1. Select the *bush* object.

2. In the Properties panel, under Transform, click the Skew tab.

3. When the numerical adjust cursor appears near the *Y* property field, scroll through the values. Set the *Skew-Y* property to -30. Notice that it's possible to set negative values. Look at the result on the Artboard.

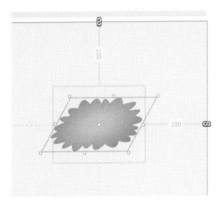

## Translate Transformation

Translation is another interesting transformation that you can apply to your objects. A translate transformation moves an object in a two-dimensional plane from one position to another. The result is that the object is offset from its original position.

### Applying a translate transformation

1. Select the *bush* object.

2. In the Properties panel, under Transform, click the first tab, which is the Translate tab.

**3.** When the numerical adjust cursor appears near the *Y* property field, drag to scroll through the values. Set the *Translate-X* property to -30. Look at the result on the Artboard. Positive *Translate-X* values cause the object to move right on the screen, and negative values move it to the left. In the same way, positive *Translate-Y* values cause the object to move down the screen, and negative values move it up the screen.

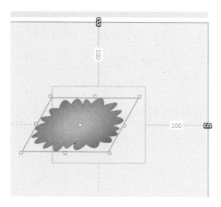

**Tip** If you don't like the result of a transformation, you can reset any value by clicking the Advanced Options icon, which appears beside the *X, Y,* or *Angle* field as a small white box, and then clicking Reset. You can also reset all properties by clicking the Advanced Options icon beside the *RenderTransform* label and then clicking Reset.

## Center Point Transformation

The fifth tab of the Transform category helps you adjust a center point for other transformations. The center point is the fixed point around which an object rotates. By default, an object's center point is located at the object's center, but sometimes you need to rotate it in a different way.

### Altering the center point

**1.** Select the second cartoon object (*tank*) by clicking on it in the Objects And Timeline panel. On the Artboard, Expression Blend marks the object's center point with a small white circle.

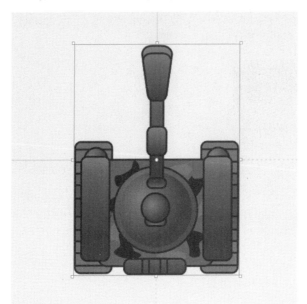

**2.** Point to one of the corner handles of the *tank* object's bounding box until the pointer becomes a rotation handle, and then, while holding down the Shift key, drag the handle to rotate the *tank* to a 30-degree angle. As you can see, it looks like the *tank* rotates around the muzzle, which is not the most natural rotation for a tank.

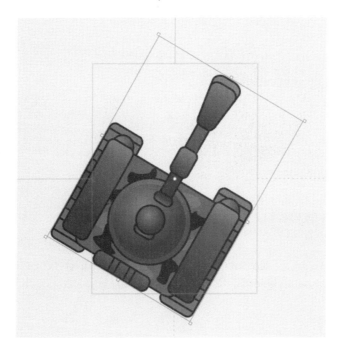

3. Press Ctrl+Z to undo the last rotation operation. In the Properties panel, under Transform, click the Center Point tab.

4. Set the *Center-X* property to 0.5 and the *Center-Y* property to 0.7, which should move the center point to roughly the center of the *tank* object's turret.

5. Use the same technique as in Step 2 to rotate the *tank* to a 30-degree angle. Do you see the difference? Now the center point is located at the center of the *tank* object's mass.

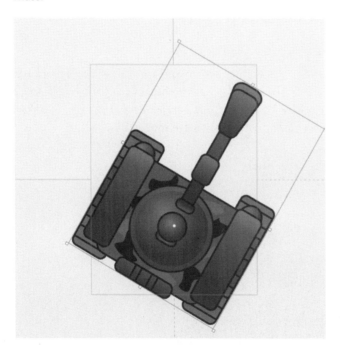

## Flip Transformation

The last tab, Flip, allows you to flip objects along their x and/or y axes. Flipping objects is useful when you want to turn an object by 180 degrees or add a duplicated mirror object.

## Applying a flip transformation

1. Select the *tank* by clicking on it in the Objects And Timeline panel.

2. In the Properties panel, under Transform, click the Flip tab.

*Flip X Axis*

3. Flip the *tank* horizontally by clicking Flip X Axis.

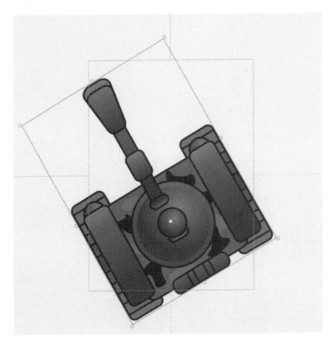

The Flip tab makes the task of scaling objects easier. In fact, flipping the *tank* converts its scale value to the *negative* of the original scale value. (If you click the Scale tab, you'll see that the scale value in the *X* field was changed to *-1* after you clicked the Flip X Axis button.)

## Simulating Three-Dimensional Space via Projection

There is no real three-dimensional space for Silverlight projects; however, you can simulate it by using an interesting type of transformation—projection. Projection lets you modify the *X*, *Y*, and *Z* projection properties of an element, which creates the appearance of rotating the object in three-dimensional space.

### Using projection to simulate three-dimensional space

1. Reset all transformations you created by clicking the Advanced Options icon beside the *RenderTransform* label and then clicking Reset. Make sure to keep the *tank* selected on the Artboard.

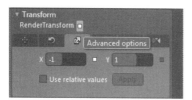

Notice the tooltip produced by pointing to the Advanced Options button.

2. In the lower part of the Transform category, under Projection, click the Rotation tab.

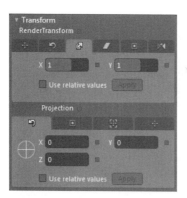

3. Drag the projection ball to the left of the axis fields to change the values. Note how the *tank* rotates around the x, y, and z axes.

4. You can also directly change the *X*, *Y*, and *Z* angles, and you can define the three-dimensional center of rotation. To do the latter, click the second tab, Center Of Rotation. Set the *Y* property to 0.7.

5. Click the Rotation tab. Set the *X* property to 50, Y to -5, and Z to -20.

*Eye icon*

6. In the Objects And Timeline panel, select the *sand* object that is hidden on the Artboard. You can show it by clicking the eye icon. Make it visible by setting the *Visibility* property to *Visible* under the Appearance category in the Properties panel.

Now your *tank* looks like it's stuck in a sand hole because of the visible, grain-oriented background and the plane projection. These transformations should give you some idea of how to simulate three-dimensional space.

You will be working with animation in the next section of this chapter, so reset all transformations to start from the beginning again.

7. Select the *bush* in the Objects And Timeline panel. Click the Advanced Options icon beside the *RenderTransform* label, and then click Reset.

8. Select the *tank* in the Objects And Timeline panel. Click the Advanced Options icon beside the *Projection* label, and then click Reset.

# Animation

When most people hear the word *animation*, they think of cartoons, but animations have a wider range of applications. In fact, animation is simply the rapid display of a sequence of images in order to create an illusion of movement. Objects can change their color, size, or opacity independently over time. They can even interact with the user and with other objects in response to actions while the animation is playing—and that might be the most interesting aspect of animation.

There are various traditional techniques for creating movement, and several types of computer animation. Expression Blend introduces animation based on *keyframes*. Keyframes define start points and end points for a smooth visual transition. A specific container type called a *storyboard* holds animation timelines in Expression Blend. In the storyboard, you specify keyframes on a timeline to mark property changes, such as color and size changes, as you're creating the animation, and you can run the animation storyboard to see how it works and make adjustments. You can also control when, where, and how your storyboard runs.

# Creating a Storyboard and Adding an Animation

The Expression Blend Objects And Timeline panel can contain a list of storyboards.

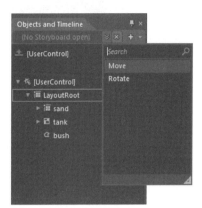

As you saw in Chapter 2, "Exploring the Expression Blend 4 IDE," the Expression Blend workspace is very compact and consists of a large number of collapsible features. The Objects And Timeline panel includes the *Storyboard Picker, a control* that is used for creating and managing storyboards.

## Adding a storyboarded animation

1. Although you had a brief introduction to the Animation workspace earlier in this book, you've worked primarily with the Design workspace. However, the most comfortable way of working with animations is to switch Expression Blend to the Animation workspace. From the Window menu, select Workspaces, and then choose Animation. Your workspace changes from Design to Animation.

2. In the Objects And Timeline panel, click New (the plus sign near the top). The Create Storyboard Resource dialog box opens.

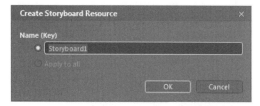

3. In the Name (Key) field, type **Moving** as a name for the new storyboard, and then click OK. The new storyboard opens in recording mode, and the Objects And Timeline panel expands to include a timeline. Also, you'll see the Recorder Indicator—shown as a red outline around the Artboard.

4. In the Objects And Timeline panel, select the *tank*.

5. In the bottom part of the timeline, change the Zoom to **200%**. Zooming lets you view the contents at a more detailed scale.

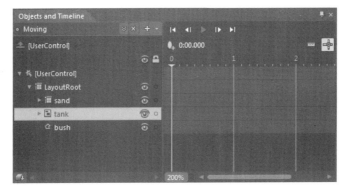

6. On the timeline, drag the play head (the yellow vertical line) to the one-second point in the timeline. The timeline displays time in seconds.

*Record
Keyframe*

**7.** Click the Record Keyframe icon to record the changes to the selected object at the one-second mark. A keyframe is a marker on the timeline that indicates when a property change occurs. After you click the Record Keyframe icon, the keyframe appears on the timeline in the row that corresponds to the *tank*.

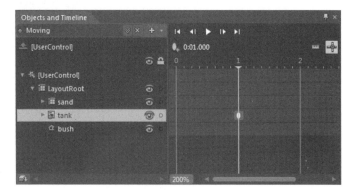

**8.** Change the vertical position of the *tank* by setting its *Y* property to **-280** on the Translate tab in the Properties panel, under the Transform category.

> **Tip** You can quickly add a keyframe by dragging the play head to the desired point in time and changing a property of the selected object, such as its position, color, or size. A keyframe automatically appears on the timeline to record the property change.

*Play*

**9.** Test your animation by clicking the Play button in the timeline. Watch how the *tank* rapidly moves upward from its original position.

*Close
button*

To close a storyboard, you click the Close button in the storyboard picker on the Objects And Timeline panel.

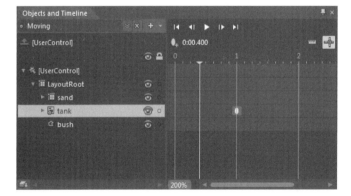

**10.** Close the storyboard now, and switch back to your Design workspace by pressing F6.

> **Note** If you run your project now by pressing F5, you won't see the animation. That's because, so far, you have created only a storyboard. To make it run, you need to add some actions to start it.

# Controlling the Storyboard

There is an easier way to control storyboards—by using *behaviors*. Think about behaviors as reusable snippets of interactivity that you can apply to any element on your Artboard by using simple drag actions. You can use behaviors for many tasks, such as setting properties, running animations, and navigating between screens. Developers might also write their own behaviors for controlling interactivity.

You will learn more about this in the next chapter, "Adding Interactivity." For now, your first step toward learning behaviors will be to start an animation.

### Adding a behavior to start an animation

1. Click on Behaviors in the Assets panel.

2. From the Behaviors category in the Assets panel, find the *ControlStoryboardAction* item.

3. Drag the *ControlStoryboardAction* behavior onto the *bush* object on the Artboard or the *bush* item in the Objects And Timeline panel. The behavior appears as a child of the *bush* item in the Objects And Timeline panel.

When you added this new element, some changes occurred in the Properties panel. It now contains Trigger, Conditions, and Common Properties sections, and there are several properties set to default values. In Silverlight, an application's animation plays in response to an event, which you define by using an event trigger. As an example, suppose that you want the *tank* to move when a user clicks the mouse button while pointing to the *bush*. You have an action, the *tank* movement, and an event trigger that causes this action to happen, the click of the mouse button. By default, when you apply the *ControlStoryboardAction* to graphic elements, Expression Blend selects the *MouseLeftButtonDown* event by default. You just need to set an action in response or choose the name of an animation to play after the event occurs.

   **4.** In the Common Properties section, set the *Storyboard* property to **Moving**.

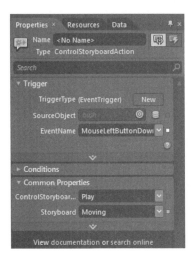

**5.** Run the project by pressing F5, and click the mouse button while pointing to the *bush*. The *tank* moves!

 **Tip** Another way to control storyboards in Silverlight applications is to create an event handler method in a code-behind file that, in turn, calls such methods as *Begin*, *Stop*, or *Pause*.

## Changing the Storyboard

Sometimes having only one moving object or animation on a page doesn't produce much of an impression. You might want to control animation repetition, auto-reverse an animation, or add some other effect. To create such changes, you need to go back to editing the storyboard.

### Editing an existing storyboard

*Open A Storyboard*

**1.** To select a storyboard to edit, click the Open A Storyboard icon in the Objects And Timeline panel.

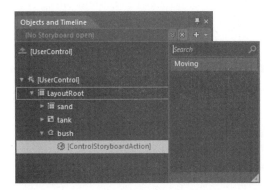

2. Click the storyboard named *Moving* so that the name is highlighted. The Properties panel now displays the common properties that you can set for the whole storyboard.

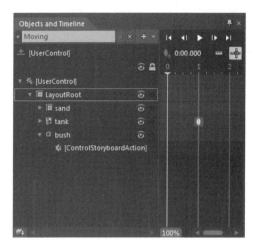

 **Troubleshooting** Storyboard properties appear in the Properties panel only when the storyboard name is highlighted in the Objects And Timeline panel.

3. Among the common storyboard properties are the *RepeatBehavior* and *AutoReverse* properties. Select the Forever option from the RepeatBehavior list, and select the AutoReverse check box.

4. Run the project by pressing F5, and click the mouse button while pointing to the *bush*. Your *tank* now moves up and down repeatedly!

## Modifying an Animation and Adding New Keyframes

At this point, your project has an animation. You can now add some interactivity. Unfortunately, the tank currently moves in an unnatural way and needs several improvements in its motion. Suppose you wanted to add a 180-degree turn to the animation. To add that behavior, you'll need to modify the animation.

## Modifying an animation

1. To modify your animation, go to the Objects And Timeline panel and click Open A Storyboard to view the storyboards that are in scope. The Storyboard Picker appears.

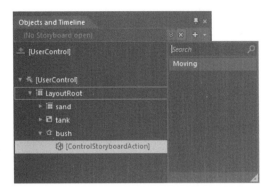

2. Select the Moving storyboard from the Storyboard Picker.

3. Press F6 to switch to the Animation workspace.

4. Click the Moving storyboard in the Objects And Timeline panel so that the name is highlighted, and clear the *AutoReverse* check box in the Properties panel.

5. Select the *tank* in the Objects And Timeline panel, and drag the play head on the time-line to the two-second point in time.

6. Click the Record Keyframe icon to record the object at the two-second mark.

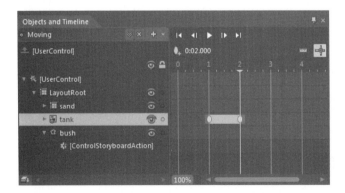

7. Click the Center Point tab in the Properties panel under the Transform category, and ensure that *X* is set to 0.5 and *Y* is set to 0.7.

**Troubleshooting** Remember, you have cleared only the Projection properties for the tank; you didn't clear the *RenderTransform* properties group.

8. Click the Rotate tab in the Properties panel, under the Transform category.

9. Set the *Angle* property to **180** degrees. Now your *tank* is rotated.

10. Drag the play head on the timeline to the three-second point in time, and click the Record Keyframe icon to record this mark.

11. Click the Translate tab in the Properties panel, under the Transform category. Set the *Y* property back to 0.

**Troubleshooting** Always move the play head first, and then make the property change.

12. Drag the play head on the timeline to the four-second point in time, and click the Record Keyframe icon to record this mark.

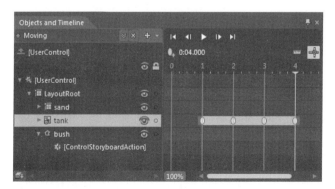

**13.** Click the Rotate tab in the Properties panel, under the Transform category. Set the *Angle* property back to 0 degrees.

> **Tip** You can change the keyframe position on the timeline by dragging it to the left or right.

**14.** Press F5 to run the project and then, in the browser, click the mouse button while pointing to the *bush*. Now your *tank* can rotate at checkpoints!

## Easing an Animation

To make your animated motions look more like natural motions, you can control how Expression Blend animates property changes in the time span between two keyframes. It's possible to simulate bouncing, accelerating from a stop, slowing down, and more. Keyframe interpolation will help you create amazing effects. You can control keyframe interpolation by selecting a suitable *easing function* from the comprehensive set that comes with Expression Blend.

## Easing an animation

1. Select the two-second keyframe in the Moving storyboard.

   In the Properties panel, under the Easing category, there is a table with three columns (In, Out, and InOut); the built-in easing modes form the rows. For example, the options in the "Back" row of the table moves the animation backward a little before continuing.

2. Select the Back Out option, and set the *Amplitude* property to 0.5.

3. Select the four-second keyframe.

4. Select the same Back Out option, and set the *Amplitude* property to 0.5.

**5.** Play the animation several times to see the difference. The *tank* rotates at both checkpoints, with easing at both points to simulate inertia.

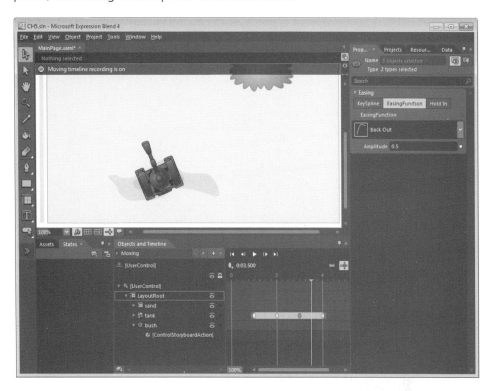

Although the differences can be subtle, animation easing functions make it a lot easier for you to animate objects and give them realistic behaviors.

# Using Storyboards

You've seen how to create a storyboard and how to start it by using behaviors. Here's another example that enables you to start an opacity animation after your application starts and the top-level *UserControl* loads.

### Building an opacity animation

*New icon*

**1.** Add a new storyboard by clicking the New icon at the top of the Objects And Timeline panel.

**2.** Type the name **Appearance** for this storyboard, and click OK.

**3.** In the Objects And Timeline panel, select the *LayoutRoot* element.

**4.** On the timeline, drag the play head to the zero-second point in time, and click the Record Keyframe icon.

**5.** Drag the play head to the two-second point, and click the Record Keyframe icon again.

**6.** Drag the play head back to the zero-second point, and in the Properties panel, under the Appearance category, change the *Opacity* property to 0. A new *Opacity* element appears in the Objects And Timeline panel, and the changes appear on the timeline in the corresponding row.

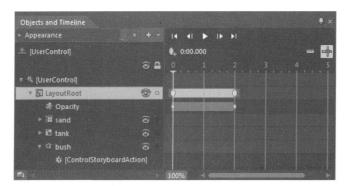

**7.** Click the Close icon at the top of the Objects And Timeline panel to close the storyboard.

**8.** From the Assets panel, in the Behaviors category, drag a *ControlStoryboardAction* behavior onto the *UserControl* in the Objects And Timeline panel.

**9.** To select the behavior, in the Common Properties section of the Properties panel, set the *Storyboard* property to Appearance by choosing it from the list that shows all the available storyboards.

**10.** Press F5 to run the project, and then click the mouse button while pointing to the yellow background. Watch how the application responds to this event. As you click the mouse button repeatedly, the storyboard runs, and the opacity changes.

**11.** A mouse click might not be the best triggering event for the opacity animation. Logically, the opacity animation needs to run only once, after the main *UserControl* loads, so here you'll change the triggering event. In the Trigger category in the Properties panel, set the *EventName* property to the name of the event that you want to use to trigger the behavior—in this case, the common *Loaded* event.

**12.** Now run the project again by pressing F5. This time you don't need to click the mouse button to start the animation; it starts automatically as soon as the top level *UserControl* loads.

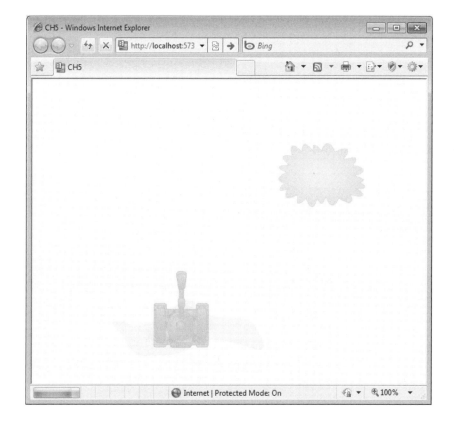

This chapter has shown you some basic techniques with which you can use animations to change property values over time and detect various types of events and apply actions (run storyboards) in response. You can create awesome effects by using transformations and animations together: translating objects, smoothly changing their size, color, opacity, and more.

# Key Points

- With Expression Blend you can resize elements easily.

- You can apply different types of transformation to simple and complex objects.

- You can change the center point of an object.

- There is no *real* three-dimensional space in Silverlight projects; however, you can simulate three-dimensional space by using plane projection.

- Storyboards are containers that hold animation timelines.

- Expression Blend animation is based on keyframes.

- It's more efficient to use the Animation workspace when adding or working with animations.

- You can use behaviors (reusable snippets of interactivity) to control storyboards.

- You can use easing functions to add more realistic physical behaviors to your object animations.

# Chapter 6
# Adding Interactivity

**After completing this chapter, you will be able to:**

- Use default Expression Blend behaviors.

- Run storyboards based on behaviors.

- Use behaviors to change properties of objects.

- Use the *ToggleButton* control.

- Modify the properties of behaviors.

- Create visual states and switch between them.

With Microsoft Expression Blend, you can add interactivity in several ways. For example, the standard developer method is to create event handlers and add code to handle the events. You were introduced to the basics of event handlers in Chapter 4, "XAML and C#." By using this method, you can have any amount of interactivity you want in your application. Another avenue to interactivity is via behaviors. Behaviors were developed expressly for designers so that they could add interactivity to applications without writing code. To use behaviors, you simply drag them onto objects in Expression Blend, set their properties, and enjoy the resulting interactivity. Expression Blend ships with several built-in behaviors, and the designers and developers of the Microsoft Expression Community actively add to that set by uploading their own behaviors to Microsoft Expression Community Gallery, which you can find at *http://cut.ms/Ylr.*

**Important** Before you can complete the exercises in this chapter, you need to install the downloadable practice files to their default location. For more information about practice files, see the instructions at the beginning of this book.

# Behaviors

The concept of behaviors was first introduced in Expression Blend 3. Behaviors are self-contained, reusable snippets of interactivity that designers can use for basic actions, such as running animations, as described in Chapter 5, "Animations and Transformations;" setting or changing properties; showing and hiding blocks of elements; opening and closing dialog boxes; navigating between screens; activating different states of elements; and much more. Expression Blend 4 has a default set of these building blocks for your most common needs. You can find them in the Assets panel. The Behaviors category shows the behaviors available for use in your project.

**Note** The list of available behaviors depends on the current project type (Silverlight application, Silverlight SketchFlow application, Windows Presentation Foundation [WPF] application, or other application type).

# The Basics of Behaviors

Before using behaviors in your project, you should know a little background. Inherently, behaviors are a logical extension of the existing concept of triggers and actions in WPF. It is immediately obvious that an action is an activity in the most general sense. Some common actions are:

- Opening or closing a window.
- Pressing a button.
- Changing a property.
- Calling a method.

Actions provide the functionality to do something—but no way to *activate* that functionality. To invoke an action, you need a trigger. A trigger is an event that occurs when something else happens. You always use actions together with triggers. Triggers provide the ability to change the look and feel of elements dynamically based on the state of the application.

In a more general sense, a trigger is an object that contains a collection of actions and that invokes those actions in response to events. It executes the actions it contains only when a condition evaluates to *true*. Take a look at these examples:

- When you *shake* the tree, apples *fall*.

- When someone *turns on* the switch, the lamp *lights up*.

- The window *closes* when you *press* the button.

All of these sentences include both an action and a trigger that causes that action to happen:

- When you *shake [trigger]* the tree, apples *fall [action]*.

- When someone *turns on [trigger]* the switch, the lamp *lights up [action]*.

- The window *closes [action]* when you *press [trigger]* the button.

With the help of triggers, actions "snap into action" when specific events occur.

The Behaviors category has a list of items that you can immediately identify as actions because their names all end in *Action*:

- **CallMethodAction**   Calls a method that is defined for a specified target object

- **ChangePropertyAction**   Changes or increments the property of a target object

- **ControlStoryboardAction**   Performs a common task with a storyboard, such as play or stop

- **GoToStateAction**   Applies a trigger that activates a specified visual state

- **HyperlinkAction**   Navigates to a website address when the hyperlink is clicked

- **InvokeCommandAction**   Specifies the target object that contains the command that you want to invoke

- **PlaySoundAction**   Plays a sound when a specified action is triggered

- **RemoveElementAction**   Removes a target object from the document

The rest of the default Behaviors category list has items that end in *Behavior*. These items aren't just actions; they are true behaviors. They are similar to actions but don't need the concept of invocation; in other words, they don't need triggers. Think of *behaviors* as functionality that can be attached to objects. There are some situations in which you can add interactivity by using behaviors more easily than you can by using triggers and actions. Some behaviors are most useful when you need to preserve the state of an object. Conceptually, a behavior's functionality is more independent and more self-sufficient than the functionality provided by actions and triggers.

Some simple examples of built-in behaviors are:

- **MouseDragElementBehavior**   Repositions an object when you drag it

- **FluidMoveBehavior**   Animates changes to the layout properties of objects inside a panel

Although it's completely possible to introduce the same effects as the *MouseDragElementBehavior* by using a set of actions and triggers, that would be a much more complex task. To implement this behavior, your application needs to "listen" for mouse down, mouse move, and mouse up events on the attached object, record the mouse position in response to the mouse down event, and so on. Sometimes, it's much easier to implement and use a behavior than it is to accomplish the same goals by using a set of actions and triggers.

Here are some examples of non-default, third-party behaviors such as those that can be found in the Expression Gallery:

- **ClippingBehavior**   Provides a rounded rectangular clipping that scales with the element

- **TransparencyBehavior**   Makes an element semitransparent when the mouse moves away from it

 **Note**  Although the Behaviors category contains both actions and behaviors, for simplicity and convenience, we'll refer to all of these entities as *behaviors* in the rest of this book.

# Using Default Behaviors

In this section, you'll use several default behaviors in your project. The most popular of these are *ChangePropertyAction*, *GoToStateAction*, and *ControlStoryboardAction*:

- **ChangePropertyAction**   By using this behavior, you can easily change or increment the property of an object and then, optionally, define a transition. A few examples of such properties are *Opacity*, *Visibility*, *Content*, or *Brushes* for *Background*, *Foreground*, *Border*, and so on.

- **GoToStateAction**   This behavior is very useful for switching visual states of your current scene. Use it to apply a trigger that activates a specified state.

- **ControlStoryboardAction**   By using this behavior, you can control and manipulate existing storyboards. You have already used this behavior in Chapter 5.

It's easy to add life to static scenes by using animations and doing things such as changing property values over time, listening for different types of events, and applying actions (running storyboards) in response. You can start animations immediately after your application loads, and then not think about them until other events occur. These animations include moving random objects, changing scene conditions, playing sounds, and so on. You can start all of these animations with the *ControlStoryboardAction* behavior.

> **Note**  Use the CH6 sample project from the CH6 folder located in the \Sample Projects folder.

## Adding life to static scenes

1. Select Open Project/Solution from the File menu. The Open Project dialog box appears. Click Browse, browse into the CH6 folder, and then double-click the CH6.sln file. Expression Blend opens your project and loads the MainPage.xaml document.

Examine the structure of the MainPage.xaml document in the Objects And Timeline panel. You'll see a *Back* container that holds the *Sky, Ground,* and *Cloud* objects; a *Grass* container; a *Hedgehog* container with *Body, Eye, Nose, Needles,* and *NeedlesFront* objects; an *Apple* container; an *InfoBar* container that holds a *TextBlock*; and an *ActionButtons* container with *Day-Night* and *INFO* buttons. All these containers help group and organize elements logically.

You can also view the list of existing storyboards in this project by clicking the Open A Storyboard button.

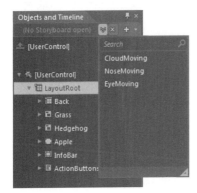

 **Note** Research the content of existing storyboards to see how the different live animations were created: moving the clouds, wiggling the hedgehog's nose, and rotating the eye.

2. Open the Assets panel. From the Behaviors category, drag a *ControlStoryboardAction* behavior onto the *UserControl* in the Objects And Timeline panel.

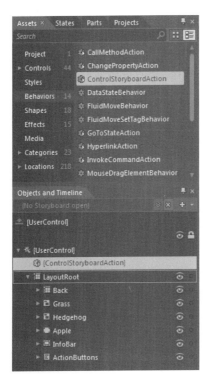

**Tip** Move your mouse pointer over the items in the list of behaviors to see what each behavior does.

**3.** In the Trigger section of the Properties panel, for the *ControlStoryboardAction* behavior you just added, set the *EventName* property to **Loaded**. The storyboard needs to run after the main *UserControl* loads.

**Note** The object to which you add a behavior provides the context within which the behavior operates.

**4.** Set the *Storyboard* property to the *CloudMoving* value by selecting it from the list in the Common Properties section of the Properties panel. Leave the *ControlStoryboardOption* value set to *Play*.

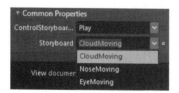

**5.** Run the project by pressing F5. The clouds start moving after the screen loads.

The game scene becomes more alive after you apply this simple behavior.

6. Return to Expression Blend and rename the *ControlStoryboardAction* behavior of the *UserControl* to **ControlCloudMoving** by double-clicking its name in the Objects And Timeline panel and then typing the new value.

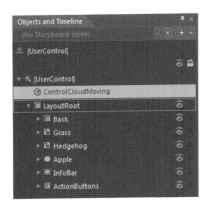

Renaming according to function allows you to easily identify the purpose of this behavior later.

Chapter 6   Adding Interactivity

**Tip** You can always identify behaviors in the Objects And Timeline panel by the small icons near their names. Behaviors always have gears as icons.

You can also start animations in response to user actions, such as clicking something, pointing to or away from elements, or dragging objects.

**Note** Continue using the CH6 sample project you opened in the previous exercise.

## Responding to user actions

1. Drag a *ControlStoryboardAction* behavior onto the *Hedgehog* in the Objects And Timeline panel.

2. Rename the *ControlStoryboardAction* behavior of the *Hedgehog* to **ControlNoseMoving**.

3. From the Storyboard property list in the Common Properties section of the Properties panel, choose the *NoseMoving* value.

4. In the Trigger section, change the *EventName* property to *MouseEnter*.

5. Run the project by pressing F5. Point to the *Hedgehog*.

   The animation starts in response to the mouse pointer entering this object's area.

   You also need a second behavior to control the *NoseMoving* animation.

6. Drag another *ControlStoryboardAction* behavior from the Behaviors category onto the *Hedgehog* in the Objects And Timeline panel.

7. Rename the *ControlStoryboardAction* behavior of *Hedgehog* to **StopNoseMoving**.

8. Set the *EventName* property to *MouseLeave* in the Trigger section.

9. Set the *ControlStoryboardOption* property to *Stop* in the Common Properties section.

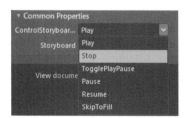

10. Choose the *NoseMoving* value from the *Storyboard* property list in the Common Properties section.

11. Run the project by pressing F5. Point to the *Hedgehog*, and then away again.

   Notice that the *NoseMoving* animation stops as soon as your mouse pointer leaves the *Hedgehog* object's area.

12. Return to Expression Blend.

Sometimes you need to start an animation for an object in response to events that happen with other objects. In this next exercise, you will see how to do that.

## Controlling the behavior source

1. Drag a third *ControlStoryboardAction* behavior onto the *Hedgehog* in the Objects And Timeline panel.

2. Rename this new behavior **ControlEyeMoving**.

**3.** Set the *ControlStoryboardOption* to *Play* and the *Storyboard* property to *EyeMoving* in the Common Properties section.

In the Trigger section, notice that the *SourceObject* property is set to *Hedgehog*. By default, the source of an object is set to the object on which you apply the behavior.

However, you can target another object by setting the *SourceObject* to a different value in the Trigger section.

**4.** Click the Artboard Element Picker (the target icon) and then click the *InfoBar* object on the Artboard.

The value for the *SourceObject* property changes automatically, and the yellow color of the Advanced Options icon in the Trigger section indicates that there is a dependent value for this property.

   **5.** Set the *EventName* property to *MouseLeave*.

   **6.** Run the project by pressing F5. Now the *EyeMoving* animation starts after your mouse
   pointer leaves the *InfoBar* object's area.

   **7.** Return to Expression Blend.

Sometimes it's logical to respond to user actions by changing properties of objects. In this
case, actions trigger something new on the screen.

### Changing properties in response to user actions

   **1.** Find the *ChangePropertyAction* behavior in the Behaviors category of the Assets panel.

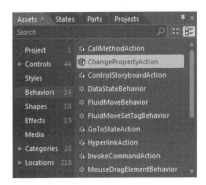

   **2.** Collapse the *Hedgehog* container, and expand the *ActionButtons* container in the
   Objects And Timeline panel.

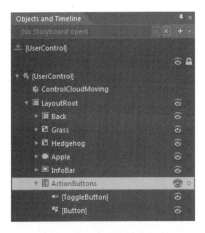

**3.** Rename the *Button* control to **Info**, and then drag the *ChangePropertyAction* behavior onto the *Info* button.

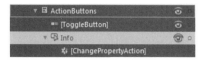

**4.** Rename the *ChangePropertyAction* to **ShowInfoBar**.

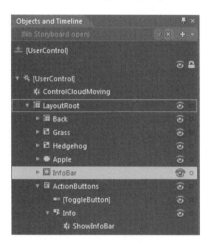

**5.** Select the *InfoBar* container and change the *Visibility* to Collapsed under the Appearance category in the Properties panel.

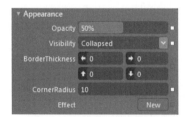

**6.** Select the *ShowInfoBar* behavior in the Objects And Timeline panel.

**7.** Leave the *EventName* set to the default in the Trigger section.

Notice that, for a *button*, the default *EventName* is *Click*.

**8.** Click the Artboard Element Picker in the *TargetObject* box in the Common Properties section, and pick up the *InfoBar* object in the Objects And Timeline panel.

You can use the Artboard Element Picker to select the target object even if that object is not visible on the Artboard.

**9.** Set the *PropertyName* field to *Visibility*.

Leave the *Value* set to its default. It should be *Visible*.

**10.** Run the project by pressing F5.

At first, the *InfoBar* is not visible. But it appears if you click the *INFO* button. Notice that the way the application is set up right now, you can do this only once. You'll fix that in the next exercise.

# Using the *ToggleButton* Control to Change Properties

As you saw in the previous example, it's easy to attach a behavior to a button, but sometimes you need opposite actions on the same event. For example, it would be nice if the first click of the button showed the *InfoBar*, the second click hid it, the third click showed it again, and so on. To implement this, you need a *ToggleButton* rather than a *Button* control. The *ToggleButton* works as a switch and has two states: *Checked* and *Unchecked*. For this reason, a *ToggleButton* is the best control for implementing a switch between any two states. In this exercise, you'll see how it works for hiding and showing the *InfoBar*.

## Implementing a *ToggleButton* to change state

1. Within the CH6 project that you've been using in this chapter, select the *Info* button in the Objects And Timeline panel.

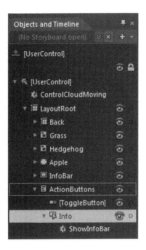

2. Switch to Split view so that you can see both the Design and XAML code panes.

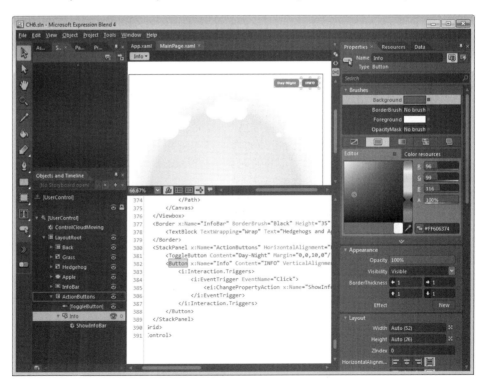

**3.** Change both the opening and closing *Button* tags to **ToggleButton**.

You don't need to change anything else.

**4.** Run your project by pressing F5.

Your *Info* toggle button still works as a simple button; it doesn't yet act like a switch.

**5.** Switch back to Design view.

In the Objects And Timeline panel, notice that your *ActionButtons* container now has two *ToggleButton* controls.

**6.** Rename the unnamed *ToggleButton* control to **DayNight**.

**7.** Select the *ShowInfoBar* behavior in the Objects and Timeline panel. Change the *EventName* value from *Click* to *Checked* in the Trigger section of the Properties panel.

**8.** Select the *ShowInfoBar* behavior in the Objects And Timeline panel. Press Ctrl+C to copy this element to the Clipboard.

9.  Select the *Info* control in the Objects And Timeline panel. Press Ctrl+V to paste the copy of the *ShowInfoBar* behavior inside the *Info ToggleButton*.

    A *ShowInfoBar1* behavior appears.

10. Rename *ShowInfoBar1* to **HideInfoBar**.

11. Change the *EventName* property from *Checked* to *Unchecked* in the Trigger section.

12. Change the *Value* property from *Visible* to *Collapsed* in the Common Properties section.

13. Run the project by pressing F5. Click the *INFO* button several times to see how it works.

    This toggle button has two states: checked (it becomes gray) and unchecked (it becomes green). It switches (toggles) the visibility of the *InfoBar* element with the help of the two behaviors.

# Switching Visual States

You can add various kinds of interactivity to your application by using behaviors, as you've seen in the preceding exercises of this chapter. You can also create interactivity by defining a different visual appearance for each visual state of an element and then adding behaviors or code to switch between those states based on user actions.

One specific behavior In Expression Blend, *GoToStateAction*, triggers visual state changes in the element to which you apply the behavior. This is a natural way to create several states for the existing game project.

Consider the common day/night visual states in games, for example. In this next exercise, you'll add day/night states to the CH6 application.

### Adding day/night states

1. Activate the States panel in Expression Blend by selecting States on the Window menu.

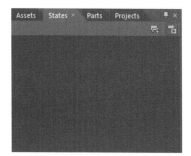

   As you can see, the States panel doesn't display anything right now.

   First, you need to create a state group for your document. A state group contains any visual states that are part of the same logical category and that cannot be displayed at the same time. In other words, only one state in a state group can be displayed at a time.

2. Click the Add State Group button in the States panel.

**3.** A default *VisualStateGroup* appears.

**4.** Rename the default *VisualStateGroup* to **Common**.

Now you need to create states within this group.

**5.** Click the Add State button.

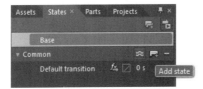

A default new *VisualState* appears. When you create and select a state, state recording is turned on, and any changes that you make will be recorded for that state.

**6.** Rename the default *VisualState* to **Day**. Then click the Add State button again and rename the second *VisualState* to **Night**.

**7.** Expand the *Back* container in the Objects And Timeline panel. Click the *NightSky* element.

**8.** Change the *Visibility* property value to *Visible* in the Appearance category.

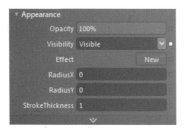

**9.** Switch back to the *Base* position in the States panel to exit from the record mode of the visual state.

10. Select the *DayNight* toggle button in the Objects And Timeline panel.

11. Find the *GoToStateAction* behavior in the Behavior category of the Assets panel.

12. Drag *GoToStateAction* onto the *DayNight* toggle button. Set the *EventName* property to *Checked* in the Trigger category, and set the *StateName* to *Day* in the Common Properties category.

13. Rename the default *GoToStateAction* behavior to **GoDay**.

**14.** Drag a second *GoToStateAction* behavior from the Behavior category of the Assets panel onto the *DayNight* toggle button. Rename this new default *GoToStateAction* behavior to **GoNight**.

**15.** Set the *EventName* property to *Unchecked* in the Trigger category, and set the *StateName* to *Night* in the Common Properties category.

**16.** Run your project by pressing F5.

**17.** Click the *Day-Night* button to see how the visual states of your document change.

Notice that the other behaviors in your project still work.

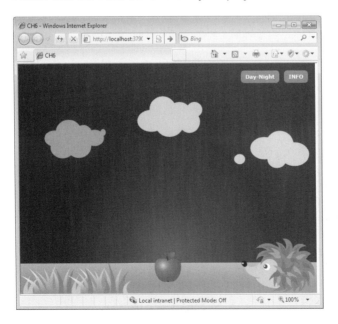

You have just completed an introduction to how Expression Blend behaviors work. More importantly, you have seen an easy way to add interactivity without writing any code. You will learn more about these and other behaviors later in this book.

# Key Points

- Behaviors are self-contained, reusable snippets of interactivity.

- Actions provide the functionality to do something but no way to activate that functionality.

- A trigger is an event that occurs when something else happens.

- Expression Blend comes with a number of commonly used default behaviors.

- The most popular default behaviors are *ChangePropertyAction*, *GoToStateAction*, and *ControlStoryboardAction*.

- Behaviors can be used to run animations.

- Behaviors can be used to change properties of objects.

- You can modify the properties of behaviors.

- You can create visual states in your application.

- You can use behaviors to switch visual states.

# Chapter 7
# Creating Design Assets

**After completing this chapter, you will be able to:**

- Use Expression Design and its tools and panels.

- Create graphic assets in Expression Design.

- Export Expression Design assets as XAML to integrate into Expression Blend.

- Import objects from Photoshop and Illustrator.

Designers can create functional and well-thought-out user interfaces for their applications within Microsoft Expression Blend. But sometimes they want to create something more than a typical interface. Designers have become accustomed to using powerful and rich graphics tools to draw awesome vector assets with full curve control, or enhance existing graphics with a wide array of preset fills, strokes, and gradients. With Expression Blend, you can integrate assets created in other tools, such as Expression Design, Adobe Illustrator, and Adobe Photoshop. The easiest way to integrate graphic assets is from Expression Design. The Expression Design + Expression Blend combination provides simple integration paths because both applications are in the Microsoft Expression Studio family. But you aren't limited to that combination. There are powerful importers to integrate assets from Adobe products as well. In this chapter, you'll learn how to integrate assets from all three of those graphics applications.

> **Important** Before you can complete the exercises in this chapter, you need to install the downloadable practice files to their default location. For more information about practice files, see the instructions at the beginning of this book.

## Using Expression Design

Expression Design 4 is a perfect companion to Expression Blend 4. It's an easy-to-use graphic design tool for creating and exporting sophisticated vector assets built for Windows Presentation Foundation (WPF)/Microsoft Silverlight applications. Within Expression Design, you work with flexible vector manipulation tools, path operators, and shape transformation capabilities to create these assets.

Expression Design also contains powerful import tools that enable you to import files from Adobe products such as Photoshop and Illustrator.

The user interface in Expression Design 4 closely matches the interfaces of the other products in Expression Studio. It has a simple workspace focused on drawing art objects, so beginners can start their design career without a huge learning curve. In this interface, you'll find an Artboard (a document frame), which you create or resize to suit your finished artwork; a Toolbox; a menu at the top; an Action Bar that appears when objects are selected; and movable panels that display editable information about the art being created.

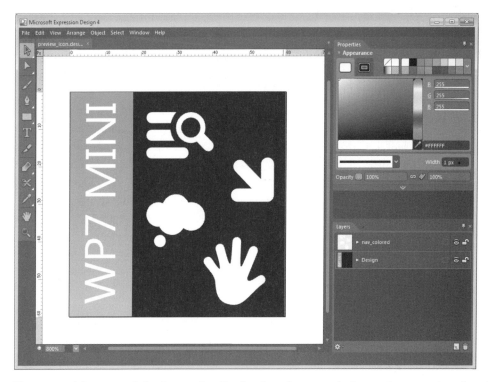

The general features of the Expression Design interface are similar to those you've already seen in the Expression Blend interface and include workspace configurations, themes, and collapsible individual panels, all of which allow you to customize or adjust your workspace. To run Expression Design, click the Start button on the Windows taskbar, click All Programs, and then click Microsoft Expression. When the Expression group opens, click Microsoft Expression Design 4 to start the program.

# Exploring the Expression Design Toolbox

On the left side of the Expression Design workspace is a vertical panel called the Toolbox, which contains a set of tools for creating new objects and modifying existing objects in your document.

The Toolbox panel is visually divided into four sections:

- Selection tools
- Object tools
- Brush tools
- View tools

SELECTION TOOLS
Selection
Direct Selection
OBJECT TOOLS
Paintbrush
Pen
Rectangle
Text
Slice
BRUSH TOOLS
Gradient
Scissors
Color Dropper
VIEW TOOLS
Pan
Zoom

The selection tools section contains the Selection and Direct Selection tools. The Selection tool lets you select elements on the Artboard so that you can directly change their properties from the Properties panel or the Action Bar. The Direct Selection tool lets you select one or more anchor points in a path or a shape.

The object tools section includes Pen tools for creating Bézier paths by positioning a series of anchor points (nodes) and manipulating their control handles and tangent handles. There are also Rectangle tools, a Text tool, and a Slice tool which enables you to cut slices of your work for export to other documents or applications.

The brush tools in the third section include Gradient tools, Scissors tools for cutting an open path into two separate paths or splitting a closed path into an open path, and a Color Dropper tool that copies a color from an existing object to another object.

The last section contains the view tools, Pan and Zoom, which enable you to adjust the portion of the Artboard that you can see by panning and zooming.

**Note**  Like the Tools panel in Expression Blend, the Expression Design Toolbox arranges related tools in tool groups that appear when you click and hold the mouse button on any tool that has a white marker in its lower-right corner.

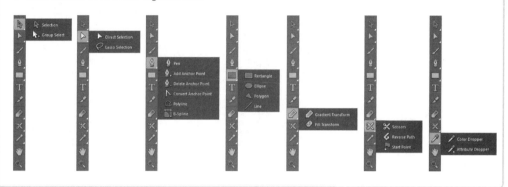

# The Properties Panel

The Properties panel displays properties for one or more selected art objects. The Properties panel organizes properties into several sections or categories, most of which appear based on the type of object selected. For example, if you select a text object, you will see a Text section. If you apply a Slice tool, you'll see an Edit Slice section. The Appearance section is always present and displays the current fill and stroke settings.

To help you become familiar with Expression Design and its Properties panel, here's a brief exercise in manipulating an icon.

 **Note**  Use the CH7 sample project from the CH7 folder located in the \Sample Projects folder.

## Using the Properties panel

1. In Expression Design, select Open from the File menu. The Open File dialog box appears. Click Browse and then browse to the CH7 folder in the sample code for this book. Double-click the CH7.design file.

   **Tip**  Expression Design files always have a .design extension. The CH7.design file displays a set of icons titled *WP7 MINI icons*.

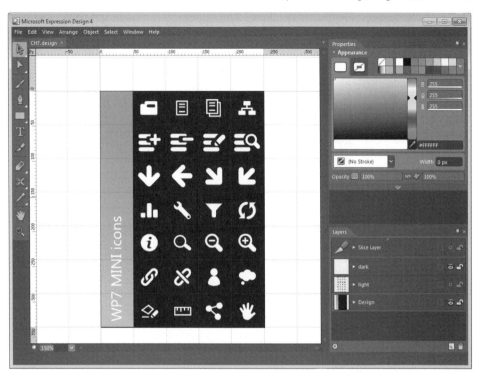

100%

*Zoom tool*

You can apply a zoom level that enables you to work with small objects on the Artboard. By altering the zoom level of the Artboard, you can either zoom out to see large artwork without having to scroll or pan, or zoom deeply into finely detailed objects so that you can work more precisely. The Zoom tool is available in the lower-left corner of the Artboard.

2. Click the Selection tool in the Toolbox panel. Select the third icon in the third row.

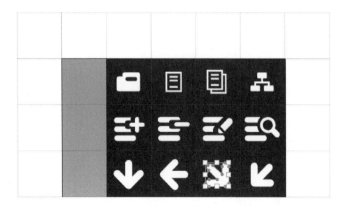

**3.** Look at the Properties panel. The Appearance category displays the current fill and stroke settings for the selected object. The first tab is used to set the fill properties and the second tab is used to set the stroke properties. A Fill Type/Stroke Type section and swatches appear to the right of the Fill and Stroke tabs.

You can set any color by using the RGB sliders or by using the Color Picker eyedropper tool to select a color from elsewhere on the screen.

**4.** Click the Color Picker eyedropper and then click the green color near the bottom corner of the *WP7 MINI icons* text block on your screen.

The *arrow* art object becomes green.

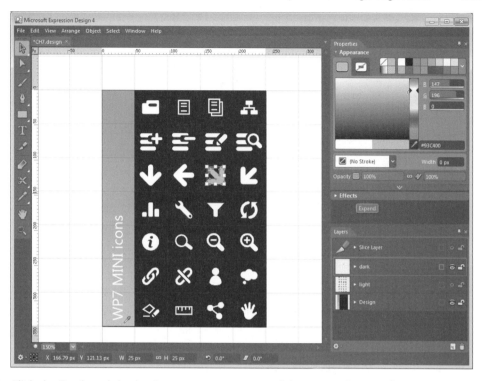

**5.** Click the Stroke tab in the Appearance category of the Properties panel.

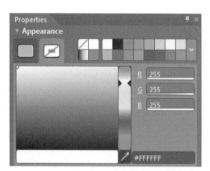

No stroke color is currently set for the stroke. You can set a solid color, a gradient, or a transparent color as the stroke for the selected object. Set the white color by using the Color Picker eyedropper tool.

6. Set the *Width* property of the stroke to **2 px**. Use the Zoom tool to look at the art object more closely.

Now your arrow has a more finished appearance.

Notice that when you use a brush stroke for an object that has a fill, the object is filled first and then stroked (the stroke always appears on top of the fill).

7. Zoom out by using the Zoom tool, and select the *WP7 MINI icons* text block .

 **Tip** Zoom in by pressing Ctrl+= (equal sign) on your keyboard, and zoom out by pressing Ctrl+ - (minus sign). Another handy shortcut, Ctrl+ 0 (zero), zooms to fit all the current objects on the screen. Your keyboard shortcuts might differ based on your input language settings.

When you select the text block, the Text category appears under the Appearance category in the Properties panel.

8. In the Type Size list, select 18 pt, or click the field to type this value.

   The text block becomes bigger.

Notice that the Properties panel also contains the Effects category. From here, you can apply different effects, sometimes referred to as filters, to any vector, text, or bitmapped object.

# The Layers Panel

The Layers panel in Expression Design looks and acts somewhat like the Objects And Timeline panel in Expression Blend. By using layers, you can organize your art objects logically, lock objects to prevent unintended changes, and hide or show other parts of your layout.

Expression Design documents always contain at least one layer on which objects appear by default. When you create a new document, Expression Design automatically creates a new empty layer named *Layer 1*.

In this exercise, you'll work with the Layers panel to select, hide, and group objects.

## Using the Layers panel

1. Select the green arrow you styled in the previous exercise, if it's not already selected.

   The Layer named *dark* becomes highlighted with a thin blue border, signifying that this is the layer with which you're currently working. Each layer displays a small thumbnail preview.

2. Click the Visibility icon (the eye) to hide the *dark* layer. Click the Visibility icon beside the *light* layer to show it.

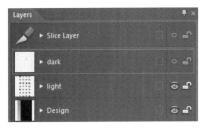

   Nothing happens on the Artboard.

3. Expand the *Design* layer so that you can see all of its objects.

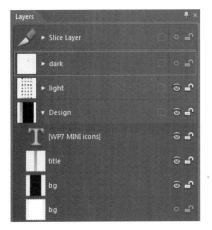

4. Click the Visibility icon to hide the black *bg* object and unhide the white *bg* object.

   Now your document displays the alternative icons.

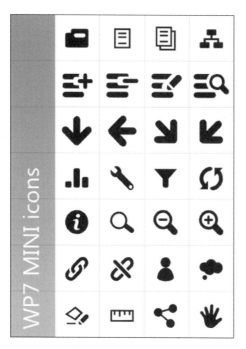

**5.** Expand the *light* layer to see all of its objects.

**6.** Scroll down and find the *arrow_left* object and select it. Press and hold the Shift key and click the three items directly beneath the *arrow_left* object to select them all.

7. On the Arrange menu, click Group, or press Ctrl+G. Now the selected objects are grouped.

You can move and work with this group as if it were a single object. You can ungroup objects by clicking Ungroup on the Arrange menu (or pressing Ctrl+Shift+G).

*Padlock icon*

**Tip** You can also lock an object or a group of objects in the Layers panel to prevent them from being accidentally changed. You do so by clicking the padlock icon.

# The Action Bar

The Action Bar displays information about selected objects and enables you to set new positions and sizes or easily make transformations.

If you select two or more objects, the Action Bar displays some additional functions that you can perform with more than one object, such as Align, Stack, and Path. When you select three or more objects, you will see the Distribute option.

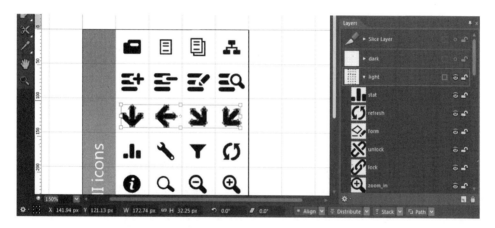

# Preparing Assets

To create artistic interfaces for your applications, it's often better to draw full screens—or at least major parts of them—with a graphic editor and then export them in a format that can be used in Expression Blend. You can then design the layout structure of your pages and organize elements and controls while taking advantage of the graphic assets created with other applications.

In the following exercises, you will learn how to export graphic assets and import them into Expression Blend. In these two exercises, you will draw two types of elements in Expression Design: a game title and a styled button.

### Creating the game title

1. From the File menu in Expression Design, select New, and then click OK in the New Document dialog box.

Expression Design applies default size and resolution settings and creates a new empty document.

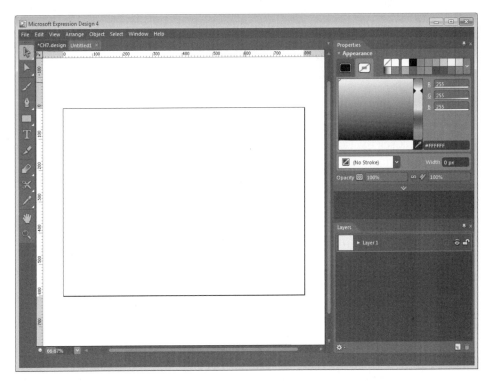

2.  Select the Ellipse tool in the Toolbox panel and drag it into the center of your document.

3.  Click the Link icon to unlink the width and height sliders on the Action Bar for the ellipse. Set the width to **300**, the height to **150**, the horizontal position of the pivot point (*X*) to **400**, and the vertical position of the pivot point (*Y*) to **300**. That places the ellipse in the center of your document. By default, the ellipse has a white background and a black stroke.

*Text tool*

*Add text to path cursor*

4.  Select the Text tool and position the pointer near the left end of the top of the ellipse.

    The pointer changes to indicate that text will flow on the edge of the ellipse.

**5.** Click the left end of the top of the ellipse.

The pointer appears on the ellipse at the position you clicked.

**6.** Type the text **HedgehoG** along the ellipse curve.

**7.** Click the Selection tool in the Toolbox, and then click the text you just typed.

**8.** In the Text category of the Properties panel, set the text size to 36. Set the font family to Segoe Print and set the Font Decoration field to Bold.

You might find that the initial position of the text on the ellipse isn't aesthetically pleasing. Because it's a separate object, you can always move it to a better location. Point to the text. Select the vertical line that appears before the first character, and drag it to move the text to the left or to the right to center the text over the top of the ellipse.

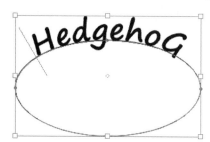

**9.** Select the text with the Selection tool. In the Appearance category of the Properties panel, set the Fill color to **#930000**.

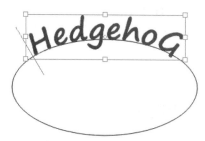

**10.** Press Ctrl+C to copy the selected text to the Clipboard. Press Ctrl+B to paste it in back of the current layer.

Expression Design pastes the group of letters behind the current letters. You can check that in the Layers panel.

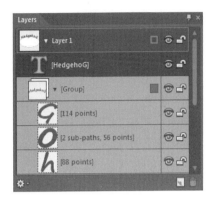

**11.** Choose the Compound option from the Path operations area of the Action Bar.

The group of objects becomes one compound path.

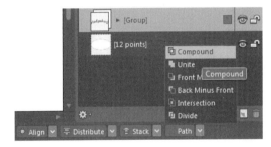

On the Layers panel, you can see the grouped objects.

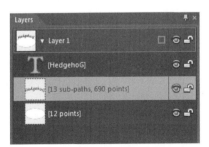

**12.** Click the Stroke tab in the Appearance category of the Properties panel. Set the stroke color to **#FFFF00** temporarily—you'll change it later.

13. Set the stroke width to **15 px**.

    Your art objects now look like red text stroked with yellow.

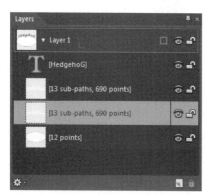

14. Press Ctrl+C to copy the selected object to the Clipboard. Press Ctrl+B to paste it to the back of the layer.

15. Set the stroke width to **30 px**.

16. At the bottom of the Color Picker, click the black gradient stop to select the gradient bar, and set its hex value to **#12A73D**.

17. Click the white gradient stop to select the gradient bar and set its hex value to **#93C400**.

*Gradient*

**18.** Click the Gradient swatch in the Stroke Type section.

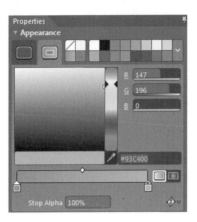

**19.** Drag the right gradient stop to position it in the center of the gradient bar.

**20.** Click the gradient bar to add a new gradient stop to the right. Set the hex value to **#12A73D**.

Now you have three gradient stops.

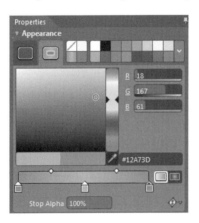

**21.** Select the yellow path in the Layers panel. Ensure that the Stroke tab is selected in the Appearance category of the Properties panel, and then set the Stroke color to **#FFFFFF**.

**22.** Select the red *HedgehoG* text. On the Object menu, click Convert Object To Path.

After you do that, the red text is no longer editable with the Text tool.

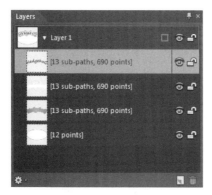

Notice that the text now appears as paths in the Layers panel.

**23.** Choose the Compound option from the Path operations area of the Action Bar panel.

**24.** Select the *ellipse* object in the Layers panel. Press the Delete key to delete the ellipse. You don't need it anymore.

**25.** Select all objects by pressing Ctrl+A or by selecting All from the Select menu.

**26.** Press Ctrl+G to group the selected objects.

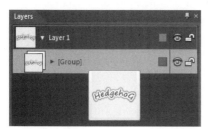

**27.** Double-click the name of this group in the Layers panel. Type **Hedgehog**, and then press Enter.

You have finished the game title.

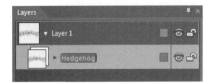

**28.** On the File menu, click Save. You are saving the file for the first time, so you'll see a Save dialog box. Type the file name **Hedgehog**, and then click the Save button.

**29.** Select your game title. On the File menu, click Export.

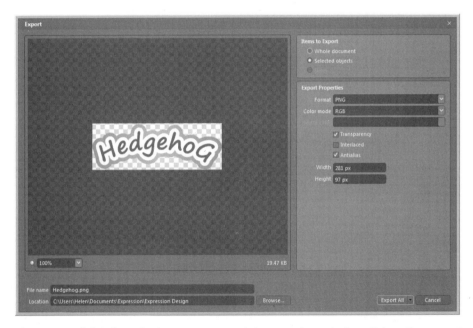

The Export dialog box displays your artwork in a preview window. Select the export option to save the Expression Design artwork as a .png file. Your selected group has a name, so you don't need to type it again.

**30.** Browse to or enter the path for the location where you want to save the output file.

**31.** Make sure that the Transparency check box is selected so that the .png file maintains a transparent background behind your artwork.

**32.** Click Export All.

You have drawn the game title and exported it as a .png file so that you can use it in the game project. Now it's time to create a styled button.

### Drawing the cloud button

1. On the File menu, click New.

2. Click OK in the New Document dialog box.

3. Select the Ellipse tool from the Toolbox panel and drag it to the center of your document.

4. If they're not already unlinked, unlink the width and height sliders on the Action Bar for the ellipse. Set the width to **50**, the height to **50**, the horizontal position of the pivot point (*X*) to **300**, and the vertical position of the pivot point (*Y*) to **200**.

   By default, Expression Design draws your ellipse with the last-used background and stroke parameters.

5. Set the fill color to **#0096FF** and the stroke color to **None** in the Appearance category of the Properties panel.

6. From the Edit menu, select Copy, or press Ctrl+C. Also from the Edit menu, select Paste In Front, or press Ctrl+F.

   Expression Design creates a second ellipse in front of the first.

7. Set this second ellipse's width to **60**, its height to **60**, the horizontal position of the pivot point (*X*) to **330**, and the vertical position of the pivot point (*Y*) to **190**.

8. Press Ctrl+C and then Ctrl+F to create a third ellipse. Set the horizontal position of the pivot point (*X*) to **360** and the vertical position of pivot point (*Y*) to **200** for this third ellipse.

9. Press Ctrl+C and then Ctrl+F once more. Set the width of this fourth ellipse to **50**, the height to **50**, *X* to **350**, and *Y* to **215**.

10. Press Ctrl+C and Ctrl+F to create a fifth ellipse. Set its *X* position to **320** and its *Y* position to **220**.

After this operation you should have five ellipses arranged in a cloudlike shape.

11. Select all the objects by pressing Ctrl+A or by clicking All on the Select menu. Choose the Unite option from the Path operations on the Action Bar panel. The selected objects become one united object.

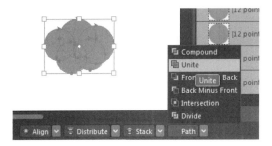

12. Click the Fill tab of the Appearance category in the Properties panel.

*Gradient*

13. Click the Gradient swatch in the Fill Type section. At the bottom of the Color Picker, click the black gradient stop to select the gradient bar, and set its hex value to **#00B6FF**.

14. Click the white gradient stop to select the gradient bar, and set its hex value to **#B6EAFF**.

The colors of your cloud object become more natural and less toy-like.

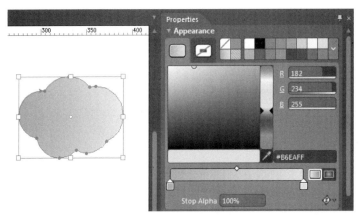

Next you will transform the gradient filling of the cloud.

*Gradient Transform*

**15.** In the Toolbox, select the Gradient Transform tool. Position the pointer near the top part of the cloud object, which will be the gradient's starting point. Drag it to the bottom part of the object and release the mouse button. This will be the gradient's ending point.

The cloud fills with a vertical gradient.

 **Tip**  Hold down the Shift key when you drag so that the angle is constrained to a vertical angle.

**16.** With the cloud selected, press Ctrl+C and then press Ctrl+F to copy it.

**17.** Select Scale As Percentage from the Transform Options menu to display the width and height parameters as a percentage of the object.

The Transform Options menu provides options on how information is displayed about the actions you take.

**18.** Set the width and height to 90% so that your second cloud object becomes a little bit smaller.

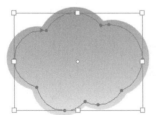

**19.** Change the gradient fill for this object so that it ranges from #FFFFFF (white) to #FFFFFF (white).

**20.** With the right gradient stop still selected, adjust the transparency at this point of the gradient to 5% by using the Stop Alpha slider.

This gradient stop point becomes almost completely transparent.

**21.** Select the Ellipse tool in the Toolbox and drag it to the center of your document.

**22.** Deselect Scale As Percentage from the Transform Options menu.

**23.** Set the width to **150** and the height to **130** for the newly created ellipse, and then set its *X* value to **355** and its *Y* value to **265**.

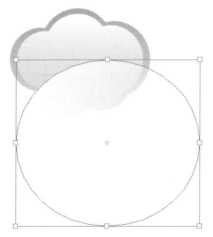

**24.** Hold down the Shift key and click the smaller cloud object to select it. You now have two objects selected.

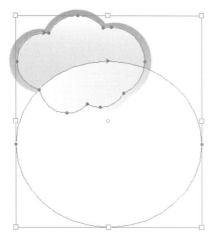

**25.** Choose the Back Minus Front option from the Path operations of the Action Bar panel.

The shape of the front object is cut out of the back object.

**26.** In the Toolbox, select the Gradient Transform tool. Position the pointer near the top part of the cut-off cloud object, drag it vertically to the bottom part of the object, and release the mouse button.

The fill looks like glass now.

**27.** Select the back cloud object. Press Ctrl+C to copy it, and then press Ctrl+F to paste it in front.

**28.** Select Scale As Percentage from the Transform Options menu and set the width to **80%**, the height to **10%**, and the *Y* position to **270**.

The form of this object looks like a shadow under the cloud, but you'll want to set a better color for the shadow.

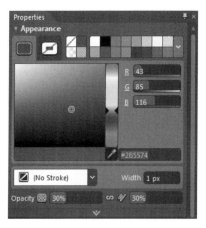

**29.** Change the gradient filling for this object to solid and set its hex value to **#2B5574** and its Opacity to **30%**.

**30.** Click All on the Select menu to select all objects.

**31.** On the Arrange menu, click Group, or press Ctrl+G to group the selected objects.

**32.** Double-click the name of this group in the Layers panel. Type the new name, **Cloud**, and then press Enter.

You have finished your first styled button.

**33.** On the File menu, click Save. Type the file name **Cloud** in the dialog box, and then click the Save button.

As this exercise has demonstrated, Expression Design has more flexible vector manipulation tools and path operators than Expression Blend.

# Exporting to XAML from Expression Design

You can export your art objects from Expression Design to Expression Blend not only in a bitmapped file format, but also as XAML files suitable for immediate use in Silverlight or WPF projects. This enables you to copy and paste objects from the exported document into another document in your projects. You can also directly copy selected objects from Expression Design to Expression Blend via the Clipboard.

**Important** If you closed Expression Blend 4, start it before beginning this exercise, and load the CH7 sample project from the \Sample Projects\CH7 folder of downloadable practice files for this book.

## Exporting the cloud button to Expression Blend

1. In Expression Design, open the Cloud file you created in the preceding exercise.

2. In Expression Blend, select Open Project/Solution from the File menu. Click Browse and browse to the CH7 folder in the sample code for this book, and then double-click the CH7.sln file.

3. Click the Project panel for your solution. In the folder list for the CH7 project, double-click the MainPage.xaml file.

4. Switch back to Expression Design and click the Cloud group to select it.

5. From the Edit menu, select Copy XAML, or press Ctrl+Shift+C.

   This allows you to copy a XAML representation of selected objects.

6. Switch back to Expression Blend and, in the Objects And Timeline panel, click LayoutRoot.

7. From the Edit menu, select Paste, or press Ctrl+V.

   Expression Blend pastes a Viewbox layout panel named *Cloud* into the *LayoutRoot*. You can expand it to see what's inside. All the pieces are grouped into the *Canvas* layout panel and are vector illustrations with saved solid colors and gradients. You can work with the exported XAML code however you want. You can leave it as is or convert illustrations to real controls, as explained in Chapter 9, "Skinning Controls."

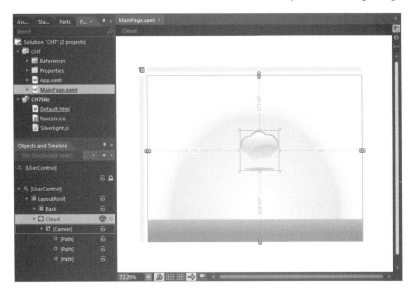

**Tip**  You can easily copy XAML code from Expression Design via the Clipboard, but you can gain more control by using the Advanced Export dialog box, which can be reached by clicking Export on the File menu with objects selected in Expression Design.

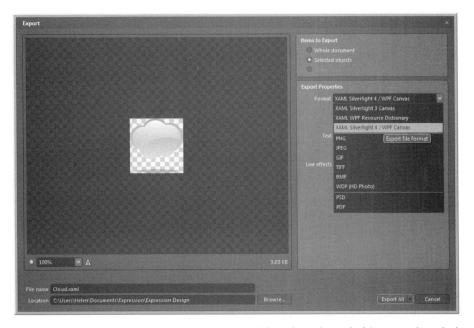

From the Export dialog box, you can export either the selected objects or the whole document, choose the format for your artwork, as well as set other parameters.

You can export illustrations as:

- XAML Silverlight 4 / WPF canvases

- XAML Silverlight 3 canvases

- XAML WPF Resource Dictionaries

- .png, .jpg, .gif, .tiff, .bmp, and WDP (HD Photo) files

- PSD and PDF files

Now that you've seen the basics of how to create graphic assets by using Expression Design and how to export them to Expression Blend projects, it's worth looking at the equivalent process for assets created in other graphic design applications, such as Photoshop and Illustrator.

# Importing Design Assets from Adobe Applications

Both Expression Design and Expression Blend allow you to import Photoshop (.psd) and PDF-compatible Illustrator (.ai) files into your documents. You don't need to have the Adobe products installed on your local computer to perform these operations. In these exercises, you will learn about the processes.

### Importing from an Adobe Photoshop file

1. Switch to the MainPage.xaml file of the CH7 project in Expression Blend.

2. In the Objects And Timeline panel, click LayoutRoot.

3. From the File menu, select Import Adobe Photoshop File.

4. In the Import Adobe Photoshop File dialog box, browse to the CH7 folder in the sample code for this book, and double-click the Sun.psd file.

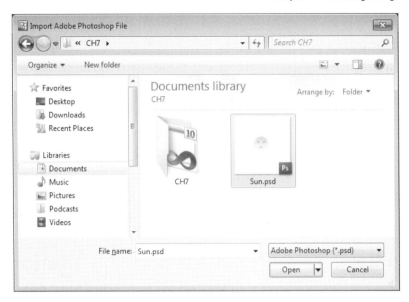

5. Click Open. Look at the dialog box that appears. Expression Blend displays a preview of the original Photoshop file on the left and preserves the layer names on the right so that you can select only the layers that you want to import.

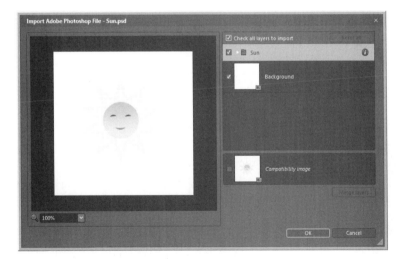

**6.** Clear the check box for the Background layer. You don't need to import it.

The preview takes on a transparent background.

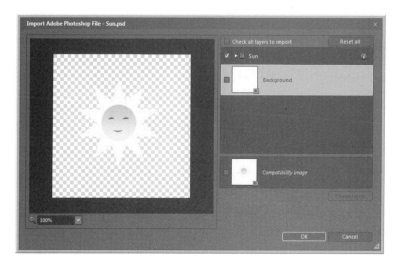

**7.** Point to the small information icon to the right of the Sun folder.

The icon displays information about unsupported features that might not import as expected. These unsupported features might be such things as layer effects applied to a layer, adjustment layers, or patterns. You can always import at least the look of unsupported features by using the Flattened bitmap import option or by merging the layer with other layers.

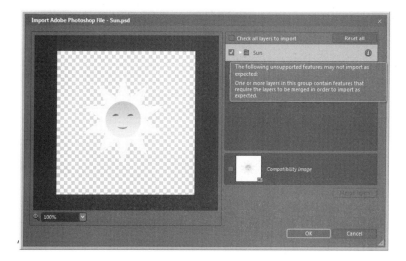

**Tip** If there are unsupported features in your Photoshop file, the Import dialog box displays information about those features as well as instructions to preserve the appearance of your document.

**8.** Expand the Sun folder on the right side.

The information icon appears near the layer named *center*. Also, the *Gradient Overlay* layer effect can't be imported as expected. Select this layer to see the available options; you can import the layer as editable content or as a flattened bitmap. If you need an editable path object, stick with the editable content option. You can add the gradient fill effect later, in Expression Blend.

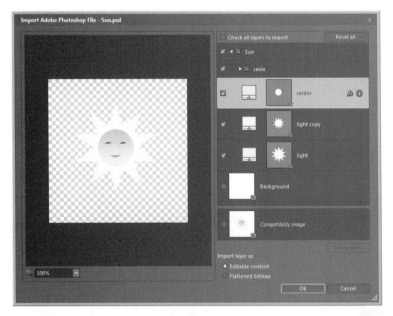

**9.** Expand the Smile folder to make sure it appears as expected, and then point to other layers to see their previews.

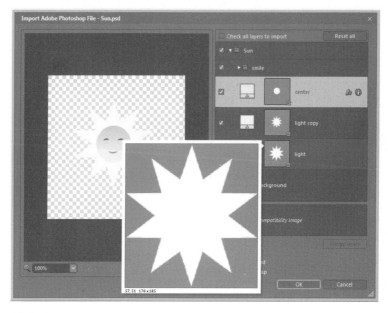

**10.** Click OK.

Expression Blend adds a *Canvas* object named the same as your imported file—*Sun*, in this case—as a child element to *LayoutRoot*, and displays it in the upper-left corner in Design view. Under this *Canvas* object you'll find your imported objects.

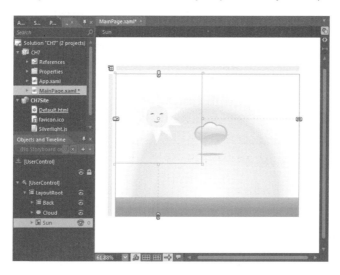

**11.** Right-click the *Sun* object and choose Ungroup.

You can reduce the number of containers and crop any unnecessary space by ungrouping the objects.

Your import and correction operations are complete. You can also import artwork created with Illustrator. Here's the procedure.

### Importing from an Adobe Illustrator file

**1.** In the Objects And Timeline panel, click *LayoutRoot*.

**2.** From the File menu, select Import Adobe Illustrator File.

**3.** In the Import Adobe Illustrator File dialog box, browse to the CH7 folder in the sample code for this book, and double-click the Grass.ai file that you are going to import.

4. Click Open to import the file. Expression Blend adds a new *Canvas* object named *Grass* to *LayoutRoot*. Under the *Canvas* object are all the imported objects.

5. Right-click the *Grass* object and then click Ungroup.

You can now reduce the top container and crop the unnecessary space.

6. Rename the *Layer_1* object to *Grass*.

7. Click the Advanced Options icon near the Margin properties in the Layout category of the Properties panel. Choose the Reset option.

Your *Grass* object relocates to the lower-right corner of your document.

You can also copy or move this object to finish the illustration.

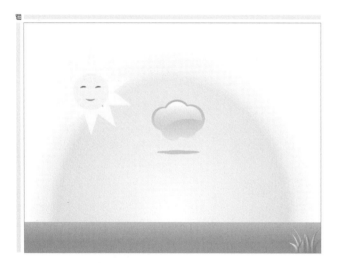

 **Tip** If there are bitmap images in your Illustrator or Photoshop file, Expression Blend creates a new folder in the project folder to contain all the converted image files.

As you have seen, you can quickly and easily import Adobe Photoshop or Illustrator files for use in your Expression Blend projects. In the next chapter, you will see how to use resources to improve the efficiency of your work and your applications.

# Key Points

- Expression Design is an excellent companion program for creating artwork to use in your Expression Blend projects.

- Assets created in Expression Design can be imported into Expression Blend as raster images, such as .png and .jpg, or as XAML code.

- You can import from Photoshop into Expression Blend while maintaining control over which layers are imported, as well as other parameters.

- You can import from Illustrator into Expression Blend while maintaining control over which layers are imported, as well as other parameters.

# Chapter 8
# Resources

**After completing this chapter, you will be able to:**

- Create color resources and use them in Expression Blend applications.

- Create and apply gradient and image brushes.

- Convert property values to resource values and apply them to properties of the same type.

- Modify existing resources.

- Organize resources by using dictionaries.

Microsoft Expression Blend increases your productivity and improves the performance of your applications by allowing the use of resources. A *resource* is an object that you or others can reuse in different places in your Expression Blend projects. Most often, reusable resources are colors or brushes that are applied to other objects. A brush can be based on a gradient, an image, or even a video. Beyond basic resources, you can reuse margins, font sizes, corner radii, alignments, and more. The concept of resources goes beyond individual properties and can include complex resources such as styles and templates (see Chapter 9, "Skinning Controls") that allow you to make controls of the same type (such as buttons) look similar and behave the same way. Instead of copying and pasting the objects or attributes multiple times, you can store, use, and change resources in one location, editing them directly in XAML files or working visually through the Resources panel, which lists all the resources used in your current project. Expression Blend also gives you a flexible way to organize resources by using resource dictionaries.

> **Important** Before you can complete the exercises in this chapter, you need to install the downloadable practice files to their default location. For more information about practice files, see the instructions at the beginning of this book.

# Color Resources

Consistent colors are important in an application. Storing colors as reusable color resources makes it easy to apply specific colors to objects throughout your application. When you use a consistent color palette in an application's elements, controls, and screens, it looks more professional and complete.

In this exercise, you'll create and store a color resource for later use.

 **Note** Use the CH8 sample project from the CH8 folder located in the \Sample Projects folder.

### Creating a color resource

1. Load the CH8 sample project from the \Sample Projects\CH8 folder.

2. Click the Project panel for your solution. In the folder list for the CH8 project, double-click the MainPage.xaml file. This document is a combination of graphic elements you have worked with in earlier chapters: a background for a game scene with imported sun, cloud, and grass objects.

Take a minute to look at this game scene. It might be a good idea to use the green, yellow, gray, and blue colors in this scene for all of the other elements in your application design. To do so, you need to convert the colors of the sky, cloud, and grass elements to color resources so that you can easily apply them many times.

**3.** Expand the *Cloud* layout panel and its child elements in the Objects And Timeline panel. Select the *Shadow* object.

**4.** Go to the Brushes category in the Properties panel.

The *Shadow* object uses the solid semi-transparent fill color #4E2B5574.

*Convert Color To Resource*

**5.** Click the Convert Color To Resource icon to the left of the hex value for the selected color. The Create Color Resource dialog box appears.

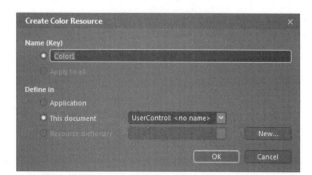

**6.** Enter **SemiGray** in the Name (Key) field for your new resource, and select Application as the location level in which the resource will be defined. Click OK.

Clicking OK changes the color to a resource, activates the Color Resources tab instead of the Color Editor for the shadow object's *Fill* property, and applies the newly defined *SemiGray* color resource as the shadow's fill.

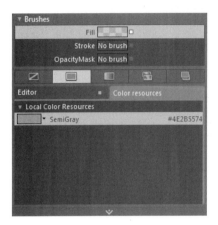

  **Note**  You can view and modify the color resources that you create on the Color Resources tab by expanding the Color Editor near the resource name.

## Understanding Resource Levels

You can define resources at various levels, creating them at the appropriate levels or *scopes* in your application. There are four levels available—*application level*, *document level*, *object level*, and external resource *dictionary level*:

- An *application-level* resource is defined in the application's App.xaml file. You can apply a resource defined at application level anywhere within your application.

- A *document-level* resource is defined in the document in which it was created and can be applied only to objects in that same document.

- An *object-level* resource can be applied only to the object used to create the resource and its child objects.

- A *dictionary-level* resource is defined in an external file called a *resource dictionary*. You can apply resources in a resource dictionary anywhere and in any application. External resource dictionaries are linked to your project in the App.xaml file.

Consider how a resource will be used when you're deciding what level or scope to save it in.

## Applying a color resource

1. Select the *InfoBar* layout panel in the Objects And Timeline panel. This element displays additional information for the game scene.

   You will set the background color a little bit lighter than the current solid color. The *SemiGray* color resource you just created is perfect.

2. Go to the Brushes category in the Properties panel. Stay on the solid color brush tab.

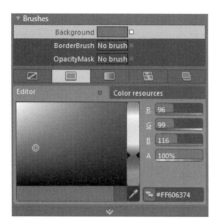

3. Click the Color Resources subtab and select the only resource currently available—the *SemiGray* color resource you created in the previous exercise—from the list.

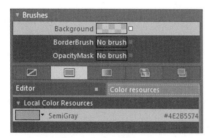

4. The *InfoBar* layout panel now uses this resource.

# Brush Resources

Creating a brush resource is similar to creating a color resource.

### Creating a brush resource

1. Expand the *Cloud* layout panel and its child element in the Objects And Timeline panel. Select the *BluePart* object.

2. Go to the Brushes category in the Properties panel.

3. Click the Advanced Options icon next to the brush property, and then click Convert To New Resource.

4. In the Create Brush Resource dialog box, enter **CloudBlue** in the Name (Key) field for your new resource and set the resource to the Application level.

5. Click OK. A created brush resource appears under the Brush resources tab (the tab on the far right).

6. You can also find and view all color and brush resources that were created and are being used in the open project in the Resources panel. At this point, you should have two: the *SemiGray* color resource and the *CloudBlue* brush resource, both stored in the App.xaml file.

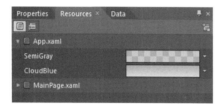

 **Troubleshooting**  If there is no Resources panel within your workspace, you can access it through the Window menu.

Resources don't display in the Resources panel if you work with your active document in XAML view.

7. Now you will create a second brush resource. Select the *Glass* object under the *CloudObj* child of the *Cloud* layout panel.

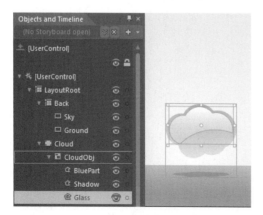

8. Go to the Brushes category in the Properties panel and convert a fill brush to a new resource. Name it *WhiteGlass* and define it at the Application level. (Remember, you can check all the available resources in the Resources panel.)

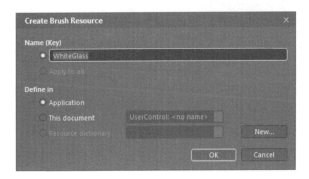

The *Cloud* object now uses resources to fill all of its graphic elements.

You can apply a stored brush resource to fill other objects using three different techniques: you can drag the resource onto the object on the Artboard, you can use the Advanced Options menu from the Properties panel, or you can use the brush resources subtab under Brushes in the Properties panel for the brush property that you want to change (*Fill*, *Stroke*, or *OpacityMask*).

### Applying a brush resource

1. Select the *light2* object inside of the *Sun* layout panel.

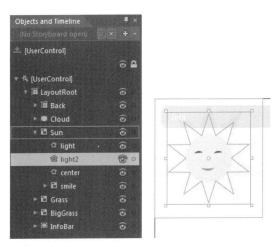

2. Under Brushes in the Properties panel, select the *Fill* property and then click the Brush Resources tab.

**3.** Under Local Brush Resources, select the *WhiteGlass* brush resource.

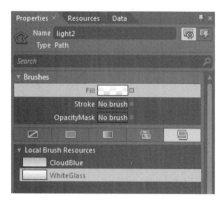

Note that the Advanced Options icon next to the *Fill* property changes to green, which indicates that the brush for the *Fill* property is linked to a local resource.

**Tip** The Advanced Options menu allows you to reapply local resources, convert and edit them as new resources, or remove any brush fill by using Reset, to return a property to its default value option.

Note that resetting a property to its default value does not delete the resource from your project.

# Image Brush Resources

Brush resources aren't limited to just solid colors or gradients. It's also possible to use images as brush resources. If there are a lot of places in your document or application where you might want to use the same image, but stretched or skewed in different ways, it's better to create an image brush resource and use it for fill, stroke, or even as an opacity mask.

 **Note** An opacity mask is a brush for which Expression Blend ignores the color but transfers its opacity to the masked object.

### Creating an image brush resource

1. You'll find two images in the Images subfolder of the CH8 sample project. Click the *LayoutRoot* container in the Objects And Timeline panel, and then double-click the Grass.png file in the Images folder. The image object appears in your document.

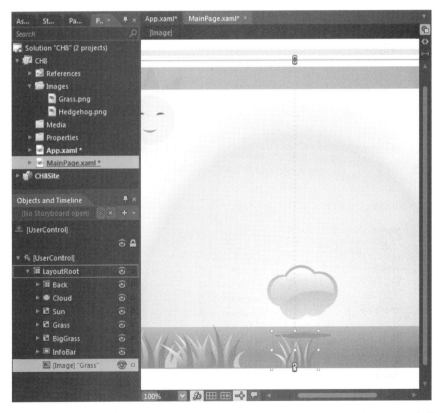

2. Set the value of the *HorizontalAlignment* property to *Center* and the *VerticalAlignment* property to *Bottom*.

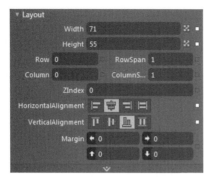

3. Select Make Brush Resource on the Tools menu, and then select Make ImageBrush Resource.

4. Enter **Grass** for the name (key) in the Create ImageBrush Resource dialog box and define the resource at the Application level.

5. Click OK. You can now delete the *Grass* image from the *LayoutRoot* container in the Objects And Timeline panel. You no longer need it, because you now have a *Grass* image brush resource. The Resources panel displays the updated list of resources.

**Note**  You apply the newly created image brush just as you would any other brush resource. Click Fill or Stroke under Brushes in the Properties panel for the selected object, and apply a brush resource from the Brush Resources tab.

# Other Resources

In addition to brush resources, you can create new resources from any existing properties. For example: margin values, font families, sizes, effects, opacities, and other properties can be converted into resources and then applied throughout the project. Consider a *Grid* container into which you place elements of different types, such as elements to create a login form. It would be useful to store a resource value to set the margins for these various elements. That way, the *Textbox* controls, *TextBlock* controls, *Button* controls, and other controls for the login form will all have the same margin values, all controlled from a single place. The following exercise shows you how to do this.

### Creating and applying a thickness resource

1. Select the *BigGrass* object in the Objects And Timeline panel.

2. Set its margin values to **10** (Left), **0** (Top), **10** (Right), and **0** (Bottom).

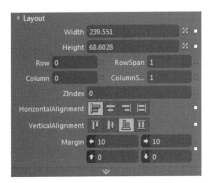

3. Click the Advanced Options icon next to the Margin settings, and then click Convert To New Resource.

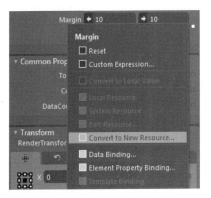

4. Expression Blend determines the type of selected resource and displays an appropriate dialog box. In the Create Thickness Resource dialog box, enter **MarginToScene** for the name (key) and define the resource at the Application scope.

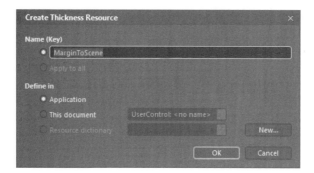

5. Select the *Grass* object in the Objects And Timeline panel. In the Properties panel, click the Advanced Options icon next to the Margin settings, point to Local Resource, and then click the new *MarginToScene* resource. Both the *Grass* and *BigGrass* objects now use the same resource for their margin settings.

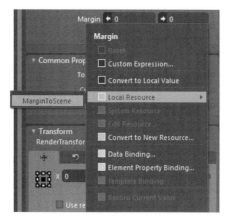

**Note** Expression Blend typically displays only resources of an appropriate type. For example, you don't see all of your color or brush resources in the list of local resources when you are setting the value for *Margins*.

## Creating and applying various resource types

1. Select the *TextBlock* object inside the *InfoBar* container in the Objects And Timeline panel.

2. Select Comic Sans MS for the Font Family setting, select 11 pt for the Font Size, and select Bold for the Font Weight.

3. Convert all of these values to new resources; give them the names **AppFont**, **FontSizeNormal**, and **FontWeightB**; and store them at Application scope.

4. Check your resources in the Resources panel.

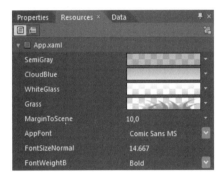

You are going to create a Welcome text block inside of the *Cloud* object.

**Note**  Although you set the font size in points, Expression Blend displays these values in pixels. In this example, 11 points translates to 14.667 pixels.

5. Select the *CloudObj* object inside the *Cloud* container. Right-click it, select Change Layout Type from the context menu, and then select Grid.

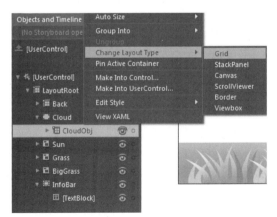

**6.** Select the *TextBlock* object inside of the *InfoBar* container in the Objects And Timeline panel, and select Copy on the Edit menu or just press Ctrl+C.

**7.** Select the *CloudObj* object inside the *Cloud* container, and select Paste from the Edit menu, or just press Ctrl+V. Text appears inside of the *CloudObj* structure.

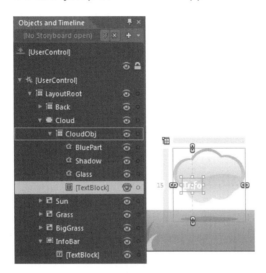

**8.** Set the HorizontalAlignment to Center, reset all margin values, and set the bottom margin property to **15**.

**9.** Set the text to **Welcome!** in the Common Properties category.

**10.** Click anywhere outside of the *Cloud* object. The Welcome text has the same parameters for font family, font size, and font weight as the text from the *InfoBar* panel because you are using resources.

# Modifying Resources

The main advantage of using resources is that you can modify them in a centralized place. You don't need to change the value of font sizes twice for different text objects if they both use the same resource; you can modify the value once, from the Resources panel.

### Modifying resources

1. Click the Resources tab beside the Properties panel to open the Resources panel.

2. Click the color chip near the *SemiGray* color resource to view the Color Editor. Change the value in the Alpha field to **40%**. The shadow under the cloud and the background for the *InfoBar* panel become less transparent.

3. Click the preview image near the *Grass* resource to view the editor. Change the value of the *Stretch* to *Uniform*. You can view the result of your actions in the preview area to the left.

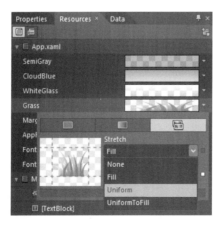

**4.** Change the left and the right margin values of the *MarginToScene* resource to **15**. Change the font family to Trebuchet MS.

**5.** You can also edit resources from the Properties panel if a property already refers to a resource. Select the *BluePart* object in the Object And Timeline panel.

**6.** Click the Advanced Options icon near the Fill property in the Properties panel, and then click Edit Resource on the menu. The Edit Resource dialog box for the *CloudBlue* brush resource appears.

**7.** Click the arrow icon at the bottom of the panel to expand the panel's additional properties. Set the values of the StartPoint to **0.5** and **0** and of the EndPoint to **0.5** and **1**. Your gradient becomes vertically straighter.

**8.** Click the arrow to hide the advanced options again. Then click the right gradient stop and set the selected gradient stop offset to **90%**. Click the left gradient stop and set the selected gradient stop offset to **10%**.

9.  Click OK to apply your changes and close the Edit Resource dialog box.

10. You can also change the names of your resources and reorganize their order any-time. Double-click the *AppFont* name in the Resources panel. Change its name to **ApplicationFont**.

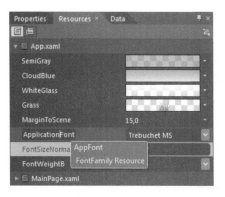

**11.** Press Enter. Expression Blend displays a dialog box and informs you that the previous name was used in several places in the project. You can update references to the new name, convert the references to local values, reset the references to their default values, or choose to not fix them at all.

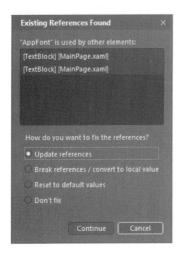

**12.** Leave the first option (Update References) selected, and click Continue.

**13.** To reorganize resources in the Resources panel, select the *WhiteGlass* brush and drag it between the *SemiGray* and *CloudBlue* resources. The order of your resources also changes in the App.xaml file. You can check and verify the changes.

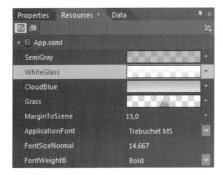

**Troubleshooting** Edit App.xaml in XAML view, or edit resources by selecting them from the Resources panel. You cannot edit App.xaml in Design view.

**14.** Save all files in your project by pressing Ctrl+Shift+S.

# Working with External Resource Dictionaries

As mentioned earlier in this chapter, there are four available levels for storing resources: the application level, the document level, the object level, and the external resource dictionary level. So far you have used only one level—application level. You can also choose to store your resources in a resource dictionary, which is a separate file that you can reuse in other projects. Resource dictionaries are linked to your project by dictionary references in the App.xaml file or by reference in another resource dictionary file.

When you create a new color, brush, or other resource, you are given the option to store them in existing resource dictionaries or create a new resource dictionary.

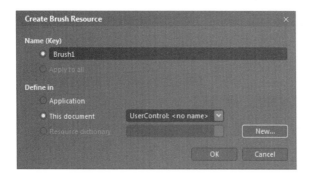

**Note**  The option to store a resource in a resource dictionary isn't available unless there is at least one existing dictionary in the project. You will create a new resource dictionary and move existing resources into it via the Resources panel.

## Creating a new resource dictionary and placing resources in it

*Create
New
Resource
Dictionary*

**1.**  In the Resources panel, click the Create New Resource Dictionary button.

2.  The New Item dialog box appears. Enter the name **Nature.xaml** for the new resource dictionary.

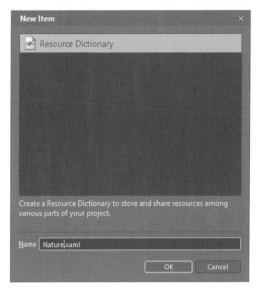

3.  Click OK. The Resources panel displays the recent changes. There is a Nature.xaml file under the App.xaml file, and you can see a link between both of these files.

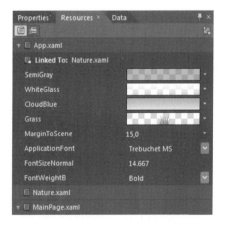

4.  Select the *BG1* object inside the *BigGrass* container in the Objects And Timeline panel.

5.  Click the Advanced Options icon next to the Fill brush property in the Brushes category of the Properties panel, and then click Convert To New Resource.

> **Note** You can convert a solid color not only to a color resource but also to a brush resource.

6. Enter **DarkGrass** as the name (key) for your new resource, and select the Nature.xaml resource dictionary as the place where the resource will be defined.

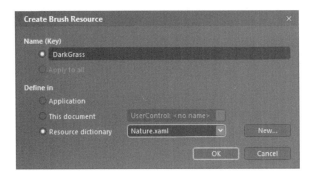

7. Click OK.

8. Select the *BG3* object inside of the *BigGrass* container in the Objects And Timeline panel, convert its Fill brush property to the *OliveGrass* brush resource, and store it in the same resource dictionary.

9. Select the *BG8* object, convert its Fill brush property to the *LightOliveGrass* brush resource, and store it in the same Nature.xaml resource dictionary.

10. Select the *BG9* object, convert its Fill brush property to the *LightGrass* brush resource, and store it in the same resource dictionary.

Now you have all the brushes for the grass elements stored in the Nature.xaml resource dictionary.

11. If you like, you can apply all these resources to other child elements of the *BigGrass* container. Using resources is a way to make your XAML code more clear and compact. Select the *BG8* object and view it in XAML view or Split view. Then select the *BG11* object, examine its code, and compare it with the code for the previous object. The *BG8* XAML code is more readable and compact because of the brush resource.

12. Save all files in your project by pressing Ctrl+Shift+S.

## Moving Resources

You can move resources between external files by dragging them to the new location.

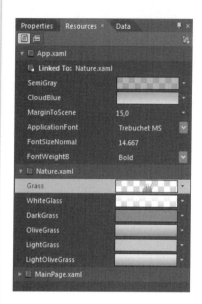

Be careful when moving resources between files or levels if those resources use other resources. For example, consider a brush resource that uses color resources for its gradient stop points. When you move resources, Expression Blend will also move the additional resources if their key names cannot be resolved in the scope of the destination.

You've now been introduced to the basics of using resources in Expression Blend projects. You'll see more about advanced resource types in the next chapter.

# Key Points

- By using color resources, designers can easily create a unified color scheme throughout an application.

- You can create a brush resource from gradients or images.

- You can save property values, such as layout properties, as resources and then use them throughout an application.

- You can save time and ensure uniformity in a project by modifying resources that are applied to elements globally.

- You can store resources in dictionaries to both organize them within a project and make them available for use in different projects.

# Chapter 9
# Skinning Controls

**After completing this chapter, you will be able to:**

- Create and use styles for controls and visual elements.
- Modify existing control templates and create custom control templates.
- Use states to change the behavior of controls.
- Create a theme for basic controls.
- Use color, brush, and other types of resources.
- Use implicit and key-based styles.
- Optimize resources and styles.
- Set template binding for object properties within custom templates.

Skinning is a common Microsoft Expression Blend task that enables designers to completely change the look and feel of default Microsoft Silverlight or Windows Presentation Foundation (WPF) controls. The tasks of skinning range from simple styling to creating and designing new control templates, which control the visual representation of elements in a unified way. With skinning, you can make controls of the same target type (buttons, sliders, and text boxes, for example) look and behave similarly throughout your application. These unified implicit styles apply to both WPF and Silverlight 4.

Expression Blend allows for easy styling of controls: default colors for the background, borders, font sizes, or drop shadow effects can all be specified by the designer. If designers need specific custom styles, they can create them with unique key/names and apply them selectively. Designers and developers can style controls that support templates, or create their own user controls, as well as define different appearances for each state of the control.

 **Important** Before you can complete the exercises in this chapter, you need to install the downloadable practice files to their default location. For more information about practice files, see the instructions at the beginning of this book.

# Structure of Common Silverlight Controls

Silverlight has many default controls that you can use and style in your applications, including:

- *Button*

- *CheckBox* and *RadioButton*

- *Slider*

- *ListBox* and *ComboBox*

- *ScrollBar* and *ScrollViewer*

- *TextBox* and *PasswordBox*

In addition, you'll find more complex controls such as *DatePicker*, *Chart*, *DataGrid*, and *DataForm* that you can style as well.

You can modify controls by changing their default appearance directly in Expression Blend, or you can focus on design by drawing everything first in Microsoft Expression Design and then importing the art or other assets into Expression Blend. When you import your artwork, you can then use the *Make Into Control* command to convert drawing objects into a template for any control.

You can modify the appearance of existing controls, or copies, by modifying the default control structure. In Silverlight, controls are built by using the "parts and states" model. For example, you might notice that the default *Button* control has different states when you run your application and test it. All default controls change their states depending on user actions.

In this chapter, we will begin by examining a simple control, *Button*, and then work toward more complex controls.

## The *Button* Control

Associated states for controls are organized into state groups, and the states within these groups cannot be displayed at the same time. For example, the *Button* control has two state groups: *CommonStates* and *FocusStates*.

Look at the states inside these state groups for the *Button* control:

*CommonStates*

- **Normal**   This is the default, normal control view that appears when there is no inter-action with the control.
- **MouseOver**   This state appears when a user moves the pointer over the control.
- **Pressed**   This state appears when a user clicks the control or when the control has focus and a user presses the Enter key or the Spacebar.
- **Disabled**   This state appears only when the *IsEnabled* property is set to *False* for the control.

*FocusStates*

- **Unfocused**   This state appears when the control does not have keyboard focus.
- **Focused**   This state appears when the control has keyboard focus.

Visually, the states in the *CommonStates* group (from left to right) look like this: *Normal*, *MouseOver*, *Pressed*, and *Disabled*.

The two states in the *FocusStates* group (from left to right) are: *Unfocused* and *Focused*.

 **Note** Only one state from a particular state group can be displayed at a time, but states from different groups can be displayed simultaneously. For example, a *Button* control can be in the *Focused* and *MouseOver* state at the same time.

## The *CheckBox* Control

The default *CheckBox* control has more state groups than the default *Button* control. Similar state and group names have the same meanings as those already discussed for the *Button* control:

*CommonStates*

- **Normal**
- **MouseOver**
- **Pressed**
- **Disabled**

In that order, the states in the *CommonStates* group look like this:

☐ CheckBox    ☐ CheckBox    ☐ CheckBox    ☐ CheckBox

*FocusStates*

- **Unfocused**
- **Focused**

In that order, the states in the *FocusStates* group look like this:

☐ CheckBox    ☐ CheckBox

*CheckStates*

- **Unchecked**    This state appears when the *IsChecked* property of the *CheckBox* control is set to *False*.
- **Checked**    This appears when the *IsChecked* property of the *CheckBox* control is set to *True*.
- **Indeterminate**    This appears when the *IsThreeState* property of the *CheckBox* control is set to *True* and the *IsChecked* property is set to *Null*.

In that order, the *CheckBox* states for the *CheckStates* group look like this:

☐ CheckBox    ☑ CheckBox    ☐ CheckBox

*CheckBox* controls also have a group called *ValidationStates*:

*ValidationStates*

- **Valid**    This state appears when the *CheckBox* control is valid.
- **InvalidUnfocused**    This appears when the *CheckBox* control is not valid and, at the same time, does not have focus.
- **InvalidFocused**    This appears when the *CheckBox* control is invalid and, at the same time, has focus.

In that order, the states of the *ValidationStates* group look like this:

☐ CheckBox   ☐ CheckBox   ☐ CheckBox  ▬

> **Note**  A red rectangle is part of the *InvalidFocused* state. This is a validation tooltip for displaying a validation message.

## The *Slider* Control

With the *Slider* control, users can select a specific value from a range by moving an indicator, also known as a *thumb*, along a track. Most commonly, the *Slider* control functions as a volume control in different types of media players.

The *Slider* control has only two state groups:

*CommonStates*

- **Normal**
- **MouseOver**
- **Disabled**

*FocusStates*

- **Focused**
- **Unfocused**

Although the state groups might seem limited, the control has some complex behaviors. It can have either a horizontal or a vertical orientation, and it consists of sets of parts. The horizontal or vertical template part contains all the elements that make up the *Slider*. The horizontal template of the *Slider* control is shown here:

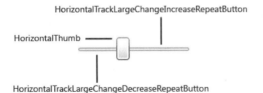

Visually, the horizontal template of the *Slider* control looks like a *Grid* with three columns. The first column contains the *HorizontalTrackLargeChangeDecreaseRepeatButton* part, the second contains the *HorizontalThumb*, and the third contains the *HorizontalTrackLarge-ChangeIncreaseRepeatButton* part. You can move a thumb along a track or click directly to the left or to the right of the thumb's position to decrease or increase the value of the *Slider*. In fact, you don't see the button itself, but the *HorizontalTrackLargeChange-DecreaseRepeatButton* and *HorizontalTrackLargeChangeIncreaseRepeatButton* provide functionality nonetheless.

The vertical slider is very similar. It looks like a *Grid* with three rows that contain smaller parts.

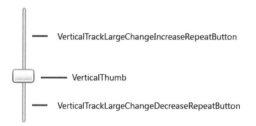

## The *TextBox* Control

The *TextBox* control enables users to enter text. The control stores the entered text in the *Text* property. This control has the following state groups:

*CommonStates*

- **Normal**
- **MouseOver**
- **Disabled**
- **ReadOnly**   This state appears when the *IsReadOnly* property of the *TextBox* control is set to *True*.

In that order, the *CommonStates* of the *TextBox* control look like this:

*FocusStates*

- **Unfocused**
- **Focused**

In that order, the *FocusStates* of the *TextBox* control look like this:

*ValidationStates*

- **Valid**
- **InvalidUnfocused**
- **InvalidFocused**

In that order, the *ValidationStates* of the *TextBox* control look like this:

The *TextBox* control has only one part: the *ContentElement*.

## The *ScrollBar* Control

The *ScrollBar* control enables users to view content that lies outside the current viewing area. A *ScrollBar* can have either a horizontal or vertical orientation and is a part of other controls such as a *ListBox*, *ScrollViewer*, or *DataGrid*. The *ScrollBar* has only one state group, *CommonStates*, which contains *Normal*, *MouseOver*, and *Disabled* states. The parts that make up this control are more interesting. Because the *ScrollBar* can be horizontal or vertical, it includes two sets of parts: one for a vertical scroll bar and another for a horizontal scroll bar. The part names are prefixed by *Vertical* or *Horizontal*, depending on the orientation of the scroll bar.

The *VerticalRoot* vertical template looks like this:

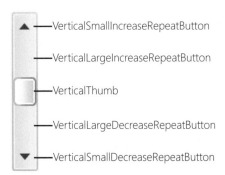

The *HorizontalRoot* horizontal template looks like this:

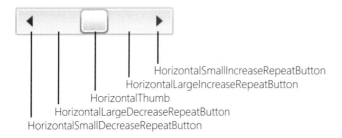

## The *ListBox* Control

A *ListBox* control is more complex than a *Button*, *TextBox*, or *Slider*. This control displays a scrollable list of items from which users can select one or more. If the number of items exceeds the number that can be displayed, a scroll bar is automatically added to the *ListBox* control. Items in the scrollable area are represented by *ListBoxItem* elements.

The control's single *ValidationStates* state group has three states: *Valid*, *InvalidFocused*, and *InvalidUnfocused*.

The *ListBox* control has only one part: the *ContentElement*. Before skinning the *ListBox*, you need to skin a *ScrollViewer* control, which also uses vertical and horizontal *ScrollBar* controls. You can skin *ListBoxItem* elements as well.

# Creating and Using Styles

Styling is the easiest and most direct method of skinning. You can create styles for visual objects, panels, and controls in your application by using several methods, the most basic of which is to set properties that relate to the appearance of the object. Style properties differ according to element type. For example, a *Border* layout panel has a different set of style properties than a *Button*, a *TextBox*, an *Ellipse*, or a *Path* element.

**Note**  Use the CH9 sample project from the CH9 folder located in the \Sample Projects folder.

### Creating a style for the *Border* layout panel

1. Open the CH9 sample project from the \Sample Projects\CH9 folder, and then open the MainPage.xaml file.

   This exercise continues the project from Chapter 8, "Resources."

2. In the Objects And Timeline panel, select the *InfoBar* object.

3. Switch to Split view to see the object's XAML code.

   The *InfoBar* layout panel has different types of properties and content.

```xaml
<Border x:Name="InfoBar" Height="35" VerticalAlignment="Top" Margin="10,10,10,0" CornerRadius="10" Opacity="0.5">
    <Border.Background>
        <SolidColorBrush Color="{StaticResource SemiGray}"/>
    </Border.Background>
    <TextBlock TextWrapping="Wrap" Text="Info" Foreground="White" VerticalAlignment="Center"
        HorizontalAlignment="Left" Margin="15,0,0,0"
        FontFamily="{StaticResource ApplicationFont}" FontSize="{StaticResource FontSizeNormal}"
        FontWeight="{StaticResource FontWeightB}"/>
</Border>
```

   You can often use a *Border* layout panel in other places in your application. For efficiency you can apply properties such as *CornerRadius*, *Opacity*, *Margin*, and *Background* as style properties so that the appearance is easily maintained and reused.

4. On the Object menu, point to Edit Style, and click Create Empty.

   The Create Style Resource dialog box appears.

**5.** Type **InfoBar** in the Name (Key) field, and in the Define In group, select Application.

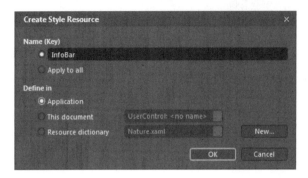

**6.** Click OK.

You are now in style editing mode. You can tell this because a breadcrumb menu bar displays *InfoBar* > at the top of the Artboard. By clicking the buttons on the breadcrumb bar, you can quickly move between style editing and object editing for a selected object. The breadcrumb bar appears for any selected object that has a custom style.

Additionally, the Objects And Timeline panel displays the objects that make up the style, and the Resources panel displays a new resource that you can view and modify.

By using the Properties panel, you can set properties such as *CornerRadius*, *Opacity*, *Margin*, and *Background*. In the Brushes category of the Properties panel you can see a selected Background brush.

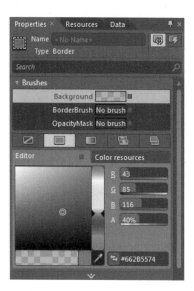

7.  Click the Advanced Options icon next to the *Background* property, and then select Convert To Local Value.

    An Advanced Options square turns white to inform you that values are set.

8.  On the right side of the Artboard, click Split to switch to Split view.

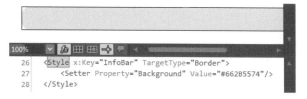

    You will see the XAML code for the style. An *x:Key* attribute shows the name of the style you entered in the Create Style Resource dialog box. Later you can apply this style to other objects of the appropriate type by using this key. A *TargetType* attribute shows the type of object for which you are creating the style. When you are declaring a style, setting its *TargetType* is mandatory, because in Silverlight and WPF, all visual elements have different properties that can be styled.

    The *Setter* line within the *Style* tag sets the value for the specified property. Setters are just lists of property-value pairs.

9.  Click the Advanced Options icon next to the *Opacity* property, and then select Convert To Local Value.

10. Click the Advanced Options icon next to the *CornerRadius* property, and then select Convert To Local Value.

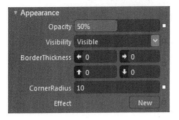

11. In the Appearance group, set all *Margin* properties to **10**. In this case, don't convert existing values to local.

    You've finished setting properties for the *InfoBar* style.

12. Click the Return Scope To arrow icon in the Objects And Timeline panel to exit the editing scope of the style.

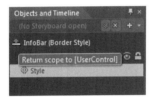

    Now you can remove unnecessary values for the *InfoBar* object, because you have created a style.

13. Click Advanced Options next to the *Background*, *Opacity*, *Margin*, and *CornerRadius* properties, and for each, select Reset.

    The visual appearance of the *InfoBar* object stays the same because of the applied style.

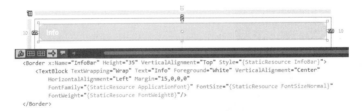

    You've finished creating the *InfoBar* style. You didn't transfer the *VerticalAlignment* and *Height* property values to the style, because additional *InfoBar* objects might have other alignment and size requirements.

Next, you'll apply the *InfoBar* style to other *Border* layout panels.

## Applying a custom style to other *Border* layout panels

1. In the Objects And Timeline panel, select the *LayoutRoot* object, and then in the Tools panel, select the *Border* object.

**2.** Double-click the control to insert the *Border* at its default size.

The *Border* layout panel appears in the upper-left corner of your document.

**3.** Right-click the *[Border]* object in the Objects And Timeline panel, point to Edit Style, and then point to Apply Resource.

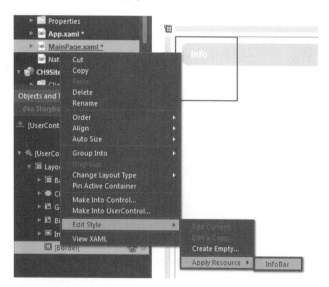

**4.** Select the *InfoBar* that you created in the previous exercise.

 **Note** You can also apply a style from the Object menu. To do so, point to Edit Style, point to Apply Resource, and then click the named style that you want to apply.

Expression Blend applies the *InfoBar* style to the *Border* object. But the selected *[Border]* object still has other predefined properties, such as *Width*, *Height*, *BorderBrush*, and *BorderThickness*.

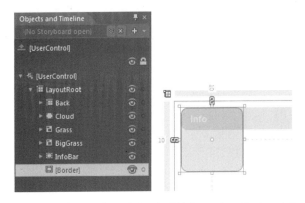

5. Reset *BorderBrush* and *BorderThickness* by clicking Advanced Options next to the corresponding properties and then selecting Reset.

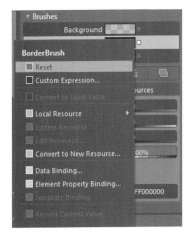

6. Set the *VerticalAlignment* property of the *[Border]* object to *Bottom* so that it moves to the bottom of your document.

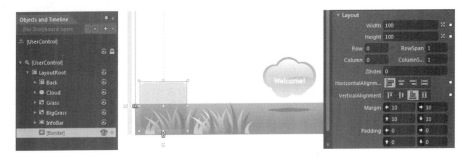

When you create styles, you can define the properties that will be common to multiple objects, and then for each property group, you can create styles that you can set directly in your document as you place objects.

You can modify existing styles in the Resources panel, or you can change them on the Artboard in style editing mode.

## Modifying an existing style by using the Resources panel

1. In the Objects And Timeline panel, select the *InfoBar* object.

2. In the Resource panel, click the Edit Resource icon next to the *InfoBar* name.

Expression Blend enters the editing scope for this style.

3. Switch to the Properties panel, and change the *Opacity* value to **70%**.

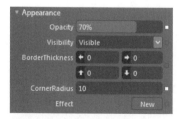

4. Click Return Scope To in the Objects And Timeline panel.

This action exits the editing scope of the style and returns you to the editing scope of the App.xaml document.

**5.** Switch to the MainPage.xaml document to see the changes.

Both *Border* layout panels have become less transparent.

**6.** On the File menu, click Save All.

Another way to edit an existing applied style is with the style editing mode on the Artboard.

### Modifying an existing style for an object on the Artboard

**1.** In the Objects And Timeline panel, select the *InfoBar* object if it's not already selected.

**2.** On the Object menu, point to Edit Style, and then click Edit Current. Expression Blend enters the editing scope for the *InfoBar* style.

 **Note** If the Edit Current option is unavailable, the object does not have a custom style applied to it.

**3.** Find the New button next to the *Effect* property in the Appearance category of the Properties panel.

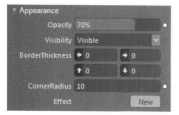

4. Click the New button. The Select Object dialog box appears.

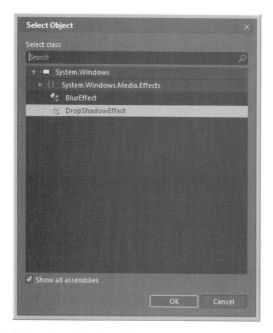

5. Select *DropShadowEffect,* and click OK.

   A new *Effect* block is added to the Appearance category and applied to the *Border* object.

6. The default values for the *DropShadowEffect* look a little rough, so set the *BlurRadius* to **3**, the *Direction* to **-90**, the *Opacity* to **30**, and the *ShadowDepth* to **3**.

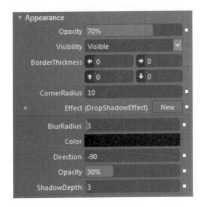

The shadow effect looks more refined now.

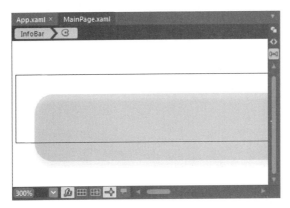

7. Click Return Scope To in the Objects And Timeline panel to exit the editing scope of the *InfoBar* style.

8. In the Zoom box at the bottom of the Artboard, select 400%. Look at the *InfoBar* object on the Artboard. The new style changes were applied to the *Border* object. The *TextBlock* object inside the *Border* object also acquired an interesting side effect.

9. On the View menu, click Actual Size, and then select Save All from the File menu.

# Templates

Sometimes, creating styles for objects is insufficient. There are many situations in which you need a specific appearance for your controls. For example, you might want your *CheckBox* controls to look like creative checks, your *Buttons* to have round or custom shapes, or your *TextBox* controls to have inside shadows or torn borders—and all of these together might need a consistent color theme. To make all of these changes, you need something more powerful than styles. Fortunately, you can customize Silverlight and WPF controls by changing their control templates in Expression Blend. With templates, you can modify the structure of the control to which the template is applied. Together, styles and custom templates give you full control over the appearance.

> **Tip** Designers cannot override template values by setting values on the control itself when it is placed on the Artboard.

## Creating Beautiful Custom Buttons

You can convert almost any art object into a *Button* control if you think it can work, behave, and appear as a button. For example, you could create a template for a button that used the cloud object in the CH9 project for the button's appearance. You can use the built-in *Button* control template to create a custom *Button* template.

### Creating a custom *Button* template

1. In the Objects And Timeline panel, select the *Cloud* object.

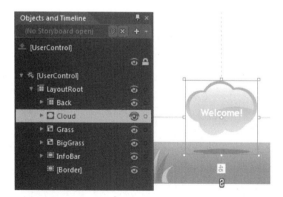

2. Right-click the *Cloud* object, and then click Make Into Control.

3. In the Make Into Control dialog box, select Button, type **CloudButton** as the name (key) for your new resource, and select Application in the Define In group.

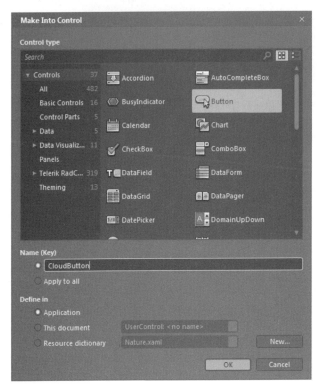

4. Click OK in the Make Into Control dialog box.

   Expression Blend switches to template editing mode.

   Expression Blend turned the *Button* control into a template for a new *CloudButton* style and applied that template to *Button*. You can see the editing mode level by pointing to the breadcrumb menu at the top of the Artboard. The first level, *[Button]*, will return you to the *Button* placed in MainPage.xaml; the second level lets you edit the style; and the third level gives you a way to modify the *Button* template.

   Take a look at the Objects And Timeline panel. It now displays the structure of the *CloudButton* template. In the preceding chapter, you placed a *TextBlock* with the text *Welcome!* inside the cloud. You don't see any *TextBlock* object inside the *CloudButton* template structure now, because Expression Blend replaced it with a *ContentPresenter* with the same properties as the original *TextBlock*.

**5.** Click the *[ContentPresenter]* object in the Objects And Timeline panel. The *Content-Presenter* displays the content. This object is used directly within the control template of a *Content* control to mark where the content is to be added.

**6.** Click the Return Scope To arrow in the Objects And Timeline panel to return to MainPage.xaml and exit the template editing scope.

**7.** Increase the size of the *Button* control. The text inside doesn't look quite as good now. It should be vertically aligned to the center and be sized proportionally.

**8.** Undo the *Resize* action by pressing Ctrl+Z.

9. Return to the *CloudButton* template editing mode by clicking the *[ContentPresenter]* item in the breadcrumb menu at the top of the Artboard.

10. Select the *CloudObj* object represented by the *Grid* layout panel in the Objects And Timeline panel. Move your pointer over the left ruler of the *Grid* layout panel on the Artboard. Your pointer changes to an arrow with a plus (+) sign, and an orange line appears where a row will be added.

11. Click somewhere between the cloud art and its shadow on the left ruler to add a row to the *Grid* layout panel at that position. Now you can separate the top part of the cloud art object and its shadow, placing them in different rows of the *Grid* layout panel.

12. Select the *[ContentPresenter]* object in the Objects And Timeline panel. Move it inside the *CloudObj* container by dragging it below the *Glass* object.

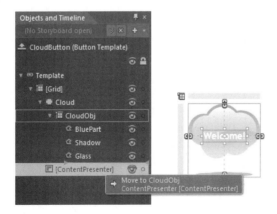

13. Click Advanced Options next to the *Margin* property, and select Reset to return the vertical alignment of the *[ContentPresenter]* object to the center.

**14.** Click the tab to view the States panel in your workspace.

As you saw earlier, the *Button* control has two state groups: *CommonStates* and *FocusStates*. The States panel displays all state groups with their states for the selected control.

**15.** Click the *MouseOver* state in the *CommonStates* group. When you select a state, state recording is turned on, and any changes that you make will be recorded for that state.

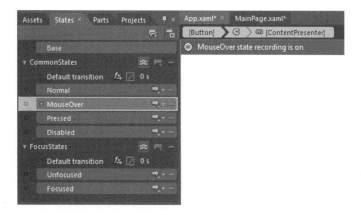

 **Note** You can turn off state recording by clicking the Record mode indicator on the Artboard or by returning to the *Base* point in the States panel.

**16.** Select the *BluePart, Glass,* and *[ContentPresenter]* objects at the same time in the Objects And Timeline panel by holding down the Ctrl key and clicking the objects one at a time. The Objects And Timeline panel also indicates that you are in *MouseOver* recording mode.

**17.** Press the Up Arrow key on the keyboard five times.

This feature allows you to nudge all selected objects while there is an active selection. Pressing it five times brings into play a render transform and subtracts five pixels from the *TranslateY* property of each selected object.

**18.** When you complete these actions, the Objects And Timeline panel displays changes made for the *MouseOver* state. Expand the *BluePart* object to see what happened. Expression Blend recorded the movement as *RenderTransform* transformation.

**19.** Select just the *Shadow* object in the Objects And Timeline panel. Stay in the *MouseOver* state. Expand the Transform category of the Properties panel, and click the Scale tab. Set *X* to **0.9** and *Y* to **0.7**.

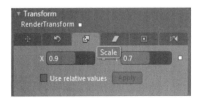

Expression Blend records these changes and displays them in the Objects And Timeline panel.

**20.** Press F5 to test your application and see the changes applied to a live button. Point to the cloud button. The cloud appears to move up, and its shadow gets smaller.

**21.** Return to Expression Blend. Select the Template level in the Objects And Timeline panel.

**22.** Right-click the *MouseOver* state in the States panel, click Copy State To, and select *Pressed*.

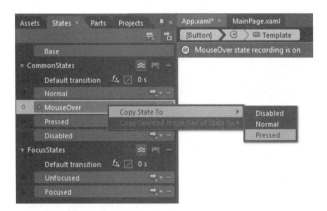

Expression Blend will copy all the changes you made for the *MouseOver* state to the *Pressed* state.

**23.** Select the *Disabled* state in the States panel, select the *CloudObj* object in the Objects And Timeline panel, and set the *Opacity* property in the Properties panel to **40**.

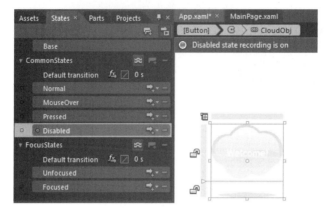

If you test your application at this point, you won't see the changes made for this state because it appears only when the *IsEnabled* property is set to *False* for the control.

Now it's time to add some nice effects to transition between states. Expression Blend allows you to create physical effects that are very natural in appearance.

*Add Transition*

**24.** Select the *MouseOver* state. Click the Add Transition icon next to the *MouseOver* state, and select * ➡ *MouseOver*.

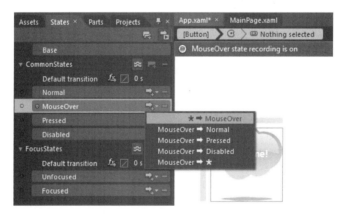

**25.** In the Transition Duration box, type **0.5**.

*Easing Function*

**26.** Click the *EasingFunction* icon in front of the Transition Duration box, and select the *Bounce: In* function from the list. Leave the default values for this function in the next box.

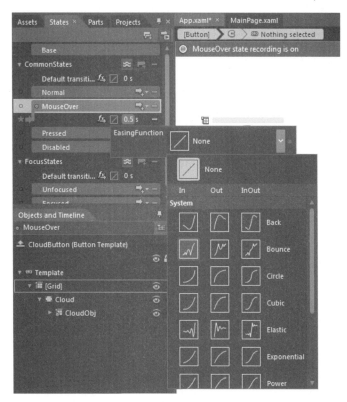

**27.** Test your application by pressing F5 to see how the *MouseOver* state changes. The cloud naturally moves up with the bounce effect.

You can also change the appearance of states from the *FocusStates* group. Before doing this though, you will make some general changes.

**28.** Select Base in the States panel. Select the *Glass* object in the Objects And Timeline panel. Set the color of the Stroke brush in the Brushes category of the Properties panel to white. Change its *Alpha* component to **0%**. The white color becomes transparent.

**29.** Set the *StrokeThickness* property to **2**.

**30.** Select the *Focused* state in the States panel. Change the *Alpha* component of the Stroke brush property to **100**. Your button now becomes more interesting in the *Focused* state.

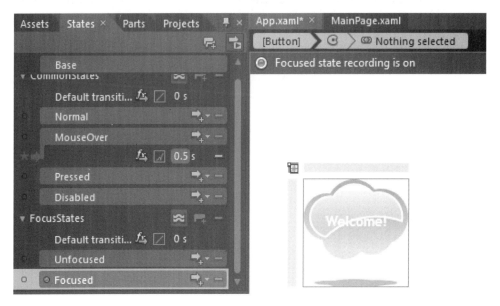

**31.** Select Base in the States panel and click Return Scope To in the Objects And Timeline panel. Save all files.

**32.** Test your application by pressing F5.

# Creating Silverlight Themes

Sometimes you need to create a complete custom theme for controls used in your application. In these cases, you need all of the application's elements—buttons, text boxes, sliders, check boxes, and others—to have the same style, the same colors, and the same behavior in similar states. You can begin by creating graphic assets in a graphic editor and then convert your work to XAML files. Then you can add these files to your project and convert art elements that look like controls to real, working controls. You can separate colors, brushes, margins, and font settings, and then use them as resources throughout all of the controls in your application to provide a unified appearance.

# Drawing Controls

The first task when you are creating themes takes place in Microsoft Expression Design, Adobe Photoshop, or another graphic editor that can work in concert with Expression Blend.

You can find the file SweetControls.design in the \Sample Projects\CH9 folder of the installed practice files. It might pique your imagination by giving you an idea of what a designer's themes might look like.

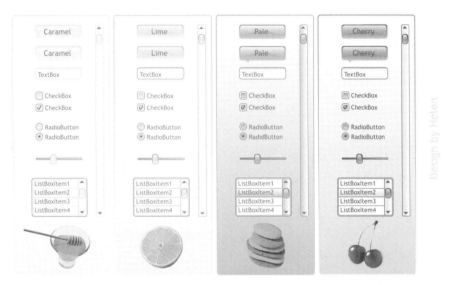

Designers or integrators can convert their complete work or just some of their design assets to XAML files and then open them in Expression Blend.

## Preparing design assets for Expression Blend

1. In the Projects panel, right-click the CH9 project level and then click Add Existing Item.

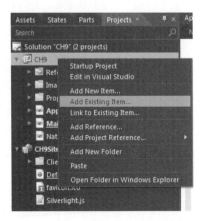

2. Select the Caramel.xaml file from the CH9 folder.

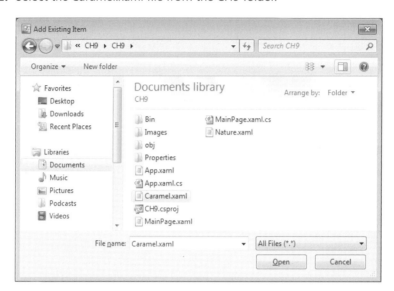

3. Click Open in the Add Existing Item dialog box. The Caramel.xaml file appears in the file list of the CH9 project. Double-click it to open and view it.

The Objects And Timeline panel shows that this XAML file contains differently named blocks, such as *Button* and *TextBox*. You can easily find visual assets that correspond with real controls.

**4.** Select the *Button*, *TextBox*, and *Slider* objects. Press Ctrl+C, or select Copy from the Edit menu.

**5.** Switch to the MainPage.xaml file, select the *LayoutRoot* in the Objects And Timeline panel, and press Ctrl+V or click Paste on the Edit menu. Drag the selected objects slightly to the right on the Artboard.

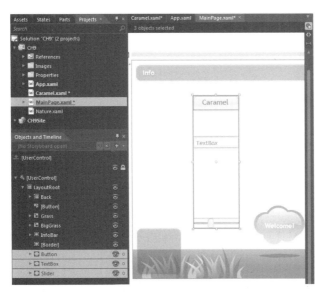

**6.** Right-click the Caramel.xaml file, and then select Remove From Project.

Because the Caramel.xaml file is no longer needed in the project, you can safely re-move it. In the next exercise, you will work with the items that you dragged onto the Artboard in step 5.

## Skinning a Control for a Theme

In one of the previous examples, you created a cloud skin for the *Button* control, which was a style with a custom template. Then you applied the skin by specifying its unique name (key) for the target *Button* control.

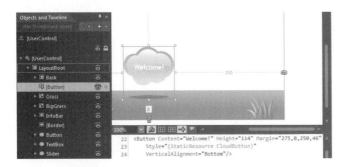

Fortunately, with Silverlight 4 and WPF, designers can create implicit styles without setting the key/name so that these styles for controls of the specified target type within the same scope can be automatically applied. This means that you can create default implicit styles with custom templates for all of the *TextBox*, *Button*, *Slider*, and other controls in your application. Implicit styles provide a unified way to apply styling over an entire application. When you want to use a non-default style, you can create a style with a key/name and apply it to any control individually.

### Creating an implicit style with a custom template for *TextBox* controls

1. With the MainPage.xaml file still on the Artboard from the previous exercise, select the *TextBox* object in the Objects And Timeline panel.

2. Right-click the *TextBox* object and select Make Into Control. Select *TextBox* for the control type, select Apply To All in the Name (Key) section, and then select Application in the Define In category.

3. Click OK in the Make Into Control dialog box.

   Now you are in template editing mode.

**4.** Press F5 to test the new style for the *TextBox* control. Type some words and see how it works.

It's not as nice as you might have expected, so you can modify an existing template so that the control will have the same look but be more stable and act as expected.

**5.** Switch back to Expression Blend and click the *TextBox* object in the Objects And Timeline panel. Right-click it, and select Ungroup. Do the same for the *[Canvas]* object.

**6.** Select the *Path_5* object. Go to the Brushes category in the Properties panel. Click the Advanced Options icon next to the *Fill* property, and then select Convert To New Resource. Type **InputShadow** for the name (key), and define the resource at Application level.

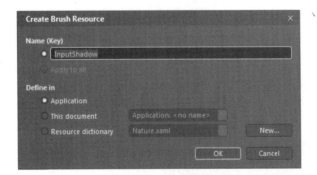

**7.** Click OK in the Create Brush Resource dialog box. Then click the Advanced Options icon next to the *Stroke* property and select Convert To New Resource. Type **StrokeBrush** for the name (key), and define the resource at Application level.

**8.** Select the *[Grid]* object in the Objects And Timeline panel. In the Tools panel, select the *Border* object, and double-click the control to insert the *Border* at its default size.

**9.** In the Zoom box at the bottom of the Artboard, select 300% to see all of the details of the custom template on the Artboard.

**10.** Click the Advanced Options icon next to the *Margin* property, and select Reset.

**11.** Set the *CornerRadius* property to **5** so that the *Border* control covers the entire *Path_5* object.

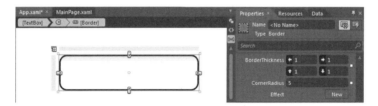

**12.** Click the Advanced Options icon next to the *BorderBrush* property, point to Local Resource, and then select *StrokeBrush*.

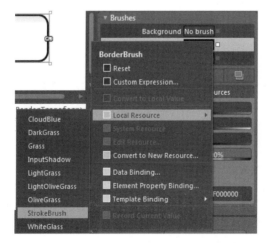

13. Click the Advanced Options icon next to the *Background* property, point to Local Resource, and select *InputShadow*.

    Now this *Border* panel looks like a path, but it has a more stable and flexible structure.

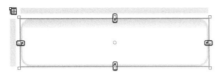

14. Select the *Path_5* object in the Objects And Timeline panel and delete it.

    You can delete it because you don't need it anymore.

15. Select the *ContentElement* object in the Objects And Timeline panel.

    This object doesn't fill the space that you have available for it, and contains some transformations as a side effect.

16. Use the Advanced Options for the *Margin, RenderTransform, RenderTransformOrigin, Height, Width,* and *HorizontalAlignment* properties to reset them to their default values.

    It's usually a good idea to use less XAML code when possible.

17. Select the *ContentElement* object and drag it inside the *Border* object.

18. Reset the *Margin* property, and set the *BorderBrush* property to *No Brush* by clicking the first tab.

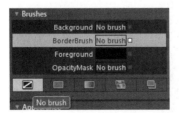

19. Test your application by pressing F5 and see how the style works now.

    It looks much better, but it still needs some modifications.

**20.** Return to Expression Blend and click the style editing level on the breadcrumb menu at the top of the Artboard to switch from template editing mode to style editing mode.

**21.** Set the *FontSize* property to **10**. Set the *MinHeight* property to **24**.

**22.** Click the object editing scope on the breadcrumb menu at the top of the Artboard.

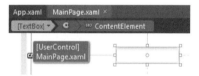

**23.** Reset the *Height* property for the *TextBox* control.

**24.** Test your application by pressing F5 and typing some words to see how it works.

The text wrapping works as expected. If you need different behavior, you can specify it by setting other properties.

**25.** Switch back to Expression Blend and select the *Path_21* object inside the *Slider* object. Click the Advanced Options icon next to the *Stroke* property in the Brushes category of the Properties panel, and then select Convert To New Resource.

**26.** Type **DarkStrokeBrush** for the name (key), and select Application level for the resource.

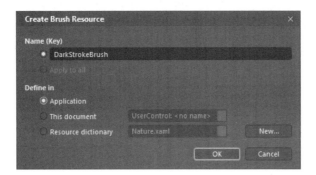

**27.** Select your *TextBox* object, and switch back to template editing mode by clicking the template editing scope on the breadcrumb menu at the top of the Artboard.

**28.** Select the *[Grid]* object in the Objects And Timeline panel. In the Tools panel, select the *Border* object and double-click the control to insert the *Border* at its default size.

**29.** Reset the *Margin* property, set the *CornerRadius* to **5**, and select the *DarkStrokeBrush* brush for the *BorderBrush* property.

**30.** Set the *Opacity* property to **0**, rename the *[Border]* to **OverState** in the Objects And Timeline panel, and switch to the States panel.

**31.** Click the *MouseOver* state, select the *OverState* property, and change the *Opacity* to **100**.

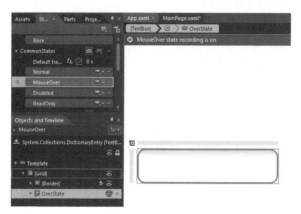

**32.** Click the *Focused* state, select the *OverState* property, and change its *Opacity* to **70%**.

**33.** Click the style editing scope on the breadcrumb menu, and choose the *DarkStrokeBrush* resource as the value for the *Foreground* property.

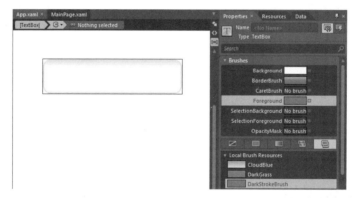

**34.** Test your application by pressing F5 and typing some text in the *TextBox* control.

The text has an appealing foreground color, and the *TextBox* control changes states and no longer looks static.

You've just created your first implicit style with a custom template for the *TextBox* control. If you need another behavior for this control type, you can specify it by setting other properties, changing the appearance of its different states, and so on.

# Optimizing an Output Theme

After you have converted all of your design assets into controls, you can optimize the theme by using colors and brushes as common resources for your control styles. For example, the *Button* foreground text color should be the same for a *TextBox* as well, and it would be beneficial if the *BorderBrush* property were the same for all *TextBox*, *PasswordBox*, and *ScrollBar* borders.

You can use the same font size, weight, and font family for your controls as well.

In addition, specifying common *Margin*, *Padding*, and *Vertical/Horizontal* alignment properties is a good practice.

## Template Binding

Sometimes custom templates require parameters that depend on the property values of the control itself. For example, suppose you need a *Border* inside a custom template to take on the same color as the *Background* of the control. That way, when you apply the template to a control with different *Background* properties, the result is a differently colored template.

To do this, Expression Blend supports a feature called *template binding*, in which a template binds to a control, using the bound control's properties as values for template objects. By binding parts of the template to a control, you effectively create parameters for the template.

### Creating a template binding for *TextBox* control properties

1. Select the *TextBox* object in the Objects And Timeline panel.

2. Click the template editing scope on the breadcrumb menu.

3. Select the *ContentElement* object in the Objects And Timeline panel.

4. Click the Advanced Options icon next to the *HorizontalAlignment* property in the Properties panel, and choose *HorizontalContentAlignment* from Template Binding.

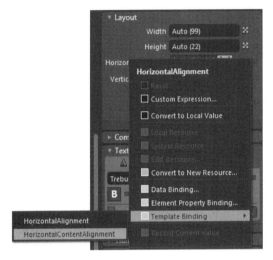

5. Test your application by pressing F5. Type **Hello** into the *TextBox* control.

Note that the content inside the *TextBox* is centered.

6. Click the object editing scope on the breadcrumb menu to return to MainPage.xaml and the *TextBox* control.

**7.** Experiment with the *HorizontalContentAlignment* property by setting its value to *Left*, *Right,* and *Stretch*. Test the result by running the application.

You've just been introduced to the basics of using styles and custom templates in Expression Blend projects, and you have seen how to use implicit styles and name (key)–based styles to apply formatting to controls. Remember to follow best practices by setting common colors and brush resources, and by using template binding.

# Key Points

- Using styles for controls and visual elements is a simple way to modify the visual appearance and behavior of elements.

- You can modify existing control templates or create custom templates for controls.

- You can use states to change the behavior of controls.

- Modify the look of controls by using a theme, which you can use throughout a project to provide a unified appearance.

- Apply color, brush, and other types of resources to project elements to alter their appearance.

- You can use implicit and key-based styles to automatically ensure uniformity in the appearance of your project elements.

- By removing unnecessary properties and assets, you can optimize resources and styles.

- You can set template binding for object properties within custom templates to further ensure project uniformity and the predictability of your elements.

# Chapter 10
# Working with Data

**After completing this chapter, you will be able to:**

- Generate sample data.

- Use styles and templates on data display controls.

- Work with sample data.

- Bind object properties to data.

- Change data templates.

- Use element property binding.

- Use Master/Detail scenarios to display data.

All applications use and interact with data in various ways. Internal data (data that exists within an application) can be based on user history or values that a user enters into a form. Some applications use external data sources such as databases, web services, or different types of files. Usually, working with data is the job of database administrators and developers. Designers create an application's user interface and styles, and they build control templates to provide a particular look and feel that presents the data in a usable way. Expression Blend provides for a process called *data binding*, which is a way to automatically connect items from a data source to user interface components (controls), populating them with data without requiring custom code. Data binding tasks can be performed by various team members: developers, designers, or integrators. An integrator has knowledge of both design and development processes and works to connect user interface components to internal or external data sources.

Microsoft Expression Blend supports data sources such as XML, objects or collections of objects, and sample data sources. An XML data source supplies data to your applications in XML format. Object data sources consist of objects that expose public properties to which you can bind target control properties. Unfortunately, you cannot see live data from external sources on the Artboard—you usually see the data only when you run your application, and only when the data is available. Because of this, it's often difficult to design the appearance of objects that display data. Expression Blend supports a third type of data source, called *sample data*, that you can use while designing or prototyping your application. Expression Blend's data binding provides a simple visual way of connecting items in a data source to controls in your application.

**Important** Before you can complete the exercises in this chapter, you need to install the downloadable practice files to their default location. For more information about practice files, see the instructions at the beginning of this book.

# Sample Data

With sample data sources, you can populate your application with temporary (but realistic) data while you design the user interface—before the application gets connected to live data. The Expression Blend Data panel provides powerful tools for generating sample data for your application from existing XML files, classes, or instantly in real time.

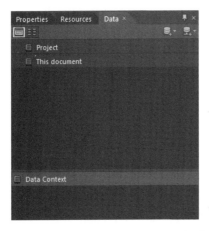

Expression Blend supports sample data of various types, including:

- **String** This data type is used for string properties and can be used for formats such as addresses, colors, company names, dates, email addresses, names, phone numbers, prices, times, website URLs, and more. If you need abstract text for prototyping, you can use a *Lorem ipsum* format for the *String* type and apply maximum word count and length values.

- **Number** This data type is appropriate for numeric properties such as IDs, counts, amounts, and similar data.

- **Boolean** This data type is used for control properties that take two values, such as check box and radio button properties.

- **Image** This data type is suitable when you need to bind images to controls. In Expression Blend, you can use your own pictures or you can generate sample images.

# Creating and Modifying Sample Data

You can capitalize on Expression Blend's ability to display sample data to help create designs that match real-life data needs.

> **Note**  Use the CH10 sample project from the CH10 folder located in the \Sample Projects folder.

### Creating sample data to display a list of vendors

1. Open the CH10 sample project from the \Sample Projects\CH10 folder.

2. Open the MainPage.xaml file from the CH10 project.

3. In the Objects And Timeline panel, select the *LayoutRoot* object, and make sure your workspace is in Design or Split view.

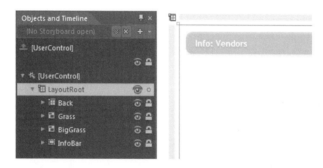

4. Find the Data panel—or display it by selecting it from the Window menu if it isn't visible in your workspace.

*Create Sample Data*

5. In the Data panel, click the Create Sample Data icon at the right end of the Data panel, and then select New Sample Data from the list.

6. The New Sample Data dialog box appears. Type **Vendors** in the Data Source Name field, and leave the Define In option set to the Project level to make the data available to all the documents in the project.

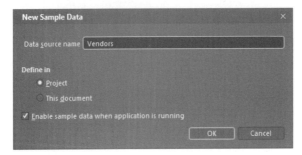

7. Click OK to close the New Sample Data dialog box.

> **Note** Make sure that the Enable Sample Data When Application Is Running check box is selected. If you don't select this option, you will be able to see sample data only on the Artboard while you are designing your documents in Expression Blend and not in a browser or when you run the application.

A new data source named *Vendors* appears in the Data panel. Expression Blend created a basic collection with multiple properties of various types. You can see the full structure of your data in the following graphic.

8. Double-click the *Property1* name to edit it, and then type **CompanyName**. Press Enter to apply the change.

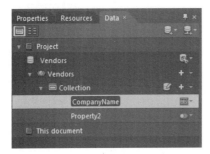

9. Click the Change Property Type icon to the right of the *CompanyName* property. In the pop-up menu that appears, leave the Type field as it is, and click the arrow next to Format. Select Company Name.

The format of this property is now changed.

10. Double-click the *Property2* name to edit it. Type **Phone**, and then press Enter to apply the change.

11. In the pop-up menu that appears when you click the Change Property Type icon, click the arrow next to Type, and then change the data type to *String*. Click the arrow next to Format, and then select *Phone Number*.

You can also add new simple, complex, or collection properties to your existing collection. The plus sign (+) icon informs you about additional available operations.

**12.** Click the + icon now and add a new simple property.

Expression Blend adds a third line to the existing collection and names it *Property1*.

 **Note** The menu that appears when you click the arrow next to the plus sign allows you to add complex, simple, or collection properties or convert the structure of an existing collection to hierarchical. You would use a hierarchical structure for displaying a recursive tree of data. For example, this option would be suitable for controls such as a *TreeView*.

**13.** Rename *Property1* to **Address**, and then choose the Address format for the *String* type.

After you rename *Property1*, Expression Blend automatically sorts the list of properties alphabetically, moving *Address* to the top in this case.

You might notice that Expression Blend added a new folder to your CH10 project. The SampleData folder contains a Vendors folder and some files.

**14.** Double-click the Vendors.xaml file to open it.

In both Split and XAML, view you can now see the structure of your sample data and generated items with appropriate properties and their values. Each item in the *Vendors* collection has *CompanyName*, *Phone*, and *Address* properties that Expression Blend populated with appropriate values.

 **Warning** You should avoid editing this file directly in XAML. Expression Blend generates it automatically with the help of various design tools. If you are unsure about the effect of editing the XAML, don't save any changes to files in the SampleData folders.

## Generating sample data in your application

1. Close the Vendors.xaml file and return to the MainPage.xaml file.

2. Select the *Collection* node in the Data panel.

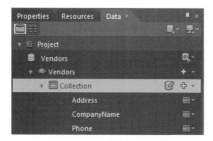

**Note**  Make sure you are in list mode. The first icon in the upper-left corner of the Data panel will be highlighted when you are.

**3.** Drag the node onto the Artboard. A *ListBox* filled with data appears on the Artboard.

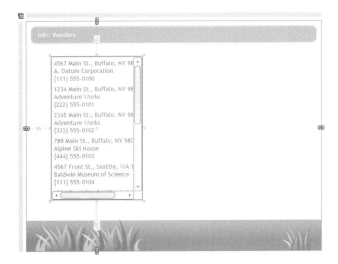

You might notice that the look of this *ListBox* differs from a default *ListBox*. That's because the CH10 project uses *custom implicit styles* that it applies automatically to controls of the target type. For more information about custom implicit styles, see Chapter 9, "Skinning Controls."

**4.** Switch to the Resource panel to see the list of available resources.

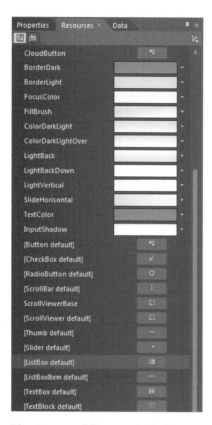

The App.xaml file now includes several brushes and custom styles for controls that are created by default, including *Button, TextBox, TextBlock, ListBox, ListBoxItem, Slider, ScrollBar, ScrollViewer, CheckBox,* and *RadioButton*. Take some time to examine the structure.

**5.** Switch back to the MainPage.xaml file and the Data panel.

**6.** Reset the *Width, HorizontalAlignment,* and *Margin* properties in the Properties panel for the selected *ListBox* control, and then set all the *Margin* values to **60**.

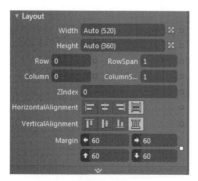

The *ListBox* now looks like this:

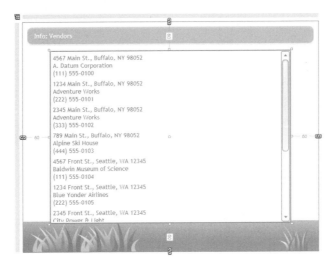

7. Test your application by pressing F5.

8. Scroll through the list of vendors to see how your data will look.

Almost everything is acceptable except the display order of the *CompanyName* and *Address* properties of each item, which are reversed. You'll see how to fix that in the next exercise.

## Changing a Data Template

In the previous exercise, Expression Blend made some changes to the MainPage.xaml file after you dragged the *Collection* onto the Artboard to connect the data to the *ListBox* control.

If you switch to Split view and select the *ListBox* control in the Objects And Timeline panel, you can see that its *ItemsSource* property is bound to *Collection*. The Data panel view has also changed.

The *ListBox* control also includes an *ItemTemplate* property. This is a data template that styles the items displayed in each row of the object itself. The data template is specific to the items bound to the object. You can change the template that Expression Blend created and make the control look very different from its default appearance.

### Changing the data template for the *ListBox* control

1. Select the *ListBox* control in the Design pane. Make sure that you are in Split view so that you can simultaneously see changes in the XAML code. Using the breadcrumb bar at the top of the Artboard, point to Edit Additional Templates and then to Edit Generated Items (ItemTemplate), and then select Edit Current.

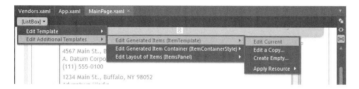

Now you are in template editing mode. Expression Blend focuses on the generated data template with the *ItemTemplate* key in the Code pane of Split view. It also adds this resource to the current document resources.

The *ItemTemplate* data template has a simple structure: a *StackPanel* layout that has three *TextBlock* controls bound to the properties *Address*, *CompanyName*, and *Phone*. Expression Blend displays the data by binding a data item to an object on the Artboard.

**2.** Select the second *TextBlock* in the Objects And Timeline panel.

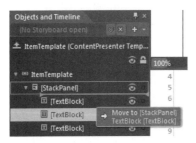

**3.** Drag the second *TextBlock* into position before the first *TextBlock*. Drag the third *TextBlock*, which is bound to the phone number, between *CompanyName* and *Address*.

**4.** Select the middle *TextBlock* for the phone number in the Objects And Timeline panel, and make a copy by selecting Copy on the Edit menu and then selecting Paste (also on the Edit menu).

**5.** Drag the last *TextBlock* (which is the new copy that you just created) so that it appears under the previous phone number *TextBlock*.

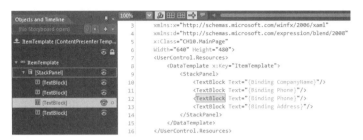

**6.** In the Data panel, add a new simple property to the *Collection*.

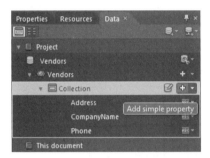

**7.** Double-click the *Property1* name to change it, type **WWW**, and then change the Format to Website URL.

**8.** Press enter to apply the changes. Drag the new *WWW* property from the Data panel onto the third *TextBlock* on the Artboard.

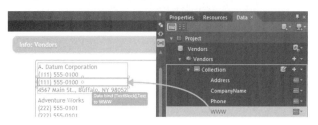

The blue border informs you that the object on the Artboard is bound to a data item.

 **Note** You can also drag properties from the *Collection* in the Data panel onto the objects in the Objects And Timeline panel to bind data items to existing or new objects.

The data displayed in the third *TextBlock* changes to web addresses.

9. Select the first *TextBlock* in the Objects And Timeline panel, and then click the Advanced Options icon next to the Bold button in the Text category of the Properties panel. Select *FontWeightB* from Local Resource.

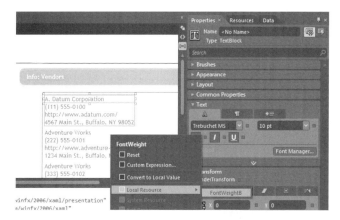

The *TextBlock* containing the *CompanyName* becomes bold.

10. Exit template editing mode by clicking the Return Scope To [User Control] button in the Objects And Timeline panel.

**11.** Press F5 on your keyboard to test the application, which should now look something like this:

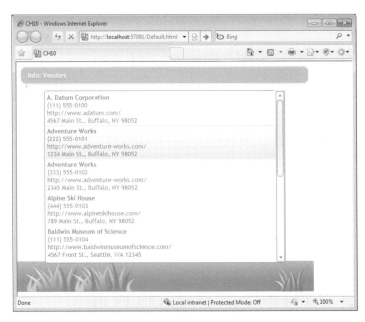

You've just changed an *ItemTemplate* for the *ListBox* control that displays the list of vendors. You also added a new property to the *Collection* and bound it to the *Text* property of a new *TextBlock* object inside the *ItemTemplate*.

You can change the *ItemTemplate* view presented as a *DataTemplate* in the Resources block of your document's XAML code in order to reorganize existing objects, change their parent layout container from a *StackPanel* to a *Grid* (or to other panels), or modify object property values, thus changing the objects' appearance. You can also add decorative elements such as borders, backgrounds, and so on to make the general appearance of the *ItemTemplate* more attractive. The Resources panel also displays this template as a resource in the MainPage.xaml file scope. You can rename it if you want.

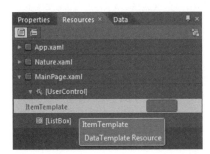

The Data panel tools let you modify existing items easily within collections by clicking the Edit Sample Values icon next to the *Collection* name.

The Edit Sample Values dialog box displays all the data in the *Collection*. You can change the number of data lines that display, alter the types and formats of existing properties, or edit specific values directly.

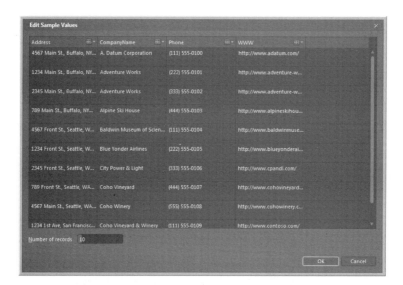

# Data Binding

As a result of the data binding process, whenever the data changes, the interface elements to which the data is bound reflect those changes. You aren't limited to binding data to complete objects; you can bind data to specific properties of an object. The sample data source lets you simulate text values, images, colors, dates, and other property types. In this exercise, you'll see how to bind data to a specific control property.

## Binding data to specific control properties

1. In the Data panel, add two simple properties to the *Collection*: *Status* and *StatusColor*.

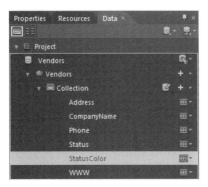

2. Click the Edit Sample Values button next to the *Collection* name, and set the number of records to **7**.

3. Double-click the first cell under the *Status* header and type **Gold**. Double-click the second cell under the same *Status* header and type **Gold** again. Modify the values of the remaining *Status* cells as you see in the following image:

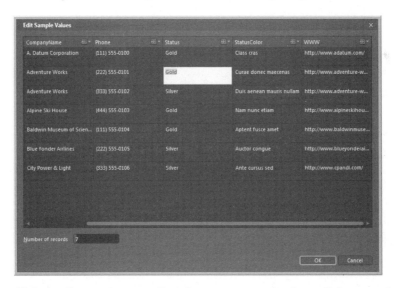

*Change Property Type*

4. Click the Change Property Type button next to the *StatusColor* name in the header line.

5. Change the value of the Format field to **Colors**.

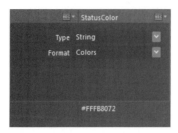

6. Double-click the first cell under the *StatusColor* header and type **#FFFCD92D**. Do the same for the other lines to which you applied a *Gold* value.

7. Change the value of the *StatusColor* cells in the lines that you changed to *Silver* to **#FFC0C0C0**.

8. Click OK in the Edit Sample Values dialog box, and then select the *ListBox* control if it isn't still selected.

9. On the breadcrumb bar at the top of the Artboard, point to Edit Additional Templates and then click Edit Generated Items (ItemTemplate). Finally, select Edit Current.

You are in template editing mode again.

10. Right-click the first *TextBlock*, point to Group Into, and select *StackPanel*.

11. In the Properties panel, reset the *Width* property of this *StackPanel,* and then change its *Orientation* to *Horizontal*.

**12.** Expand this *StackPanel* object in the Objects And Timeline panel.

**13.** In the Tools panel, select the *Border* object, and double-click the control to insert the *Border* at its default size.

In the Objects And Timeline panel, the *Border* appears inside the *StackPanel* container with the *TextBlock* object.

**14.** Drag the *Border* object above the *TextBlock*.

**15.** Set the *Width* and *Height* properties to **16**, the right *Margin* property to **5**, and *BorderBrush* to **#FFC2C2C2**.

**16.** Select the *Background* property in the Brushes category for the selected *Border* object.

**17.** Click the Advanced Options icon next to the *Background* property, and then select Data Binding.

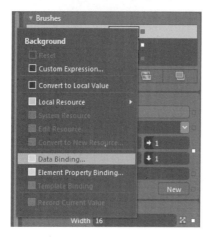

The Create Data Binding dialog box appears.

**18.** Select the *StatusColor* field from the fields available on the Data Context tab. This tab lets you bind to a data source in the context specified for the current object. It displays only compatible data items.

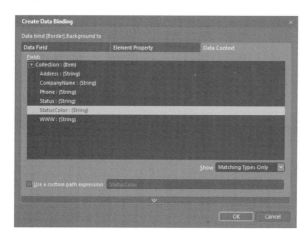

**19.** Click OK.

A yellow bounding box appears around the *Background* property to indicate that the property is now data bound.

**Note**  A yellow bounding box always appears around properties when they are bound to data. This behavior is unrelated to the colors used in this exercise.

20. Now press F5 on your keyboard to test the application and view the changes. Note how the sample data displays in the current view.

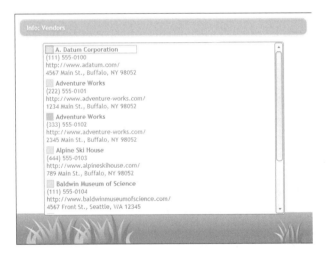

Notice that a gold or silver square appears but doesn't inform you about its meaning. In the next few steps, you will add a tooltip to this element.

21. Return to Expression Blend and select the *Border* object if it isn't still selected.

**22.** Access the Advanced Options for the *ToolTip* property in the Common Properties category.

**23.** Select Data Binding. Then select the *Status* field from the available fields on the Data Context tab.

**24.** Exit template editing mode by clicking the Return Scope To [User Control] button in the Objects And Timeline panel.

**25.** Press F5 to test the application again. Point to the color squares to see how the tooltips change depending on the underlying data.

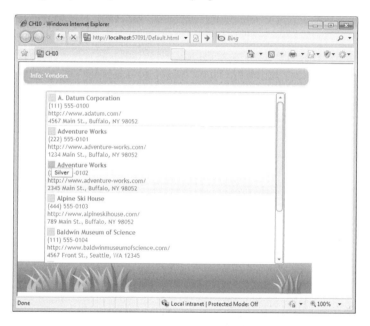

# Element Property Binding

In addition to the scenarios you saw in the previous examples it's also possible to bind the value of one element property to the value of another element property to synchronize the two.

## Binding one element property to another

1. Unlock the *InfoBar* object in the Objects And Timeline panel by clicking the lock icon.

2. Select the *TextBlock* object inside the *InfoBar* object.

3. Click the Advanced Options icon next to the *Margin* property in the Properties panel.

4. Select Element Property Binding.

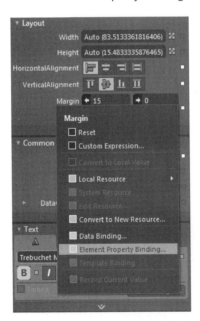

   The cursor changes to the Artboard Element Picker.

5. Click the *InfoBar* object on the Artboard.

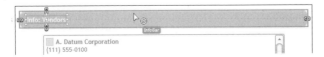

**Note** If you can't pick up the proper element on the Artboard, you can click the object in the Objects And Timeline panel.

**6.** In the list in the Create Data Binding dialog box, select the *Margin* property.

**7.** Click OK. A yellow bounding box appears around the *Margin* property of the *TextBlock* object to indicate that the property is now data bound and depends on the *Margin* property of the *InfoBar* object.

Using Element Property Binding is an easy way to bind element properties together, but there's another way to accomplish this type of binding.

**8.** Click the Advanced Options icon next to the *Margin* property of the *TextBlock* object, and select Data Binding.

The Create Data Binding dialog box appears, with the Element Property tab selected. You can bind internal values to properties on this tab as well.

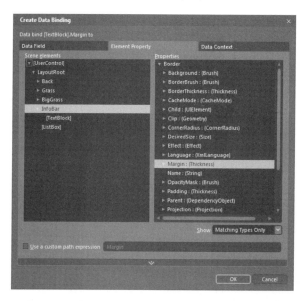

In the preceding image, you can see that the *InfoBar* object is selected on the left and its *Margin* property is selected on the right. The Create Data Binding dialog box gives you an advanced and flexible way to bind element properties together.

# Using a Master/Details Scenario to Display Data

The master/details scenario is an often-used screen pattern in efficient user interfaces. It allows the user to stay on one screen while still being able to navigate between items and view detailed information about selected items.

You can create a master panel by using a list (*ListBox*), a tree (*TreeView*) or a *DataGrid*. The details panel displays the extended information and/or scaled image data for the item a user selects from the master panel.

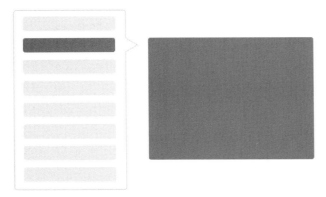

The master/details screen pattern can be vertical or horizontal; the functionality is the same for both layouts.

In this exercise, you will implement this scenario and display detailed information for items selected from the vendors list.

### Adding a details panel to create a master/details scenario

1. Select the *ListBox* object in the Objects And Timeline panel, and then set the *HorizontalAlignment* property to *Left* and the left *Margin* property to **20**.

2. In the Data panel, add two simple properties to the *Collection*: *Price* and *ContactPerson*.

3. Change the format of the *Price* property to **Price**.

4. Change the format of the *ContactPerson* to **Name**.

5. In the Data panel, click the Details Mode icon.

6. Select the *CompanyName*, *ContactPerson*, *Price*, and *Status* properties in the *Collection* by holding down the Ctrl key and clicking each one in turn.

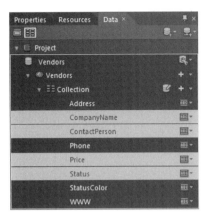

**7.** Drag the selected properties from the *Collection* onto the Artboard to the right of the *ListBox*.

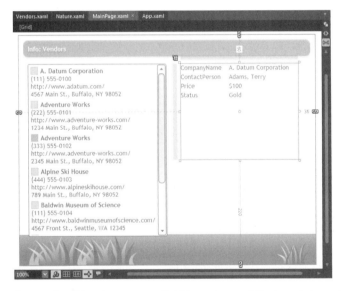

Expression Blend creates a *Grid* layout panel that contains a *TextBlock* control to display the name and value of each property.

**8.** Press F5 to test your application. Click items in the *ListBox* control. The details view will update accordingly.

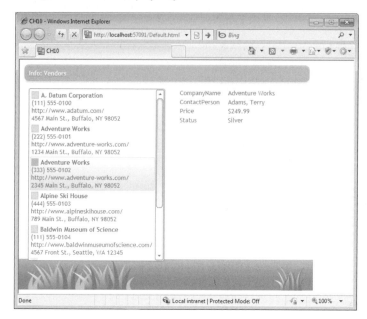

9. Return to Expression Blend and select the *CompanyName TextBlock* object on the Artboard.

   This block displays only the title for the neighboring field.

10. Remove the *Name* portion of this text.

11. Select the *ContactPerson TextBlock* object on the Artboard and insert a space between the two words.

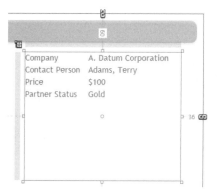

**12.** Select the *Status TextBlock* object on the Artboard and change it to **Partner Status**.

Now all of the fields have properly modified titles. You might notice that there is no data (except titles) displayed in the details block when you start the application without selecting an item from the list. In the next few steps, you will refine the interface so that the details block is hidden unless it has something to display.

**13.** Select the *ListBox* in the Objects And Timeline panel.

**14.** Drag the *ChangePropertyAction* behavior from the Assets panel onto the *ListBox* control in the Objects And Timeline panel.

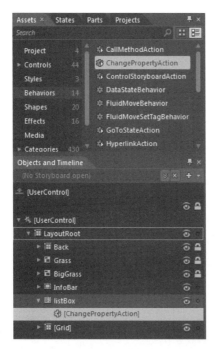

**15.** In the Properties panel, select the *SelectionChanged* value for the *EventName* property. Then choose the Artboard Element Picker near the *TargetObject* property, and select the *Grid* layout container (which is the last item in the Objects And Timeline panel and is the element that displays the details). Directly on the Artboard or in the Objects And Timeline panel, choose the *Visibility* value for the *PropertyName* property and select the *Visible* value for the *Value* property.

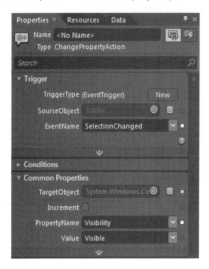

 **Note**   When you pick up the *Grid* layout container that displays details, Expression Blend automatically names it *grid*.

**16.** Select the layout container named *grid* in the Objects And Timeline panel, and set its *Visibility* property to *Collapsed*.

**17.** Press F5 to test your application.

Now the details block appears only when you select something in the list.

This master/details view is only two levels deep. You can create three or more levels to display data that has a complex and hierarchical structure.

## Important Data Display Concepts

### Data Context

During the process of data binding, you dragged data items directly from the Data panel or created a data binding by using the Advanced Options features of the Properties panel. Expression Blend then added lines of code to make your design work more easily. If you work in Split view, you can see all the changes that Expression Blend makes to the XAML code.

In addition to the property binding, Expression Blend also sets the data context during the process of data binding. The data context identifies the data source. Creating the master/details scenario was simplified because Expression Blend automatically created the relationship between the list view and the details view.

You can see in Split view that the *DataContext* property of the *Grid* layout container was set to the *SelectedItem* property of the *ListBox* object. Expression Blend also automatically gave the name *listBox* to the *ListBox* control.

If you click the *LayoutRoot* object in the Objects And Timeline panel, you'll see that the *DataContext* property is also present.

### The Structure of Sample Data

Sample data is used only for prototyping, temporarily filling your application with data and displaying data at design time on the Artboard. Sample data helps you test different scenarios for displaying data in your application.

Before switching from sample data to live data, make sure that your sample data source has the same structure as the live data source that your production application will use.

# Key Points

- Sample data helps designers visualize data in an application at design time.

- You can create styles and templates for data display controls to provide them with appearances specific to data controls.

- You can bind object properties to data, making their appearance change depending on the specific data to which they're bound.

- You can easily change Expression Blend's default data templates.

- Use a master/details scenario to display related data efficiently.

# Chapter 11
# Using SketchFlow

**After completing this chapter, you will be able to:**

- Create and run a SketchFlow application.

- Navigate between SketchFlow screens.

- Create an application flow.

- Add controls and use sample data for prototyping.

- Make your SketchFlow projects interactive.

- Modify the SketchFlow Player settings.

- Package your application prototype.

- Use the feedback functionality to collect new ideas and comments.

- Generate documentation in Word format.

With Microsoft Expression Blend, you can do more than just design and develop applications; using its built-in dynamic prototyping tools, you have the freedom to experiment with ideas without having to build the entire application. Expression Blend's exciting prototyping tool is SketchFlow. With SketchFlow, you can sketch and quickly prototype applications, including all interactivity. You can create a working "initial prototype" of an application in just a few hours without writing any code, thus improving productivity and letting you experiment with multiple ideas. You can import scanned paper sketches, use the power of sample data, include built-in navigation between screens, switch between states, and add animations so that you and your clients can test how the prototype behaves.

 **Important** Before you can complete the exercises in this chapter, you need to install the downloadable practice files to their default location. For more information about practice files, see the instructions at the beginning of this book.

## Sketching

Sometimes you have a really great idea, and you say "Eureka! That's what I need!" Your mind begins working more intensely, and you think about how to implement and evolve the idea. Sometimes you want to share your idea and get input from others. Often, such ideas are born on scraps of paper or napkins and are nothing but pencil sketches. Then you might take these rough sketches and draw everything out more cleanly on larger paper, perhaps drawing several screens or parts of screens that you evaluate as the idea transforms into a rough draft, and then you experiment with the details. Often, if something doesn't result in what you envisioned, you start over from scratch.

All of this sketching becomes the first draft of your idea. But the idea is still on paper and looks static, even if you arrange all the sketches in the order that they might appear in an actual application. At this point, you're ready to take your rough sketches to the next stage: a prototype.

Prototyping adds life and functionality to your idea; you can feel how buttons click and how and when screens change, you can preview sample data in lists and fill out forms, and more. In a well-done prototype, the application looks almost finished. And that's key, because after a prototype is finalized, it's much easier to create a real application because almost all of the interactive parts of the application—the screens, the elements, the behaviors, and the parts—are polished and integrated.

# Creating and Running a SketchFlow Project

The process of creating a prototype is similar to that for creating a real Microsoft Silverlight or Windows Presentation Foundation (WPF) application in Expression Blend. It starts from the New Project dialog box, where you can create either a Silverlight SketchFlow application or a WPF SketchFlow application, depending on the type of application you want to build after the prototype phase. It's worth noting that a SketchFlow prototype actually *is* a Silverlight or WPF application.

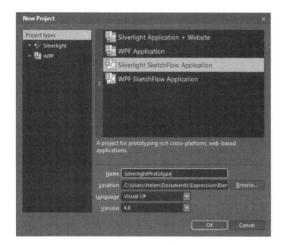

In this exercise, you'll work with an existing SketchFlow project. For the exercise, imagine that you are going to create an application for an online shop that sells guitars.

 **Note**  Start Expression Blend 4 before beginning this exercise. Use the CH11 sample project from the CH11 folder located in the \Sample Projects folder.

### Opening and running a SketchFlow project

1. From the File menu, select Open Project/Solution. In the Open Project dialog box, browse to and open the CH11 sample project from the \Sample Projects\CH11 folder.

2. Expression Blend will show you the *Start* (Screen_1.xaml) page of this project, which displays a shop logo, a picture of a guitar, and some menu items.

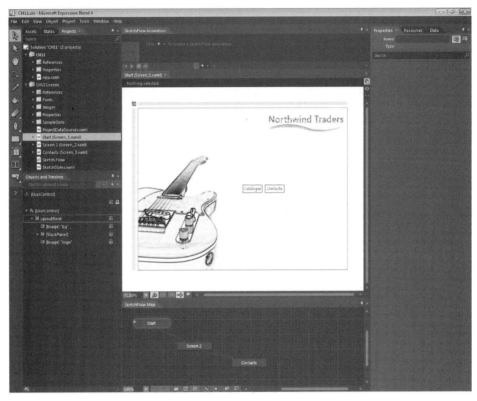

**3.** The main difference between the SketchFlow project workspace and the workspace of a standard Expression Blend project is the SketchFlow Map that appears at the bottom of the workspace. This panel provides a visual representation of the application's flow and its available screens.

**Troubleshooting** If you can't see a SketchFlow Map panel in your workspace, you can display it by selecting SketchFlow Map from the Window menu or by pressing Ctrl+F12.

**4.** Press F5 to run the project.

Expression Blend launches your project in the SketchFlow Player, which plays the application flow in the sequence in which you designed it. In the SketchFlow Player, the first screen appears in the middle of the Artboard, and navigation tools and a feedback panel are displayed on the left side. The navigation tools are particularly useful when you are just starting to design your application and haven't created internal navigation to enable users to move between screens.

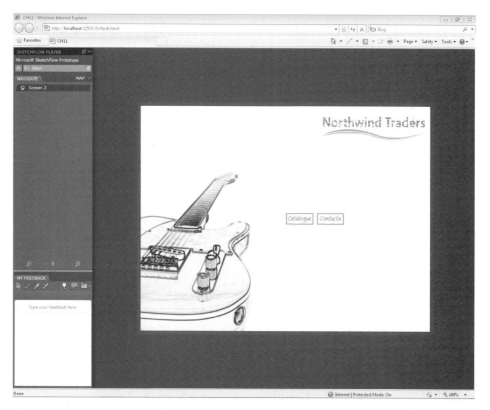

**5.** The Navigate tab in the SketchFlow Player panel displays a list of screens available from the currently active screen. Click the *Screen 2* item.

**6.** In the SketchFlow Player panel, click the Map tab. The application flow appears in the Map window. You can also navigate from one screen to another by clicking the nodes in the graph.

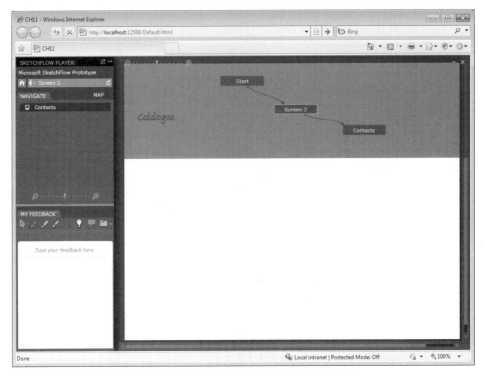

7. Click the *Contacts* node to see its content, and then click back to *Screen 2.*

8. Use the Zoom control at the top of the Map window to zoom into or out of the SketchFlow map. Click the close button in the upper-right corner of the Map window to hide it.

9. Click the home icon in the top part of the SketchFlow Player panel. You are returned to the home screen of the application.

10. Close the SketchFlow Player and return to Expression Blend.

Now that you've seen how to run a SketchFlow program and navigate between its various screens, you'll explore how to create and control application flow.

# Creating an Application Flow

When you first create an empty SketchFlow project, you'll see only one empty screen. It looks like a piece of white paper onto which you can sketch your ideas. You can add any number of additional "papers" to your application from the SketchFlow Map panel, filling them with content and defining the navigation between them, connecting existing screens with new screens. Every screen in your prototype appears as a node in the SketchFlow Map panel. The connections between these nodes simulate the navigation. You can have both connected and unconnected screens in a SketchFlow application.

### Creating a new navigation screen and connecting it to existing screens

1. In Expression Blend, open the SketchFlow Map panel if it's not already open.

2. Point to the first node, the one with the green triangle icon. A group of icons appears at the bottom of the node.

3. Point to the leftmost icon in the menu (a screen icon with a plus sign [+] on it). Drag the icon to where you want the new screen to be on the SketchFlow Map.

   A new node appears.

4. Click in this new node, type **About**, and then press Enter to give the new node a name.

   Note that the *About* screen is highlighted, connected with the *Start* screen, and activated for editing on the Artboard.

**5.** The *Start* screen has two direct connections: to the *About* node and the *Screen 2* node.

**6.** Press F5 to run the application.

Both items now appear on the Navigate tab of the SketchFlow Player.

**7.** Next you will return to Expression Blend and rename the *Screen 2* node. To do so, select the *Screen 2* node, double-click it, and then type the new name **Catalogue** directly into the node.

 **Note** You can also rename the node by right-clicking it and then clicking Rename.

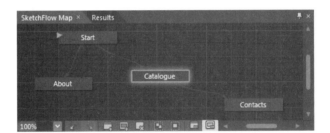

**8.** Point to the *Start* node.

The node becomes highlighted and an icon menu appears at the bottom of the node.

**9.** Point to the Connect An Existing Screen icon (the second icon from the left).

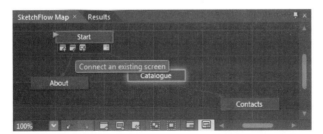

**10.** Drag the icon to the *Contacts* screen to connect these two screens.

A new line with an arrow appears. Now you can navigate to three screens from the *Start* screen when you run your prototype application.

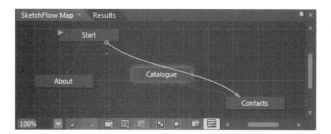

 **Note** To remove a connection, right-click the arrow and then click Remove.

By default, all nodes and connections are blue, but you can apply different colors to different types of screens and connections by setting visual tags on the SketchFlow Map.

**11.** Point to the *Start* node and then to the Change Visual Tag icon on the menu (the icon on the right). Click the icon, and then select Red.

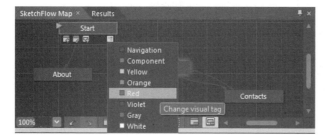

The *Start* node becomes red. By setting different colors to group nodes, you can quickly identify the types and purposes of screens.

## Navigation and Component Screens

The SketchFlow Map panel displays two types of screens: navigation and component. You worked with navigation screens in the previous example. Component screens are similar to navigation screens but contain content that you can reuse on multiple screens. A component screen can also be part of a navigation screen. These *Component* screen nodes do not have incoming navigation connections on the SketchFlow Map panel.

You can organize content that you want to reuse on multiple screens into component screens. Such content might include a header with the company logo, menus, footers, and so on. Component screens are similar in functionality to an HTML website's templates.

## Creating and using component screens

1.  Activate the *Start* screen to see it on the Artboard. Click the logo to select it.

2.  Right-click the logo, and then select Make Into Component Screen.

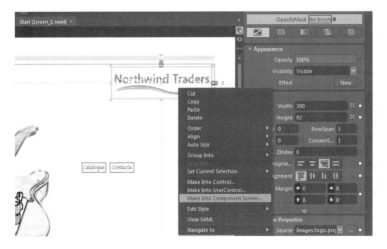

The Make Into Component Screen dialog box appears.

**3.** Type **Logo** into the Name field.

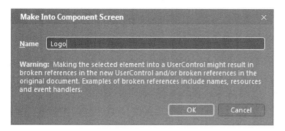

**4.** Click OK.

Expression Blend creates a new *UserControl* the size of the selected object before completing the conversion, and then it adds the Component Screen to the project and to the SketchFlow Map panel and opens it for editing on the Artboard. The *Logo* component screen appears as a green rounded rectangle on the SketchFlow Map panel. This element is connected with the *Start* navigation node by the green dashed line in one direction only.

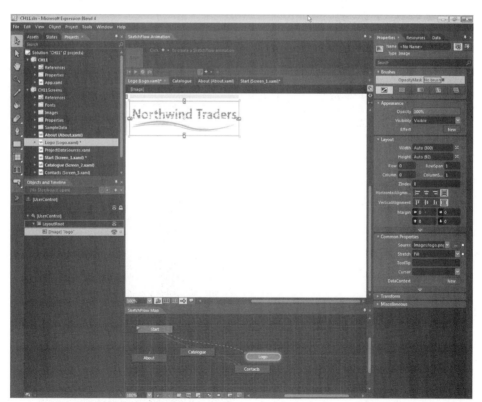

**5.** In the SketchFlow Map panel, Activate the *Start* screen.

After the previous operation, you need to rebuild your application to see the correct view of the created component screen on the navigation screen.

**6.** Press Ctrl+Shift+B or select Build Project from the Project menu.

**7.** Point to the *Logo* node on the SketchFlow Map panel. Point to the Insert A Component Screen icon in the menu (the third icon from the left).

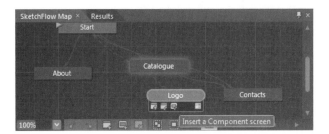

**8.** Drag the icon to the *Catalogue* screen to connect these two nodes.

A new line with an arrow appears. The *Logo* component is now also added to the *Catalogue* screen. It appears in the upper-left corner by default.

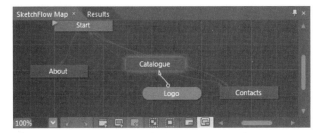

**9.** Drag the Insert A Component Screen icon from the *Logo* node to the *About* and *Contacts* nodes to add the *Logo* component to these screens too.

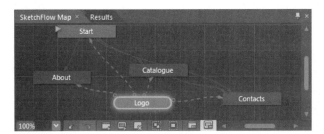

Now the *Logo* node is connected to all the screens in your application. You can move the *Logo* node a little bit to the left on the SketchFlow Map panel to create more space between the nodes.

10. Test your prototype application by pressing F5. Navigate through all the screens to make sure that the *Logo* component appears throughout your application.

11. Close the SketchFlow Player and return to Expression Blend.

By using these techniques, you can add any number of component screens to your prototype, grouping objects and reusing them on multiple screens. Both navigation and component screens appear on the SketchFlow Map panel so that you can quickly interconnect them.

# Adding Controls and Data

Adding new controls to your SketchFlow application is similar to adding them to other applications. The difference is that controls in SketchFlow prototypes have a hand-sketched look and use special Sketch styles. You might notice that the two buttons on the *Start* screen in this chapter's example have this odd look.

Microsoft chose the Sketch style for controls to help users focus on ideas rather than appearance at this early stage of the application design process. At the prototype stage, you should concentrate on thinking and experimenting with ideas, and postpone skinning for the next phase of the application's development.

## Adding Controls to Your Prototype

Expression Blend automatically uses a hand-sketched style when you add a control to the screen. You can see this even when selecting a control from the Tools panel. All the default controls have a *-Sketch* suffix.

### Adding a Sketch control to the screen

1. Select the *StackPanel* object in the Objects And Timeline panel for the *Start* screen.

2. Double-click Button-Sketch in the Tools panel to insert a button control into the selected *StackPanel* container.

   A third button appears below the two buttons in the Objects And Timeline panel and in line with them on the Artboard.

3. Change the *Content* property of this button to **About**.

4. Click the tab above the Artboard to open the *About* navigation screen. Select the *BasicTextBlock-Sketch* control from the Tools panel.

5. Draw the area for the *TextBlock* control in the center of the screen to define the boundaries.

   This area will contain information about the guitar shop.

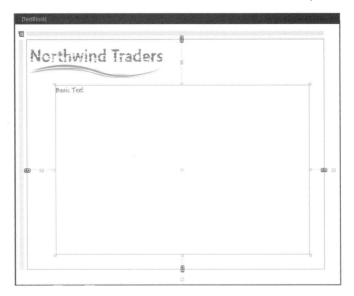

The process of adding new controls to a prototype is simple and fast. Even if you directly write or copy XAML code to add elements, you can apply Sketch styles later from the Resources panel or by using the Expression Blend breadcrumb bar at the top of the Artboard. You can also remove the Sketch styles to use the default Silverlight and WPF appearance of controls.

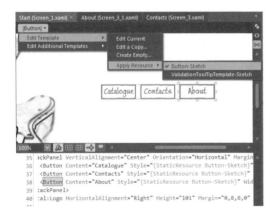

# Using Sample Data

The main purpose of sample data is to quickly fill prototype applications with temporary but realistic data, which you saw in Chapter 10, "Working with Data".

Again, at this prototype stage, you should concentrate on ideas, not on production data. You can fill your completed application with real data later, at the appropriate point in the development cycle.

## Obtaining and displaying sample data

 **Note**  This exercise is a continuation of the previous exercises.

1. Activate the *Catalogue* screen.

   You will add some data to this screen to display a list of guitars.

2. Open the Data panel.

   You already know how to generate different types of sample data from Chapter 10. The *Guitars* sample data source contains a *Collection* with *Description*, *Price*, and *Title* properties.

3. Add a simple property to the *Collection* and name it **Image**.

4. Select the *Image* type and click the Browse button.

   The Browse For Folder dialog box appears.

5. Select the Guitars folder within the CH11 folder that contains the current sample project.

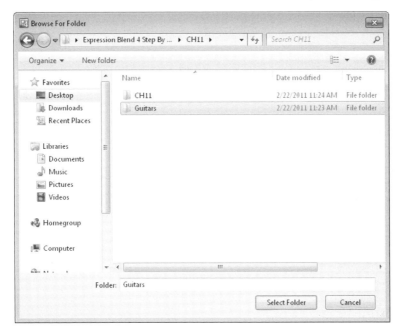

6. Click the Select Folder button and then expand the Guitars_Files folder inside the SampleData\Guitars folder.

   You can see a list of images that were added automatically by Expression Blend, with names running from image01.png to image05.png. You can also see several images that were added manually, with names running from 1.png to 6.png.

7. Delete the files named image01.png through image05.png from the project, leaving only the files 1.png through 6.png. These are sketched images of guitars that you will use for your prototype application.

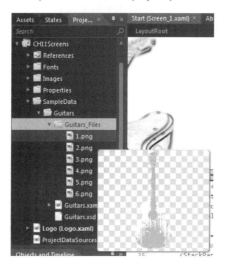

 **Tip** You don't need image01.png through image05.png for this project, because they are sample images that Expression Blend adds.

8. Activate the *Catalogue* screen.

9. Switch to list mode. Select the *Description*, *Title*, and *Price* properties in the *Collection*. Drag these properties onto the Artboard. Expand the width of the *ListBox* control so that it takes up about half of the screen (approximately 350 pixels).

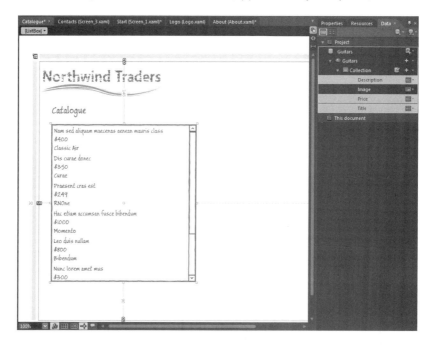

10. Use the Expression Blend breadcrumb bar at the top of the Artboard to change the *ItemTemplate* for the *ListBox* control. Select the *GuitarItemTemplate* resource.

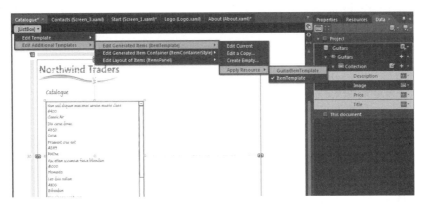

The *ListBox* control looks more attractive now.

11. Switch to details mode in the Data panel and drag the *Image* property to the right side of the *Catalogue* screen on the Artboard.

**12.** Press F5 to test the application and see the result of your work on the *Catalogue* screen.

**13.** Select any item in the list to see the corresponding image on the right.

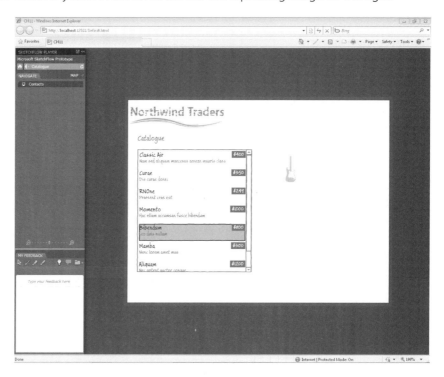

**14.** Switch back to Expression Blend and select the *Grid* object that contains the *Image* object. Set its *Bottom Margin* property value to **0** so that the bottom boundary of this *Grid* now aligns with the bottom boundary of the page.

**15.** Select the *Image* object in the Objects And Timeline panel. Set its *Width* property to **160** and its *Height* property to **415**.

**16.** Press F5 to test the application and see the result.

Now the guitar image looks larger.

## Sketch Illustrations

When you design an individual screen for a prototype application, you can also draw by using Expression Blend's vector tools, scan paper sketches, or import graphic assets from Microsoft Expression Design, Adobe Photoshop, or Adobe Illustrator. Additionally, you can use the custom shapes from the Assets panel. The shapes also have Sketch styles appropriate for use in SketchFlow projects.

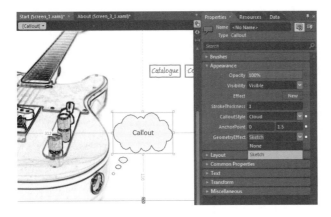

The Sketch styles in SketchFlow applications are intended to help designers and viewers focus on the interactive design of the prototype rather than the visual design. You can even create a hand-sketched look for images and photos you use in prototype applications.

Expression Design provides numerous effects suitable for converting photos to sketch images. Try using *Note Paper*, *Graphic Pen*, *Crosshatch*, and combinations of these to create sketch effects.

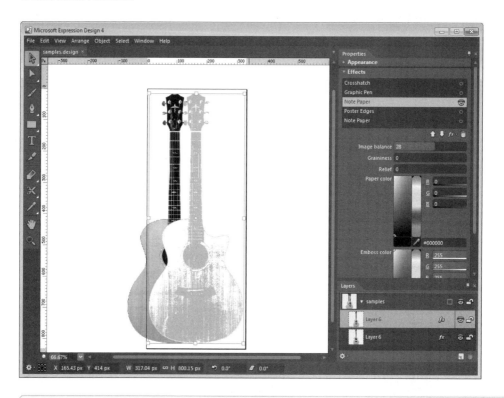

 **Tip** If you don't want to use Sketch styles for controls in your prototype application, or when you're ready to move your application to the next design phase, you can clear the Sketch styles. In the Assets panel, under Styles, right-click Sketch Styles, and then clear the Set As Default Style check mark.

# Adding Interactivity to a SketchFlow Project

Interactivity provides a feeling of realism to the user interface (UI) elements in your SketchFlow prototype. SketchFlow provides tools for creating true interactivity and for simulating it. Applying behaviors to elements in your prototype, using states to switch between different scenes, and adding specific navigation to elements all enable you to include real interactivity. Simulated interactivity works by using animations instead of behaviors.

# Adding Additional Navigation

The SketchFlow Player's Navigation panel and the connections you create between nodes provide you with a manual method of navigating between screens. But in a real application, screens typically change when users press buttons, select something from a list, enter data in fields, and so on. SketchFlow includes tools with which you can include these more realistic ways to navigate between screens. Providing these interactive features enables users to interact with UI elements much as they would in the finished application.

### Adding additional navigation

1. Activate the *Start* screen and right-click the *Catalogue* button.

2. Point to Navigate To and click *Catalogue*.

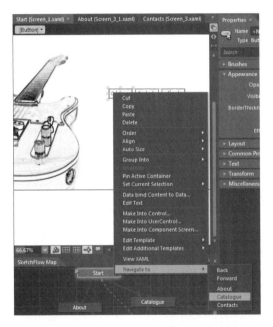

This action creates a connection between the *Catalogue* button and the *Catalogue* screen so that the user will be taken to that screen when he or she clicks the button.

3. Expand the *Catalogue* button in the Objects And Timeline panel.

Expression Blend added the *NavigateToScreenAction* behavior to this object. This behavior and other similar navigation behaviors are available only for SketchFlow projects.

4. Click the *NavigateToScreenAction* behavior to see its properties.

   You can change the values for some of the behavior properties, such as *EventName* and *TargetScreen*.

5. Right-click the *About* button on the Artboard. Point to Navigate To, and then click *About*.

6. On the Artboard, right-click the *Contacts* button, point to Navigate To, and then click Contacts.

   Now all three buttons have navigation to their specific screens, so you can navigate to the screens by clicking the buttons in addition to using the built-in SketchFlow Player navigation.

> **Note**  Use the *NavigateBackAction* and *NavigateForwardAction* behaviors to navigate back to a screen that you were previously viewing or to navigate forward to a screen that you were viewing before navigating back to a previous screen. These options are available through the list of available connections in the Navigate To menu.

You have completed the actions for the three menu buttons on the first screen. Now it's time to place those buttons on the other screens of your prototype application.

**7.** Select the *StackPanel* object in the Objects And Timeline panel.

**8.** Right-click the *StackPanel* object and click Make Into Component Screen.

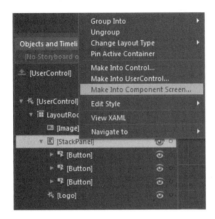

**9.** Type **Menu** in the Name field of the Make Into Component Screen dialog box, and then click OK.

A new component node appears on the SketchFlow Map.

**10.** Move the *Logo* component and the *Menu* component to convenient places on the map.

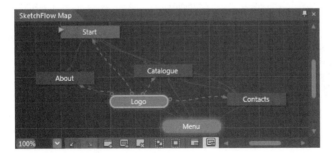

**Note** You can undo or redo your actions on the SketchFlow Map by clicking the buttons on the menu bar at the bottom of the SketchFlow Map panel.

11. Rebuild the project to see the change on the *Start* screen.

12. Select the *Menu* object in the Objects And Timeline panel. Press Ctrl+C to copy the object to the Clipboard.

13. Activate the *Catalogue* screen and select the *LayoutRoot* container in the Objects And Timeline panel.

14. Press Ctrl+V to paste the *Menu* object into the selected container, and then reset its *Width* and *Margin* properties.

15. Set the *HorizontalAlignment* property to Right and the *VerticalAlignment* to Top, and set the right and top *Margin* properties to **40**.

16. Press Ctrl+C to copy the *Menu* object to the Clipboard again.

17. Go to the *About* screen, select the *LayoutRoot* container, and press Ctrl+V to paste this object onto the screen.

18. Go to the *Contacts* screen, select the *LayoutRoot* container, and press Ctrl+V to paste it again in the same place.

After you perform all of these operations, new green dashed lines appear from the *Menu* component node to all of the navigation screens.

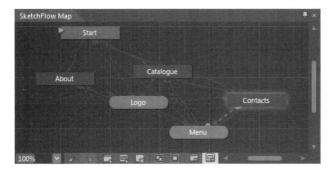

**19.** Press F5 to test your application and see the menu in action on all the screens of your prototype.

You've just implemented additional navigation between all of the screens in your project and created separate menu buttons in a component node that you can use on multiple screens throughout the prototype.

## Using States and Behaviors

You learned about states for controls in Chapter 9, "Skinning Controls." You can also use the states model for screens when you are designing a prototype application.

States help you demonstrate interactivity and can help provide different design alternatives for a single screen. For example, you can display different states for the contact form, login, or cart screens of your shop. Adding animation between the various screen states provides additional realism.

### Adding screen states

**1.** Activate the *Contacts* screen and open the States panel from the Window menu if it isn't already present in your workspace.

**2.** Under States, click the Add State Group button.

3. Type **Common** for the state group name, and then press Enter.

A state group contains visual states that are part of the same logical category.

*Add State*

4. Click the Add State button next to *Common* on the States panel.

5. Type **Normal** for the visual state name, and then press Enter.

Expression Blend turns state recording on. The red border around the Artboard and the red icons let you know that recording is in progress. Changes you make to the appearance of objects in this document will be recorded for the selected *Normal* state.

6. Click the Add State button again and add another state with the name **Sent**. Stay in the *Sent* state.

7.  Select the *ContactForm* object in the Objects And Timeline panel.

8.  Change the value of the *Visibility* property to *Collapsed* to hide the *ContactForm* in the *Sent* state.

9.  Select the *Thanks* object in the Objects And Timeline panel, and change the value of the *Visibility* property to *Visible*.

    Now the *Thanks* text will be visible only in the *Sent* state.

10. Switch between the *Normal* and *Sent* states to see the difference.

11. Press F5 to run the project, and then go to the *Contacts* screen.

    You can see new items on the Navigate tab. The two states for this screen are high-lighted by color and icons.

12. Click each state to see how your screen changes.

    Everything works as expected, but what if you want to switch states interactively, without having to use the SketchFlow Player navigation? To do that, you'll need to activate the states in response to user interaction.

13. Return to Expression Blend and select *Base* in the States panel.

    State recording is now turned off.

**14.** On the Artboard, select the *Send* button from the *ContactForm* container.

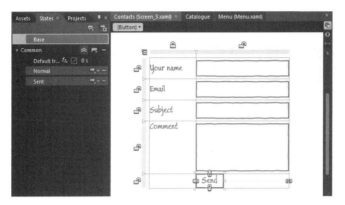

**15.** Right-click the *Send* button, point to Activate State, and then select Contacts / Sent.

**16.** Run the application and navigate to the *Contacts* screen. Type something in the form, and then click the *Send* button.

The form disappears, and the thank-you text becomes visible. Note that the state changed in response to your interaction.

**17.** Expression Blend used the *ActivateStateAction* behavior when you activated the *Sent* state. Select the behavior in the Objects And Timeline panel, and then check its properties.

This behavior applies a trigger that switches between visual states.

Just as you did in this exercise, you can add other state groups and states to define various design alternatives for the screen, and you can use behaviors to activate those states in response to user actions.

You can easily create a smooth transition between states by using Expression Blend's FluidLayout feature and by adding some transition effects to create an even more interesting impression.

## Adding transition effects between states

1. In the States panel, click Turn On FluidLayout for the *Common* state group.

2. Switch between states to see the changes.

3. Set the default transition duration to 1 second.

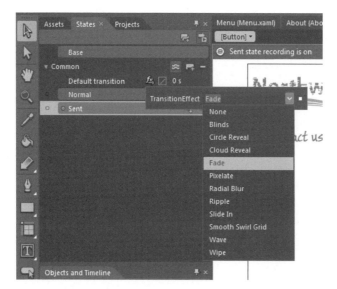

*Transition Effect*

4. Click the TransitionEffect button and select the Fade transition effect from the TransitionEffect list.

5. Test the changes by switching states in the States panel and by running the application to see them in action.

# Changing SketchFlow Player Settings

You can customize the SketchFlow Player runtime environment by changing the SketchFlow project settings. By default, the SketchFlow Player includes a *branding area* that displays text and has active Navigation and Feedback panels.

You can customize the branding area to suit your needs: enter a new title for a project, add versions, or include a custom image by using special tags.

### Changing the SketchFlow Player settings

1. Select SketchFlow Project Settings from the Project menu.

   The SketchFlow Project Settings dialog box appears.

2. Type **Northwind Traders Guitars Prototype. Version 1.0** into the Branding Text field.

3. Click OK. Press F5 to test the application and see the changes in the branding area of the SketchFlow Player, and then return to Expression Blend.

In addition to changing SketchFlow Player settings, you can define settings for both current and future SketchFlow projects by selecting Options from the Tools menu.

For example, on the SketchFlow page of the Options dialog box, you can set a default size for new navigation and component screens in SketchFlow projects.

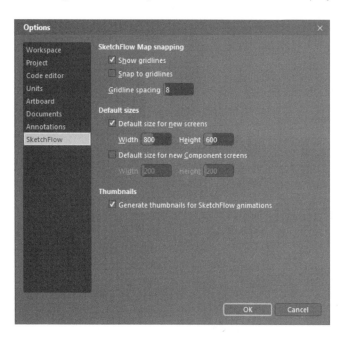

# Packaging a Prototype

When you have finished your prototype application, or when it reaches one of the final phases, you might want to show it to your friends, colleagues, team, or customers. Creating a SketchFlow package enables you to include all the required files to view the project without source files, making it easy to share with others.

## Packaging a SketchFlow project

1. Select Package SketchFlow Project from the File menu.

2. Select the location for your package. Leave CH11 as the folder name, and select the Open Windows Explorer When Complete check box.

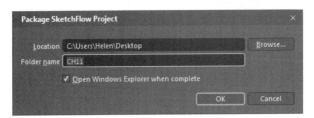

3. Click OK in the Package SketchFlow Project dialog box and wait for the packaging operation to complete.

   When the packaging operation is done, the contents of the CH11 folder appear in Windows Explorer in the location you specified.

4. Double-click the Default.html file to run the project in a browser.

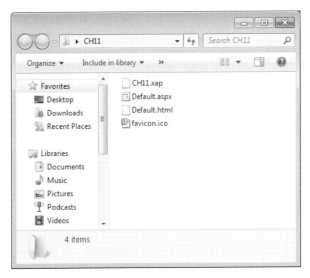

You can copy the contents of this folder to a web server, send the folder via FTP to a publically visible hosting location, compress the folder and send it in an email message, or use numerous other distribution methods.

# Getting Feedback

While viewing your prototype, your friends, colleagues, team members, or customers might want to provide comments or feedback. Feedback is a valuable way for users to inform you about what they liked, about needed changes or missing features, and so on. By collecting these comments, you can improve your prototype to make the final application better—before investing the work to build the final application.

### Adding feedback capabilities to your prototype application

1. Press F5 to run the prototype application.

   By default, the SketchFlow Player displays the My Feedback tab, which allows users to add text or ink-based feedback on each screen throughout the prototype. Users type their text feedback in the My Feedback box. They can also choose to draw directly on the prototype screens to provide ink-based feedback.

2. To enable ink-based feedback, click the Enable Ink Feedback button (the second icon from the left) and select red for drawing. You can set the brush size for drawing as well.

3. To test the Feedback settings, run the project and draw a double-ended arrow between the *Contacts* and *About* buttons.

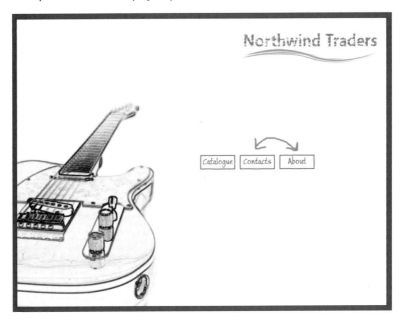

> **Note** If you draw something incorrectly, you can use the Erase Ink Feedback tool to erase the result.

4. Click inside the text box of the My Feedback tab and type the comment **Rearrange these buttons.**

> **Note** You can add new comments or delete existing comments by using the icons that appear at the right of each comment.

Reviewers can provide both text and ink-based feedback on any screen of your prototype application. The SketchFlow Player saves all feedback automatically. You or your team members might want to save user feedback as a file that you can later import into Expression Blend and use to help fix errors and to redesign the prototype application.

You'll save and import feedback in this exercise.

## Saving SketchFlow prototype feedback and importing it into Expression Blend

1. Click the Show Feedback Options button in the My Feedback tab, and then click Export Feedback.

2. The Feedback Author Information dialog box appears. Type the author name and initials.

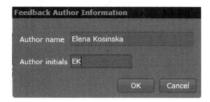

3. Click OK in the Feedback Author Information dialog box.

   The Save As dialog box appears.

4. Browse to the location where you want to save the file and type the file name.

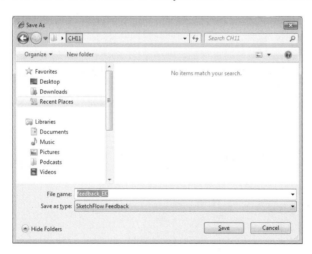

5. Click Save.

   When others view your project, they can send the saved file to you. You can import the feedback file to Expression Blend and view it while you work on the prototype.

**6.** To import the saved feedback file, return to Expression Blend and display the SketchFlow Feedback panel by selecting it from the Window menu.

**7.** Click Add (+) in the SketchFlow Feedback panel.

The Add Existing Item dialog box appears.

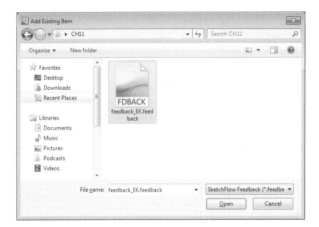

**8.** Locate the required feedback file, select it, and then click the Open button.

The feedback file now appears in the SketchFlow Feedback panel, and the text displays when you select an item from the list.

The SketchFlow Map displays a special icon indicator that informs you which screens contain feedback.

**9.** Double-click the *Start* screen to activate it.

You'll see the red arrow ink-based feedback you drew earlier on the screen, and the text feedback appears in the SketchFlow Feedback panel.

 **Note** You can show or hide feedback by clicking the Show or Hide Feedback buttons, and you can delete feedback by using the Delete (-) button.

# Generating Documentation

Expression Blend supports the creation of documentation about your prototype application. The report file, which Expression Blend exports in Microsoft Word format, includes a table of contents, a list of figures, the SketchFlow Map, navigation and component screens, the screens' states, and user feedback.

### Creating documentation for your prototype project

**1.** Select Export To Microsoft Word from the File menu. In the Export To Word dialog box, select the location where you want to save the file. Select both the Include Feedback and the Open Document When Complete check boxes.

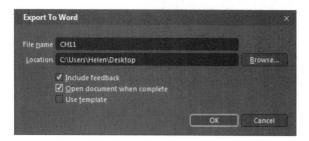

**2.** Click OK in the Export To Word dialog box.

Expression Blend performs the documentation process and opens the document in Microsoft Word when the documentation is complete.

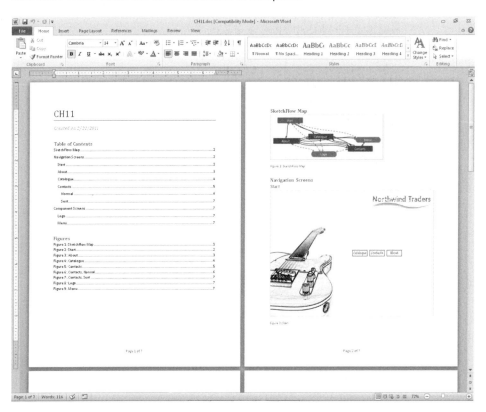

The report is a Microsoft Word document. You can edit the report, send it to team members and clients, and work with it as you would any other Word document.

In this chapter, you received an introduction to creating, modifying, and delivering prototype applications in Expression Blend.

As you've seen, the process works fairly intuitively. You can start with just a series of screens and proceed logically to develop a complete prototype by using the powerful SketchFlow tools. As part of Expression Blend, SketchFlow enables you to quickly experiment with dynamic user experiences in a very simple and visual manner, collect feedback from others, and create output documentation.

# Key Points

- You can rapidly create an application prototype by using a SketchFlow application.

- In SketchFlow, you can build an application flow by adding screens and navigation.

- You can increase the realism of your prototypes by adding controls and using sample data.

- Use states and behaviors to make your SketchFlow projects interactive.

- You can modify SketchFlow Player settings for an individual project or for all projects you create.

- Expression Blend provides an easy way to package your prototype to share with others.

- Use the feedback capabilities in SketchFlow projects and the SketchFlow Player to collect ideas and comments from users.

- Generate output documentation for your SketchFlow application in Word format.

# Chapter 12
# Designer/Developer Collaboration

**After completing this chapter, you will be able to:**

- Identify key points in a typical design workflow.
- Differentiate between designer and developer tasks and roles within the workflow.
- Identify mixed tasks.
- Share projects between Expression Blend and Visual Studio.
- Understand the benefits of using source control.

> *"Always code as if the guy who ends up maintaining your code will be a violent psychopath who knows where you live."*
>
> *- Martin Golding*

Most professional applications are the product of collaboration between designers and developers. The collaboration is made possible by a shared file format (XAML) and a shared solution/project format. Designers use the tool designed for their tasks, Microsoft Expression Blend, which has the same solution/project format as the developers' tool, Microsoft Visual Studio, and enables designers to manipulate the same XAML and code-behind files that the developers can. Throughout this book, you explored a lot of Expression Blend design features, so you know how to create parts of a great user experience from the designer's point of view. *Parts* is an accurate term because of the different tasks within the designer/developer collaboration process.

 **Important** There are no exercises in this chapter, so no accompanying practice files are required.

## A Typical Design Workflow

Design should be a basic part of an application's development lifecycle. Of course, the application can and should have great functionality, solid architecture, stability, and provide functionality that improves the user's productivity. But applications created solely by developers often have no "wow" effect and suffer from a low user adaptation rate. That's not to say that developers don't have the ability to do design work, but they typically don't have the same training, mindset, and project interests as designers. Similarly, a program conceived primarily by designers might have a carefully designed user interface (UI) with a lot of fancy elements—but if developers were not consulted, the application will probably be limited to a role as a "cool demonstration mockup/prototype" at best. Or, at worst, it will be diagnosed as a solution that can't be implemented. An application reaches a happy medium only when both designers and developers are involved in the process of its creation.

Typical designer/developer collaboration scenarios depend on various factors, including the size and complexity of the project. If a project is small, there might be only one person who performs both design and development work. This person must have the background, skills, and tools to do the job.

When one person acts as both designer and developer, he or she would use both Expression Blend and Visual Studio. This person might be focused more on the design end of the spectrum, with a great design background and yet some knowledge of how to code correctly and how to solve development problems. Or this might be a person with a great development background who has expanded his or her skills into image processing, drawing with vector tools, design principles, and color theory.

However, when a project is complex, it's likely to require a team with several members, including a project manager, an architect, and one or more designers, developers, and testers. In such cases, it's better to separate the designer and developer roles between different people. In this case, the collaboration scenario takes a hybrid form. The designer starts by making static mockups or creating dynamic mockups directly in Expression Blend with help of SketchFlow, then works on the design and theme of the application, and then creates XAML fragments that the developer can import into the project.

Designers use Expression Blend to create color resources, brush resources, and other types of resources; styles and templates for elements in the application's UI. They then use Expression Blend to package these elements into resource dictionaries. Developers import the resources into Visual Studio and apply them to the UI. Additionally, designers can create their own user controls as customized controls that can be reused multiple times in a project. Adding states and state groups helps to change the appearance of user controls. Developers can manipulate and change these states in response to user interaction and add event handler methods.

Sometimes a third specialist appears in the designer/developer collaboration process for complex projects. This person, often called the *integrator*, has broad knowledge of both design and development. In this case, the team can have a developer who focuses solely on development, a graphical designer who does only graphic design work, and an integrator, who converts design assets into resources, styles and templates for elements; creates custom user controls; and is responsible for data binding and connecting user interface components to internal or external data sources. In small and medium-sized projects, the integrator's role can be shared between designers and developers.

Good designers and developers tend to extend their knowledge into related areas because it's difficult to find people who are experts in the integrator role. Therefore, designers should know about the structure of controls and their properties, understand how to work with behaviors and event handlers, and grasp the basics of data binding implementation. Similarly, developers should have some knowledge about composition, layout, templates, styles, and identifying and converting commonly used values into project resources.

In Chapter 1, "Welcome to the Silverlight and WPF World," you saw a typical set of steps for a design process, which is repeated here.

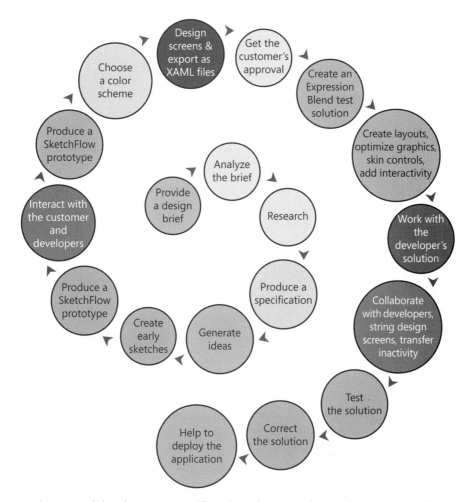

In this part of the chapter, you will explore the steps shown above in more detail:

1. **Provide a design brief to the client.**   A design brief is a document focused on business objectives and design strategies for a project. It provides a common understanding about the goal of the project, the target audience, and the expected business out-comes. The document does not address the aesthetics of the application. Its purpose is to let the client focus on what he or she wants to achieve before any designer or developer starts working on the project. Describing the goal of the project provides designers with an understanding of the main differences between the client and their

competitors. The design brief should also provide designers with some examples of what the client considers to be effective or relevant designs and also inform them about aspects that they should avoid in the project. The brief should also include information about the overall project schedule, and it should set due dates for milestones that mark important completion dates for the project. Finally, it's useful to include a budget so that team members can avoid wasting valuable time and resources on ideas that would simply cost too much to implement in the final product.

2. **Analyze the brief and understand the client's needs and goals.**   After agreeing with the client about the information in the design brief, you should analyze this document carefully to understand the client's final needs and goals before producing any ideas. The purpose of this analysis is to come up with relevant research questions. Prepare a list of questions, asking about the client's existing products, similar products, the function and aesthetics of the new products, and so on. You can start with simple questions, such as who, what, where, when, why, and how. The analysis stage helps to provide correct specifications later in the process.

3. **Research design solutions that address needs similar to the client's.**   The analysis phase gradually morphs into the research phase—the process of searching for new knowledge and facts. During the research phase, you collect, sort, and prepare the information you discover. This should be a time when possible solutions come to you. Write them all down. Research similar design solutions, but don't spend too much time doing so, because the research process can easily expand to take up countless hours unless you stick to a schedule.

4. **Produce a specification or list of design requirements.**   A specification is an explicit set of requirements to be satisfied by the final product. This document should list only the requirements that must be addressed. The specification doesn't describe how to address them.

5. **Generate a range of ideas to satisfy the requirements.**   Designers typically generate a range of possible ideas that satisfy the specification. Consult with developers as early in the idea-generating process as possible to avoid "can't be implemented" situations. Try to come up with five or more different initial designs that solve the problems set out in the specification. Describe how each design meets the requirements, and highlight its most impressive features.

6. **Create early sketches with pen and paper.**   Create your initial sketches with pen and paper. Rough sketches in their basic form, done in a few minutes, are very effective for visualizing ideas. Written ideas can be misinterpreted when they exist only in text form; detailed, sketched ideas produce better results and also more effectively elicit emotions and an overall impression from reviewers. The following images show an initial sketch and a fragment of a sketch example for the "Hedgehog and Apples" game and a detailed sketch idea for the main screen of the Northwind Traders Guitar Shop site.

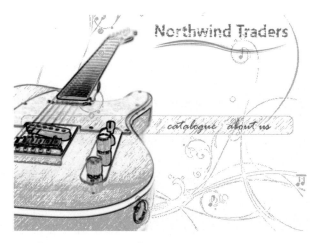

7. **Produce a prototype by experimenting with ideas in SketchFlow.**    Sketched ideas and detailed static mockups look fine on paper, but they need interactivity and animation when they are transferred to the computer. You can scan all the best ideas and import them into SketchFlow projects. Dynamic prototypes enable you to navigate

between screens and states, generate sample data, add hand-sketched controls, and interact with the application. The following picture shows the previous Northwind Traders Guitars image scanned into a SketchFlow project, with working controls added.

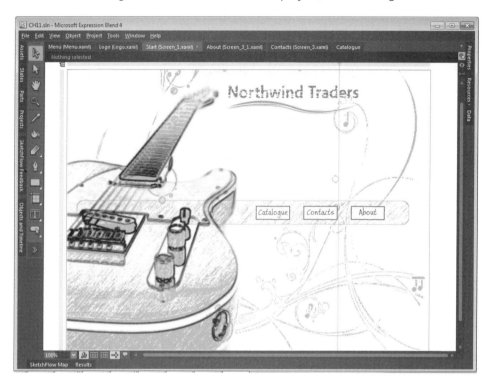

Create several branches in your prototype or segregate different ideas into independent projects. Add several navigation screens connected to the *Start* screen in the SketchFlow Map panel. Mark your ideas with color visual tags. The following example shows one project with several branches.

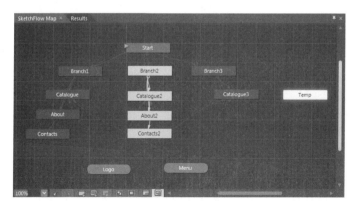

8. **Interact with clients and developers to choose the best idea.**   Interact with your team members. Show them your ideas and the implemented branches of your proto-types. Both designers and developers should be involved in the process of creating dynamic prototypes. Developers can specify which sketched ideas can't be implemented or would be too expensive to implement. You can work iteratively, going back to the previous sketching phase when you discover that an idea doesn't work as expected. Choose the three best ideas and show them to your client. Don't forget to collect feed-back from your team members and clients. You can see some typical feedback in the following image.

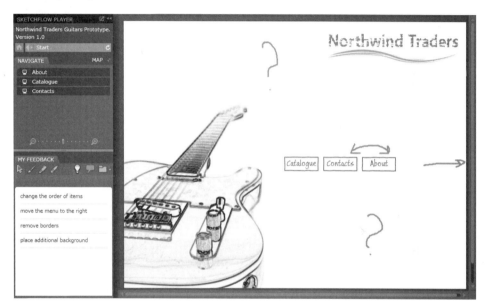

9. **Correct and finalize the SketchFlow prototype.**   Make changes to your prototype based on the feedback you receive. Remove unusable branches, but leave the two best ideas in order to improve them. Use states to show the different phases of the screens. Add transition effects and animations to make your prototype appear more realistic. You can also involve developers to help implement features and behaviors. For example, developers can create custom panels for displaying items, quick filtering, sorting, and instant search. An example of an instant search screen appears in the following image.

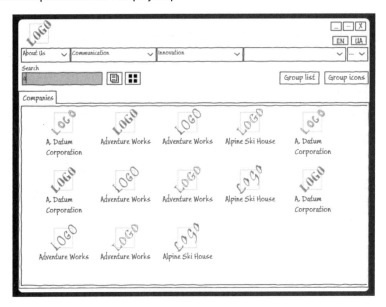

Obviously, features always depend on the client's requirements. Sometimes, implementing such features helps you choose the best scenario and the right idea. Later you can copy the code from the prototype to the production application so that developers only need to write the code once.

10. **Choose an application color scheme to meet the client's requirements or reflect the corporate identity.**   Choose an application color scheme based on your client's requirements and/or corporate identity. If your client already has a corporate color palette and style for their products, use that as the starting point and follow the rules of color combination from the corporate identity specifications.

If the application doesn't require the use of a pre-existing color palette or style, you can propose a new color scheme for the application. Before starting to choose palette items, determine your client's likes and dislikes. Optimally, the design brief should contain this information. If you are new to color selection, it's wise to spend some time understanding color theory. Be careful when selecting colors; they carry emotions and have different meanings in different cultures.

There are several ways to define a new color scheme. Here are a few:

❑ Use a paper color palette or color books to define five RGB (and CMYK) values for the product color scheme.

❑ Use natural photos and pick up the colors with the help of such graphic tools as Microsoft Expression Design. For example, you can use the Color Eyedropper tool to select colors from scanned or digital photos and apply them to a set of rectangles to see the results.

❑   Use online sites or desktop applications of special interest to the graphics community (for example, *http://www.colourlovers.com/*, shown in the following image).

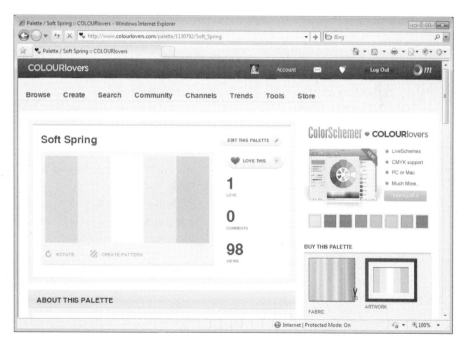

❑   COPASO is an advanced color palette tool that can help you create your own custom color palettes (also available at *http://www.colourlovers.com/*).

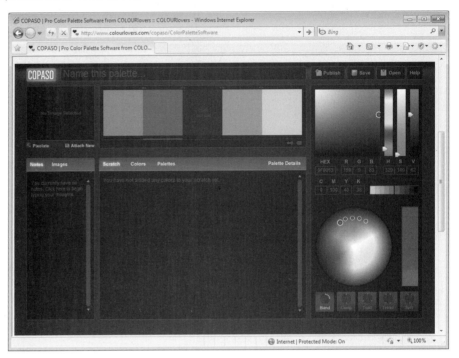

After selecting items for your color scheme, you can create a new swatch library in Expression Design and add the colors. Some online services enable you to download a color palette as an Expression Design Swatch (XML) file, WPF Resource Dictionary, Microsoft Silverlight XAML file, or other type of file. If you can, get your color scheme as an Expression Design Swatch—it's the easiest type to import and use in Expression Design. Regardless of where the initial swatches were created, you can pick up additional colors with the Expression Design tools and add them to the Swatch Library.

11. **Design application screens and control styles in Expression Design and then export the work as XAML files.**   After selecting a color scheme for your application, design the required application screens, control styles, and various other visual elements in Expression Design, and then export them to XAML files. You can use scanned sketches as a starting point for drawing outlines of objects and object details. For example, the following shows a background and basic elements for the "Hedgehog and Apples" game.

The following image shows some of the design assets used to create control styles for the game.

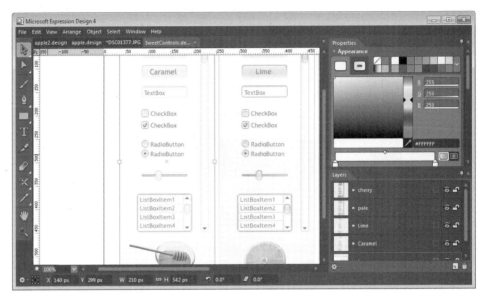

12. **Get the client's approval on the design screens.**   Test your XAML files by importing them into Expression Blend. Be careful with applied effects, shadows, and strokes. Compare them with your mockups in Expression Design and fix any differences. Be sure that the XAML files look the same as your design screens. Print the design screens, export them to .png files, and share them with the client to get approval. Collect feedback and finalize the design screens, elements, and the appearance of the controls.

13. **Create an Expression Blend test solution and import the XAML files.**   After getting design approval, create a test solution in Expression Blend where you can evaluate a more complete view of the approved design elements, controls, and their behaviors. Import the final approved XAML files.

**14. Create layouts for the application screens, transfer and optimize background graphics, skin controls, and add interactivity.**   Create pages for the application's screens, set their sizes, add layouts, and create a composition. Add and segregate secondary elements such as graphic and image backgrounds, shapes, and other non-active elements that aren't involved in user interaction, such as the clouds, grass, and sky for the game. Check vertical and horizontal stretching and alignment of these objects. Define and separate color and brush resources for these elements. The following image shows a few of the color and brush resources for graphic and image background elements defined for the game.

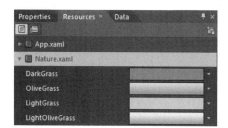

At this point, you perform the project skinning, convert design assets into real controls, and create implicit styles for all the controls used in the application. Don't forget about defining states. Add additional styles with names (keys) so that you can use them in nondefault situations. You can also define additional styles based on existing styles, cascading or inheriting them in Silverlight applications.

**Note**  To use styles based on existing styles, you can simply add the *BasedOn* property when defining the style for controls or elements. For example, for the *Button* control, the first line of the style would look like this:

```
<Style x:Key="ButtonSmall" TargetType="Button" BasedOn="{StaticResource ButtonClear}">
```

It is efficient to store resources by organizing them into resource files and adding a link to the resource file from the application's App.xaml file. You can easily copy and include the resource files in other projects.

The following image shows the color and brush resources and implicit styles for the most frequently used controls in the sample applications.

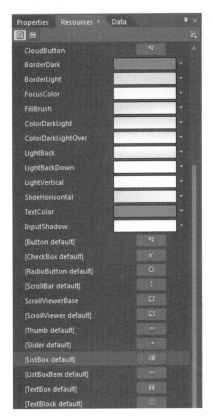

When designing a large application or set of applications that use many controls and different styles and templates, it's easier to define the styles, templates, and other resources for each type of control in a separate file. In this case, your App.xaml file will include links to all of these files and be tied to the control type, as shown in the following screen.

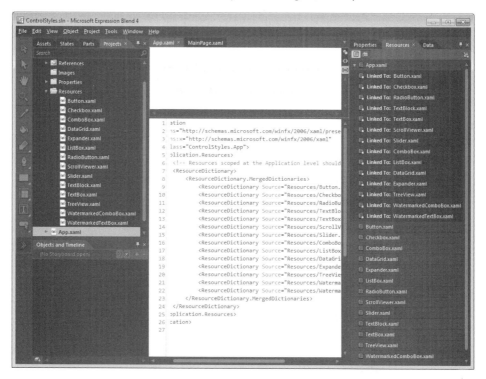

> **Tip**  To organize resource files, place them in one location, ideally in a separate folder with a meaningful name, such as *Resources*. This makes it easy to copy the Resources folder for use in other projects.

Separating control styles into different files is a good practice when several designers work on the same project. Skinning controls such as *DataGrid*, *RibbonBar*, *Menu*, and *Chart* takes a significant amount of time, so designers can focus on independent controls and work simultaneously on different parts and resources.

**15. Connect to the source control system and work with the developer's solution.**
Successful teams use special high-quality tools to work productively and effectively. Developers who create solutions based on Microsoft .NET technologies mostly use Visual Studio. When developers need to collaborate, they use Microsoft Visual Studio Team Foundation Server 2010, which is the collaboration platform for all team members. Team Foundation Server provides the single store for all assets associated with a project as well as a history of everything that has happened during the project creation process and lifecycle. It provides centralized storage of various work item types, including requirements, tasks, user stories, bugs, test cases, and the project source code.

After the designers have created a theme for the controls of an application, separated independent background elements, and added states for user controls, it's time to get the developer's solution—usually from a source code repository such as Team Foundation Server. There's always a question about when to start using source control. The answer is that it depends on your team's needs. It's possible to use source control from the beginning. You can even drop your SketchFlow prototypes into the Team Foundation Server source version control. You can add a new Team Foundation Server with help of Visual Studio 2010. Ask your administrator about the Team Foundation Server name or URL and connection details.

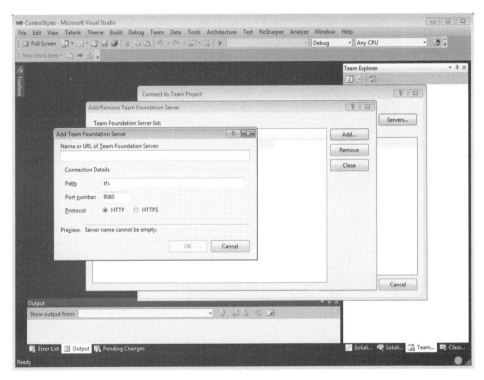

Connect to Team Foundation Server and get the team project from source control. Map the server folder of the solution to a local folder where you want to store the project, as shown in the following two images.

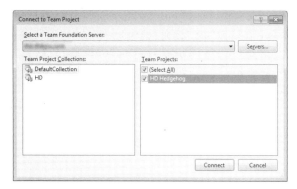

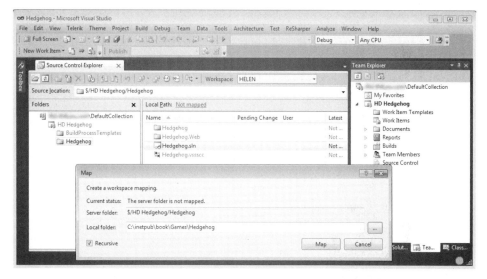

Now you can open the solution connected to Team Foundation Server in Expression Blend.

**Note**  When you open a solution connected to Team Foundation Server, the Windows security dialog box appears, and you'll need to enter your user credentials before you can connect.

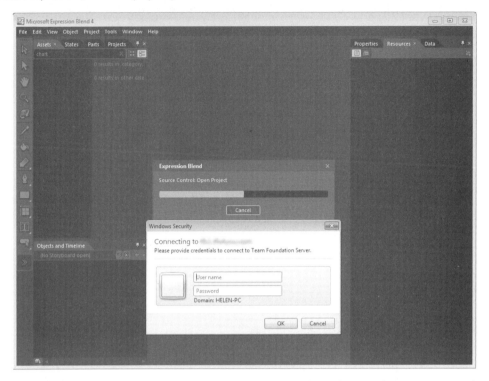

After a successful connection, Expression Blend opens the solution. The source control status for each file is represented by an icon next to the file name.

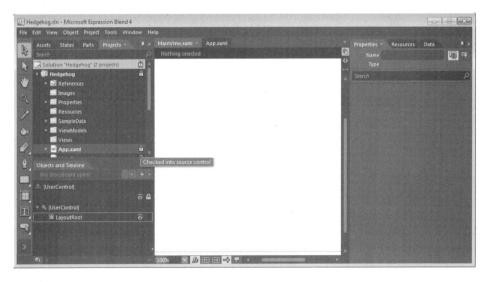

Now that the connection is complete and the project is open in Expression Blend, you can continue using the developer's solution. Run and test the project to ensure that it works.

16. **Collaborate with developers, string design screens, transfer interactivity, and implement data binding.**   This phase involves active collaboration with developers. Ask them where to place folders with resources. Copy all resource files and images from the test solution you created earlier to folders within the developer's solution. Make sure that the App.xaml file is linked to all these resource files and that the paths to images used in brushes, styles, and templates are correct.

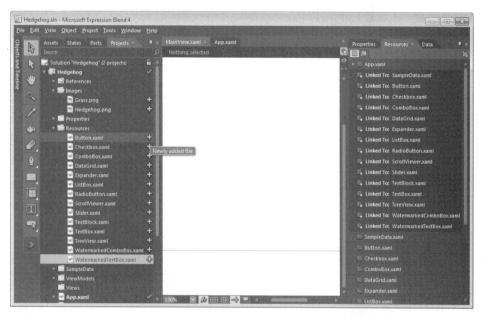

Run and test the developer's application to see the result of applying implicit styles. Make sure you don't break anything that worked *before* you begin applying your changes.

**Troubleshooting** If something *does* break, you always can undo your pending changes. Right-click the solution name in the Projects panel and then select the Undo Pending Changes option from the list.

The Undo Pending Changes operation will undo all pending source control changes for the selected files, reverting those files to their prior state.

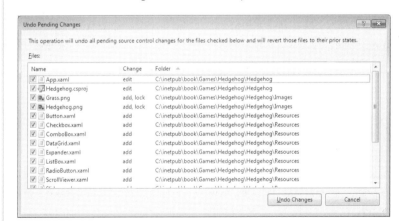

You can perform this Undo operation for individual files when editing the appearance of user controls and other elements.

After you have made all of the resource changes with the Check In operation from the context menu for the solution folder, the other team members can use the Get Latest Version operation to see your changes. Include comments for your check-in. You can also associate your changes in source control with the work item—task, bug, user story, and so on—defined for you by the project manager.

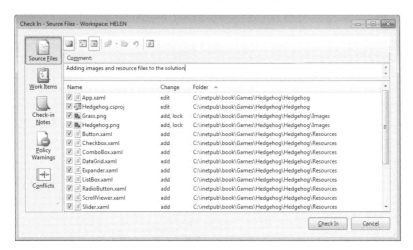

The next steps involve transferring background and secondary elements used for screens, adding custom user controls and states, copying sample data and data templates from your prototype and test applications, and adjusting data binding parameters.

Check-in your changes into source control so that developers can use your custom user controls and check data binding in data templates. In all likelihood, the sample data from your prototype and test applications will not have the exact same structure as the live data that the production application uses, so developers will replace the sample data bindings with live data bindings or adjust your sample data schema.

> **Note**  In some cases, the live data schema *does* match your sample data schema. In this case, the sample data bindings can still exist, stored in design-time properties. The sample data will display on the Artboard at design time, and the live data will display in the running application.

17. **Test the solution.**   Test the solution and see how the live data loads, how the application responds when data changes, how controls behave, what happens with the application on different computers and at different screen resolutions, and so on.

18. **Modify and correct the solution.**   Modify and fix problems that you find with control behaviors and layout compositions. Collaborate actively with developers to solve problems. Organize feedback from clients and testers from all phases of the design and development process. Verify that the production application meets the requirements and solves the problems set out in the original design specification.

19. **Help to deploy the application to the client's environment.**   Deploying an application involves moving the application from a development environment to a production environment. After deployment, your clients and the application users will have full access to the application.

    If you've developed a WPF desktop application, make sure that the production application works on the client's machines; don't rely solely on testing within your design and development computers. The clients will need all of the additional software used by the application, including the .NET Framework runtime. Use "clean" machines for testing, preferably with just operating systems installed. You should test all of the steps—from setup to running the application.

    If you've built a Silverlight application, make sure that the end users can view it properly. Watch out for situations in which clients don't have the Silverlight plug-in installed on their computers or have an out-of-date version installed. Also make sure that users can easily install and update the plug-in.

    You can customize the Silverlight installation experience and change the default image to a custom image. You can also provide additional information about why users need to install the plug-in as well as information about viewing and using your application. For example, the following images show the default Silverlight installation prompt and a customized version.

# The Designer's Role

Although you should have a reasonably clear idea of the designer's role at this point, it's worth briefly recapping it here. A designer's tasks include sketching, dynamic prototyping, creating custom backgrounds and vector graphics, creating styles and templates, adding animations, and defining states for custom controls. The basic tools designers need to perform these tasks are Expression Design and Expression Blend with SketchFlow. Additionally, they can also use Adobe Photoshop and Adobe Illustrator as preliminary tools. Beyond that, designers should install Visual Studio, because it's often helpful for developers to debug the application on a designer's computer.

Designers should create vector UI elements, except under certain circumstances in which the assets can be raster images. It's a bad practice, for example, to create a gradient background for buttons and use it as an image. Such incidents occur fairly often when designers are used to working with bitmapped graphics and print media. Don't forget, XAML enables you to display different types of gradients by setting simple and editable parameters. At the same time, it's better to use raster images for such UI elements as rich three-dimensional icons that have a complex layer structure and whose exported XAML code is often very large.

Always optimize and organize your XAML code in Expression Blend. Create clean XAML code for readability and maintenance. To paraphrase the quote at the beginning of this chapter, "Always code XAML as if the designer/developer who ends up maintaining your code and resources is a violent psychopath who knows where you live."

# The Developer's Role

Developers have a completely different set of requirements for creating and using UI elements and layout composition. They focus primarily on the architecture and patterns used to build applications, getting data from the data layer efficiently, and ensuring overall application performance, security, unit testing, and deployment of the production application.

Visual Studio is the primary tool used by developers for Silverlight and WPF applications. In many cases, they don't have Expression Blend installed. In fact, they rarely use any graphic tools, except perhaps some screen-capture software. Developers often use default controls with default styles when creating an application, or they create custom generic-looking controls and layout panels when they need more functionality. One of the primary tasks for developers when working in tandem with designers is the need to provide a high level of compatibility with Expression Blend. The process doesn't make any sense if a designer can't open a custom control in Expression Blend at design time to create or modify the styles and templates.

Mixed tasks that can be accomplished by either designers or developers include the creation of data templates and presentation of the data in the application, data binding, analysis and determination of which controls are best suited to solve specific layout compositions, and so on.

At this point, you have a solid overview of how the design process should work, what role designers play in this scenario, and at which points collaboration with developers should occur. Remember, good communication is the key to developing great applications.

# Key Points

- Completing the entire process embodied by a typical design workflow involves many steps and several specialists.

- The designer role in the project team has specific visually oriented tasks suited to designers' skills and tools.

- The developer role in the project team has specific tasks oriented toward developers' particular knowledge, skills, and tools.

- Some tasks are mixed in that they bridge the design and development specialties.

- Because Expression Blend and Visual Studio both use the same project/solution format, the project can be opened, modified, and manipulated in the tool best suited to the specialist's needs.

- Using Team Foundation Server as the collaboration platform and source control, the whole team can work on the same project from the same location, benefiting from true collaboration with the added benefits of assignable work items, easy rollback of changes, and the maintenance of notes about each team member's work.

# Index

# Author Bios

### Elena Kosinska

Elena Kosinska is a UX/UI designer focused on prototyping, designing, and developing Microsoft Silverlight and Windows Presentation Foundation (WPF) applications. She is a Microsoft Certified Trainer (MCT) and Most Valuable Professional (MVP) in Microsoft Expression Blend. Elena has more than nine years of experience in design (graphic, web, UI), including four years specifically with Silverlight and WPF. She has used Expression Blend professionally since the very first version, is a community supporter, writes blog posts and articles for UI designers, and has spoken at Microsoft events as well as taught WPF/Silverlight courses.

### Chris Leeds

Chris Leeds is a long-time digital photographer and web enthusiast who has been a MVP for Microsoft Office FrontPage and now Microsoft Expression Web for eight years. He is also a Network Partner with Microsoft's WebsiteSpark program (*http://www.microsoft.com/web/websitespark/*), a commentator at Lockergnome (*http://www.Lockergnome.com*), and a software reviewer on Bright Hub (*http://www.BrightHub.com*). Chris developed a software product called ContentSeed (*http://www.ContentSeed.com*) with which users can create webpages that can be edited and managed using only a browser. Chris is also the author of *Microsoft Expression Web 4 Step by Step* and two previous books on Expression Web, and has developed several tutorials about FrontPage and Expression Web. He hopes to continue helping the user community through the site at *http://www.ExpressionBlendStepByStep.com*, where he'll try to answer questions regarding this book and Microsoft Expression products.

# What do you think of this book?

We want to hear from you!

To participate in a brief online survey, please visit:

**microsoft.com/learning/booksurvey**

Tell us how well this book meets your needs—what works effectively, and what we can do better. Your feedback will help us continually improve our books and learning resources for you.

Thank you in advance for your input!

**R.C.L.**

**SEP. 2011**

**G**

# Stay in touch!

To subscribe to the *Microsoft Press® Book Connection Newsletter*—for news on upcoming books, events, and special offers—please visit:

**microsoft.com/learning/books/newsletter**